The UNIX™ C Shell
Field Guide

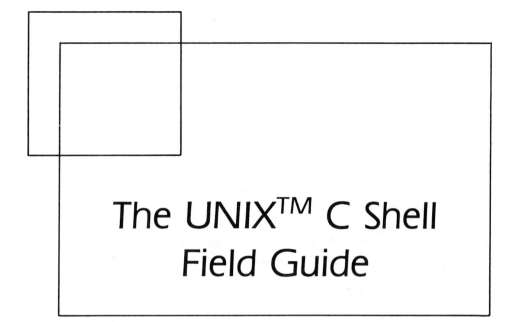

The UNIX™ C Shell
Field Guide

Gail Anderson
Paul Anderson

P T R Prentice Hall, Englewood Cliffs, New Jersey 07632

Library of Congress Catalog Card Number: 83-63102

Editorial/production supervision: Sophie Papanikolaou
Interior design: Sophie Papanikolaou
Cover design: Bruce Kenselaar
Cover illustration: Linda McVay
Manufacturing buyer: Gordon Osbourne

UNIX is a trademark of AT&T/Bell Laboratories.
XENIX and MS-DOS are trademarks of Microsoft Corporation.

Printed in the United States of America

20 19 18 17 16

ISBN 0-13-937468-X NBZI

PRENTICE-HALL INTERNATIONAL (UK) LIMITED, *London*
PRENTICE-HALL OF AUSTRALIA PTY. LIMITED, *Sydney*
PRENTICE-HALL CANADA INC., *Toronto*
PRENTICE-HALL HISPANOAMERICANA, S.A., *Mexico*
PRENTICE-HALL OF INDIA PRIVATE LIMITED, *New Delhi*
PRENTICE-HALL OF JAPAN, INC., *Tokyo*
PRENTICE-HALL OF SOUTHEAST ASIA PTE. LTD., *Singapore*
EDITORA PRENTICE-HALL DO BRASIL, LTDA., *Rio de Janeiro*
WHITEHALL BOOKS LIMITED, *Wellington, New Zealand*

For Sara and Kellen

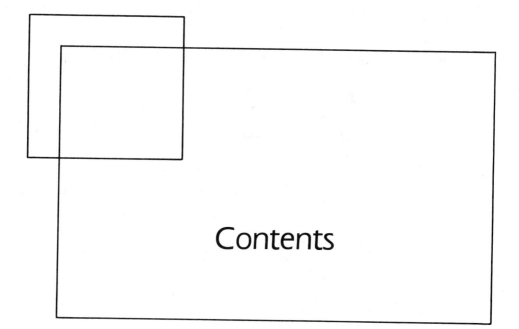

Contents

2. Climbing into Your Shell: A Tour of the C Shell   **24**

5. Job Control

6. History and Alias Mechanisms

10. Inside the C Shell

11. Example C Shell Scripts   **288**

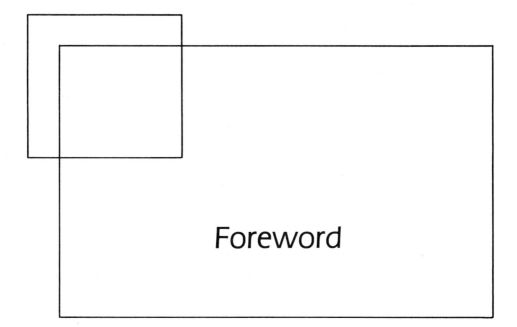

Foreword

The C shell was written while I was at U.C. Berkeley, with the aim of providing aid to the interactive use of UNIX. The shells that existed at the time provided few creature-comforts for the user, and most of the contemporary work on shells was aimed at making the shells more programmable. Features such as the history mechanism, job control, and command aliases' are at the heart of what the C shell provides. These features were not relevant to shell programming, but that did not distract from their importance.

The history mechanism of the shell was inspired by the History and DWIM features of Interlisp, invented by Warren Teitelman, then at Xerox, now at Sun Microsystems. The aliasing mechanism was my own invention, patterned roughly on Lisp reader macros. Job control was added to the C shell by Jim Kulp, then at IIASA in Austria, now at Symbolics, Inc. The shell would not have existed without the inspiration of these and other people, and the cooperation of the many people at Berkeley and in the UNIX community that existed because of the essentially free licensing of UNIX in source form to Universities. I have been proud to work in this community.

I am glad that the features that UNIX and the C shell provide are being made widely available through books such as this field guide, and through the widespread availability of UNIX made possible by microprocessors.

Bill Joy
Sun Microsystems
Mountain View, California

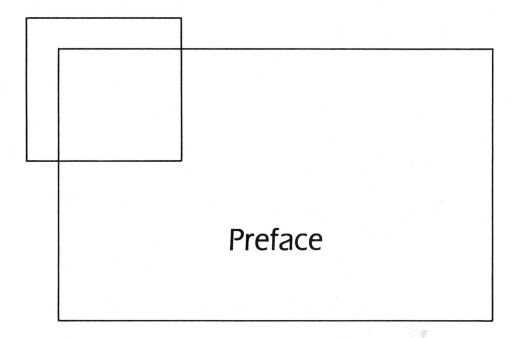

Preface

The C shell is a program that executes under the UNIX operating system. It is a command interpreter—the gateway to other programs and utilities running under UNIX. *The UNIX C Shell Field Guide* is an in-depth guide to this powerful interface. Its purpose is to show you how to use the C shell effectively, to explain the practicality of its features, and to offer guidelines to using the C shell based on our own experiences (found in the "Hints and Cautions" sections of many of the chapters).

Both the experienced and novice UNIX user will find this book useful. We emphasize situations typical to the software developer, but those interested in word processing, accounting, database manipulation, or data entry will also benefit from the material presented in this book.

We have organized the book as follows: Chapters 1 and 2 introduce the C shell. Chapter 1 discusses what it is, what it does, and how you use it. Chapter 2 gives a brief tour of the C shell with a sample terminal session.

Chapters 3 through 6 present the C shell as an interactive command language. Chapter 3 presents the C shell's basic command forms. Chapter 4 shows the C shell's power—its command shorthand. Chapter 5 shows how to juggle your commands using job control. Finally, Chapter 6 covers the history and alias mechanisms—the C shell's claim to fame.

Chapters 7 and 8 present the C shell as a programming language. Chapter 7 covers the basic language forms, and Chapter 8 discusses more advanced techniques. Both chapters contain example scripts to illustrate the material.

Chapter 9 shows how to customize the C shell to accommodate your terminal type, working habits, login and logout procedures, and custom commands.

Chapter 10 explains how the C shell works and how it interfaces to the UNIX system. We include diagrams to show you how the C shell executes commands.

Chapter 11 is a collection of C shell scripts that illustrate a particular technique, perform an interesting task, or solve a problem. Most are "real" scripts in use on production UNIX systems.

Each chapter (except chapters 1, 2, and 11) contains a "Key Point Summary." In addition, many contain a "Hints and Cautions" section (based on our C Shell experiences) and a "Putting It All Together" section that solves a problem using the material presented in the chapter.

The appendices provide a reference guide to the C shell. Of particular interest is Appendix E, a collection of C shell summary tables, and Appendix G, a guide to using the C shell under XENIX.

Since *The UNIX C Shell Field Guide* is not an introduction to the UNIX system, we present a listing of Common UNIX Commands before Chapter 1. We organize these commands into four categories:

   I. File and Directory Management Commands
  II. Text Processing Commands
 III. System Status Commands
 IV. Software Development Commands

This summary will help readers who are not familiar with terse UNIX command names (e.g., **cp** for copy, **cd** for change directory). This listing contains all commands that appear in the examples we use.

In presenting the examples, we use **boldface** to distinguish the text you type from the output.

Our approach is to teach by example. You may want to key in the examples as you read along. With any major project, you must choose the right tool for the right job. In writing this book, we used many of the C shell's features (and discovered a few new ones along the way). We hope you find the C shell to be as valuable a tool as we did.

Gail and Paul Anderson
San Diego, California

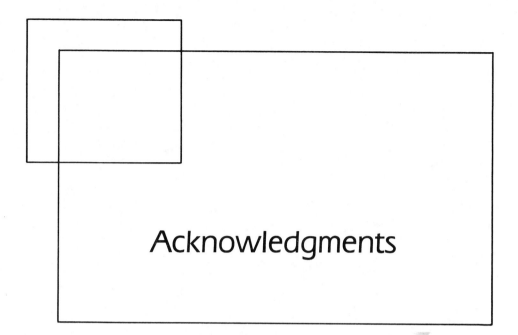

Acknowledgments

We'd like to thank the following people who contributed in so many ways to the project: Bill Barton, Walt Morton, and Cipher Data Products, who provided time and encouragement; Marty Gray, for his unbounded UNIX "zeal"; Tom Korb, Cal Williams, and Stephen Koehler, who all provided many valuable suggestions for the manuscript; Lance Leventhal, for his constructive editing; Linda McVay, for her cover illustration and design suggestions; Bill Joy, for making this all possible; and last, but not least, Jean Campbell, for baby-sitting the kids.

The UNIX™ C Shell
Field Guide

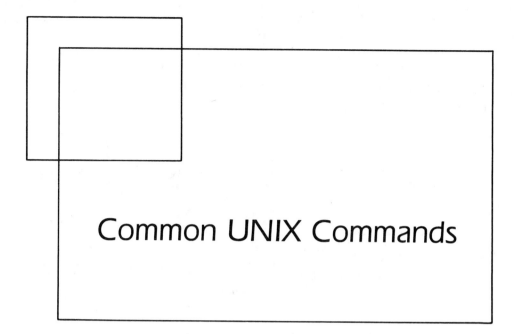

Common UNIX Commands

This listing describes common UNIX commands. We use the following symbols to define a command's syntax:

[item]   **item** is an optional argument.

item(s)   Must specify one or more **items.**

*   Command reads from standard input if file argument is omitted.

I. FILE AND DIRECTORY MANAGEMENT COMMANDS

cat   concatenate and print

```
cat [options] [file(s)]*
```

Useful Options

- **-** Read from standard input first.
- **-n** Number lines (BSD only).
- **-u** Output is unbuffered.

Examples

cat /etc/motd
Displays file **/etc/motd** on the screen.

cat dict1 dict2 > dictionary
Concatenates files **dict1** and **dict2** to file **dictionary.**

cat > memo
Reads from keyboard (standard input) until user types **control-D** and places output in file **memo.**

cd, chdir   change working directory

```
cd [dir]
```

Change working directory to **dir.** If no arguments specified, change to home directory **($HOME).**

Examples

cd japanese
Change to subdirectory **japanese.**

cd /u/eric/dbms/source
Change to directory **/u/eric/dbms/source.**

cd
Change to home directory.

See index entries **cdpath, pushd, popd, dirs, pwd.**

chmod   change access permission (mode) for files or directories

```
chmod absolute-mode file(s)
chmod symbolic-mode file(s)
```

Useful Options

Absolute
4 Read access.
2 Write access.
1 Execute (search) access.

Symbolic
r Read access.
w Write access.
x Execute (search) access.

u user (owner)
g group
o others
a all

Examples

chmod 755 .
Make current directory (**.**) read, write, and searchable by owner, read and searchable by group, and read and searchable by others.

chmod +x loc
Make **loc** executable by everyone.

chmod o-r logfile
Remove read permission on **logfile** for others.

chmod o-r,o-w *
Remove read and write permission for others on all files in the current directory.

chmod a=r *.c
Make all files ending in **.c** read-only for everyone (all).

cp   copy file(s)

```
cp file1 file2
cp file(s) directory
```

Copy **file1** to **file2.** Copy one or more files to a directory.

Examples

cp .cshrc save.cshrc
Copy file **.cshrc** to file **save.cshrc.**

cp /u/scott/network/include/* .
Copy all files in **/u/scott/network/include** to the current directory.

doscp   DOS disk copy (XENIX only)

```
doscp file1 file2
doscp file(s) directory
```

Copy files between a DOS format disk and a XENIX file.

Examples

doscp A:spec.doc spec
Copy file **spec.doc** from DOS disk in device in **A** to file **spec.**

doscp spec* A:
Copy all files starting with **spec** to DOS disk in device **A.**

doscp A:spec1.doc A:spec2.doc /u/kellen
Copy files **spec1.doc** and **spec2.doc** from DOS disk in device **A** to the directory **/u/kellen.**

file   determine file type

```
file file(s)
```

file attempts to classify its arguments' file types. Some typical classifications are **directory, ascii text, commands text** (i.e., shell scripts), **c program text, executable not stripped, English text,** and **empty. file** is not always accurate.

Example

file *
Classify each file in the current directory.

find find files

```
find pathname-list expression
```

Find all files in **pathname-list** that match **expression.**

Useful Options

Options may be combined.

-name filename	True if **filename** matches the current file name.
-perm octnum	True if the permission matches the octal number **octnum.**
-print	Display the file name.
-type t	True if the type of file is **t**, where **t** is **d** (directory), **f** (file), **c** (character special file), or **b** (block special file).
-exec command	True if the executed command returns a zero exit status. Replace {} with the current pathname. An escaped semicolon follows **command.**
-size n	True if the file is size **n** (greater than **n** is **+n** and less than **n** is **−n**).
-mtime n	True if the file has been modified in **n** days.

Examples

find ~ -name "*.c" -print
Display all file names in the user's directory hierarchy ending in **.c.**

find / -size 0 -exec rm "{}" \;
Remove all zero-length files in the file system.

find ~ -type d -print
Display all directory names in the user's file system.

head display in front of file

```
head [-count] [file(s)]*
```

Display the first (10 or **-count**) lines of **file(s)**.

Examples

head /etc/passwd
Display the first 10 lines of the password file.

head -20 report
Display the first 20 lines of file **report**.

grep jun.85 *.taxrec | head
Display the first 10 lines of all **jun 85** entries in **taxrec** files.

ln   make links

    1. ln file1 [file2]
    2. ln file(s) directory
    3. ln [-s] file1 [file2] (BSD only)

In form 1, **ln** creates a link called **file2** to an existing **file1**. If **file2** is not specified, the link is created in the current directory with **file1**'s file name. In form 2, **ln** creates a link in **directory** to each file named. You cannot link to directories or across file systems. In XENIX, you must specify **file2**. Form 3 (BSD only) allows symbolic links (**-s** option), which may be made across file systems.

Examples

ln /usr/data/base /usr/data/lock
Create a link **/usr/data/lock** to **/usr/data/base**.

ln com1 com2 com3 ~/bin
Create three links in ~/**bin** to files **com1, com2,** and **com3.**

ls   list directory content (BSD version may be called **lc**)

    ls [options] [name(s)]

List the content of each directory name or status information of each file name. If **name** is omitted, use current directory.

Useful Options

    -l List in long format (mode, links, owner, size, time of last modification).
    -a List entries including those starting with . (dot).
    -F Mark directories with a trailing /, executable files with *.
    -R List subdirectories recursively.
    -1 Force output to consist of one entry per line.

Examples

ls -l
Give long listing of current directory.

ls *.c
List all files ending in **.c** in current directory.

ls -RF1 /u
List all entries in **/u** recursively, marking directories and executable files. Output is one entry per line.

mkdir   make a directory

```
mkdir dir(s)
```

Examples

mkdir project1
Make subdirectory **project1.**

mkdir project1/{source,doc,bugs}
Make directories **project1/source, project1/doc,** and **project1/bugs.**

more   page output to screen

```
more [options] [file(s)]*
```

Display files on screen. Type **q** to quit display, **SPACE** to continue, **h** for help.

Examples

more /etc/termcap
Display the **/etc/termcap** file.

nroff document | more
Format **document** using **nroff** and display on screen using **more.**

mv   move or rename a file; rename a directory

```
mv oldname newname
```

Moves or renames file **oldname** to **newname.** If **newname** exists, it is replaced by **oldname.** If **oldname** is a directory, only a rename is possible.

Examples

mv /tmp/workarea new.data
Move file **/tmp/workarea** to **new.data** in current directory.

mv /u/george /u/bg
Rename directory **/u/george** to **/u/bg.**

rm   remove files

```
rm [options] file(s)
```

Useful Options

-f Do not attempt to verify removal (force removal).

-i Interactive—prompt to remove each file.

-r Delete each file and subdirectory recursively.

Examples

rm .history
Remove file **.history**.

rm -r book
Remove directory **book** and all its subdirectories.

rm -i *
Prompt to remove each file (no directories).

rmdir   remove directory

```
rmdir dir(s)
```

Example

rmdir book project1
Remove directories **book** and **project1**. These must be empty.

tail   display tail end of file

```
tail [options] [file]*
```

Examples

tail /etc/passwd
Display the last 10 lines of the password file.

tail -20 report
Display the last 20 lines of file **report.**

history | tail -5
Display the last five commands from the history list.

tee   read standard input and write to standard output and file(s)

```
tee [options] [file(s)]
```

Useful Options

-i Ignore interrupts.

-a Append to **file(s).**

Examples

date | tee stat1 stat2 stat3
Write the date to the standard output as well as files **stat1, stat2,** and **stat3.**

spell ch8.* | tee errors
Write spelling errors to file **errors** and display.

spell ch9.* | tee -a errors
Append spelling errors to file **errors** and display.

II. TEXT PROCESSING COMMANDS

awk   search text for patterns and perform operations (named after the authors, Aho, Weinberger, and Kernighan)

```
awk string_[file(s)]*
```
Execute **awk** commands in **string** on text in **file(s).**

```
awk -f program_file [file(s)]*
```
Execute **awk** program in **program_file** on text in **file(s).**

Examples

awk 'length > 8 { print $1 }' data
Display field 1 of each line that is longer than 8 characters in file **data.**

**awk '{s += $2 } \
END { print "sum is", s, "average is", s/NR} ' data**
Display the sum and average of field 2 in file **data.**

awk -F: '{ print $1, $5, $6 }' /etc/passwd
Display the first, fifth, and sixth fields of each line of the password file. **-F:** changes the field separator character to **:.**

awk -f awkprogram data
Read **awk** statements from **awkprogram.**

diff   list differences between two files

```
diff [options] file1 file2
```

Useful Options

-e Produce a script for the editor **ed,** which will create **file2** from **file1.**
-b Causes trailing blanks to be ignored.

Examples

diff scanner35.c scanner36.c
List differences between **scanner35.c** and **scanner36.c.**

diff -e ch3-1.man ch3-1a.man
Produce **ed** script to make **ch3-1a.man** from **ch3-1.man.**

ex   ex text editor

```
ex [options] [file(s)]
```

ex is a superset of the **ed** line editor.

grep   global regular expression parser; search a file for a pattern

```
grep [options] expression [file(s)]*
```

Search **file(s)** for **expression.**

Useful Options

-v Print all lines but those matching **expression.**
-c Print the number of matching lines.
-l Print the names of files having at least one match.
-n Print the line and the line number.

Examples

grep -c /bin/csh /etc/passwd
Display the number of users whose login shell is **/bin/csh.**

grep -l MAXPROP *.c
List the names of the C source files that contain the identifier **MAXPROP.**

grep -v "ˆ[0-9]" report
Display all lines in file **report** that do not begin with a digit.

lpr   line printer spooler

```
lpr [options] [file(s)]*
```

Prints named files (or standard input if no files) on off-line printer.

Examples

lpr document
Prints file **document.**

nroff -ms report | lpr
Formats **report** using **nroff** and prints.

nroff   text formatter

```
nroff [options] [file(s)]*
```

nroff uses in-line text formatting commands.

Examples

nroff -ms doc/∗.man > doc/man.out
Format (using **ms** macro package) all files ending in **.man** in **doc** subdirectory. Place output in file **man.out** in **doc** subdirectory.

nroff memo
Format file **memo.** Output appears on screen.

pr   paginate and print

```
pr [options] [file(s)]*
```

Useful Options

-n Produce **n-**column output.
+n Begin with page **n.**
-h Use next argument as page header.

Examples

pr -4 guestlist
Print file **guestlist** in four columns.

pr -h "Minutes of Weekly Meeting" minutes
Print file **minutes** using title **"Minutes of Weekly Meeting".**

pr +5 specification
Print file **specification** starting with page 5.

sed   stream editor

```
sed [options] [file(s)]*
```

Noninteractive text editor.

Useful Options

-f Use next argument as a file of editing commands.
-e Use next argument as an editing command.
-n Display parts of a file.

Examples

sed -f cmnds list > newlist
Edit **list** using editing commands in the file **cmnds.** Modified text stored in **newlist.**

find . -type f -print | sed "s/ˆ.∗/cp & &.bak/" | csh
Select only files in current directory to be backed up with the name **filename.bak. sed** is used as a filter to create copy commands (**cp**) for the C shell.

sed -n 10,30p getrec.c
Displays lines 10 through 30 of **getrec.c** on standard output.

sort sort or merge files

```
sort [options] [file(s)]*
```

Sort files.

Useful Options

- **-** Read from standard input first.
- **-b** Ignore leading blanks.
- **-d** Dictionary order: only letters, digits, and blanks are significant.
- **-n** Sort by arithmetic value.
- **-o** Put output in file specified in next argument.
- **tc** Fields are separated by character **c.**
- **+n** Skip **n** fields.

Examples

sort -d dict[1-6] -o dict1
Sort files **dict1** through **dict6** by dictionary order. Store output in **dict1.**

sort -t: +2 /etc/passwd
Sort the password file by user ID (the third field).

spell find spelling errors

```
spell [options] [file(s)]*
```

Find spelling errors in named files (or standard input if no files) and write to standard output.

Examples

spell document
Display spelling errors in **document.**

spell text?.doc | pr -h "Spelling Errors" | lpr &
Find all spelling errors in files **text1.doc, text2.doc,** etc.; paginate list; and print it (all in the background).

split split large files

```
split [-n] [file]*
```

Split file (or standard input) into **n**-line files (default 1000 lines). The files are named **xaa, xab,** continuing in dictionary order.

Examples

split bigfile
Splits **bigfile** in as many 1000-line files as necessary.

split -66 document
Splits **document** into 66-line files (i.e., one page per file).

tr   translate characters in a file

        tr [options] [string1 [string2]]

Copies standard input to standard output, substituting or deleting characters based on **string1** and **string2.** Input characters in **string1** are mapped to the corresponding characters in **string2.**

Useful Options

-d Deletes input characters in **string1.**
-s Squeezes multiple occurrences of characters in **string2.**

Examples

tr "[a-z]" "[A-Z]" < inputfile > outputfile
Translates all alphabetic characters in **inputfile** to uppercase and stores output in **outputfile.**

tr -s "" "\012" < dbl.report > sngl.report
Squeezes out blank lines in file **dbl.report** and stores output in file **sngl.report** (**string1** is empty).

tr -d "\015\024\035\037" < special.ch > plain
Deletes all characters corresponding to octal 15, 24, 35, and 37 from file **special.ch** and stores output in file **plain.**

vi   visual (screen) editor

         vi [options] [file(s)]

vi is a screen text editor based on **ex.** The correct terminal characteristics must be in **/etc/termcap,** and environment variable **TERM** must be correctly defined.

wc   word, character, and line counter

        wc [options] [file(s)]*

Counts lines, words, and characters in the named files or in the standard input.

Useful Options

-l Give line count only.
-c Give character count only.
-w Give word count only.

Examples

wc /etc/passwd
Give line, word, and character count of password file.

who | wc -l
Give the number of people logged into UNIX (count the lines in the output of **who**).

III. SYSTEM STATUS COMMANDS

date   give the system date and time

        date

du   disk usage

            du [options] [dir(s)]

Summarize disk usage for directory **dir** or for **.** if **dir** is not specified.

Useful Options

-s Give total only.
-a Give size of each file.

Examples

du
Disk usage for current directory and everything below it.

du -s ~
Disk usage (summary only) for home directory and everything below it.

env   display the current environment variables

            env

id   (non BSD) give user and group identification

        id

kill   terminate a process

            kill [-signal_number] process_id(s)

Terminate process **process_id.**

Examples

kill 546
Terminate process number 546.

kill -9 546
Send a signal 9 to process 546.

mail   send or read mail

Different versions of this program exist on different systems.

Examples

mail
Read your mail.

mail sara kellen < **letter**
Send **letter** to **sara** and **kellen.**

mail scott
Type letter to **scott** (read from standard input) and end input with **control-D**.

news   read system news

Different versions of this program exist on different systems. **news** may include a network bulletin board as well as local items.

ps   process status

```
ps [options]
```

Report process information for user or system processes. Options allowed may vary.

Examples

ps
Give process status on user's current processes.

ps -efl (non-BSD), **ps -ax** (BSD)
Give process status on all processes in system (use long format).

pwd   print working directory

Give full pathname of current working directory.

stty   set or display terminal characteristics

```
stty [options]
```

Examples

stty
Display current terminal settings.

stty -echo
Turn off echoing.

stty nl2
Pad **newline** characters.

stty intr ˆc
Set interrupt character to **control-C.**

tset   terminal set program

        tset [options] terminal-id

Tell UNIX what kind of terminal you have.

Useful Options

  - Write the name of the terminal to the standard output.
  -ec Set erase character to **c.**
  -kc Set kill character to **c.**

Examples

tset vt100
Set terminal to **vt100.**

setenv TERM `tset - -m dialup:vt100`
A hardwired terminal is set properly from data in file **/etc/ttytype.** A terminal on a dial-up port is set to a **vt100.** The terminal type is written to standard output (and captured with command substitution to set environment variable **TERM**).

tty   display special device corresponding to current terminal

        tty

whereis   (BSD only) give pathnames corresponding to command

  Example

  whereis who vi
  Tell where commands and documentation for **who** and **vi** are.

who   who is logged onto UNIX

        who

write   write to another user

        write user [ttyname]

write sends lines of text from your terminal to **user**. If **user** is logged on more than once, you may specify a **tty** identification. **user** responds by executing **write** concurrently. **write** terminates when it reads an **EOF.**

Examples

write eric
Initiate written communication with **eric**.

write tom tty15
Write to **tom** on terminal **/dev/tty15**.

IV. SOFTWARE DEVELOPMENT COMMANDS

ar   archive and library maintainer

```
ar key [position] library member_name(s)
```

Archive according to **key** using archive file **library** and constituents **member_name.**

Keys

d Delete
r Replace
q Append quickly
t Produce a table
p Print the named **member_names**
m Move
x Extract

Examples

ar r mylib scanner.o mailer.o
Replace files **scanner.o** and **mailer.o** in library **mylib.**

ar x mylib
Extract all files from **mylib.**

cb   C beautifier

```
cb
```

cb reads the standard input and produces a C program with appropriate spacing and indentation to indicate its structure.

Example

cb < mailer1.c > mailer2.c
Produce a beautified C program from **mailer1.c** and write it to **mailer2.c.**

cc   C compiler

```
cc [options] file(s)
```

Compile **file(s)** using named **options.** Files must be of the form **file.c.**

Useful Options

-c Produce an object file but don't call the loader.
-o out Name the output file **out** instead of **a.out.**
-s Strip the symbol table.
-O Optimize object code.

Examples

cc -c driver.c
Compile module **driver.c** (but omit loading step).

cc driver.c -O -s -o driver
Compile module **driver.c,** optimize, strip symbol table, and place object file in **driver.**

cmp   compare two files

```
cmp [options] file1 file2
```

Compare files **file1** and **file2.** If **file1** is **-,** the standard input is used. Exit code 0 means the files are the same, 1 means the files differ, and 2 means a file is not accessible or an argument is missing.

Useful Options

-l Display the byte number and the differing bytes for each difference (long listing).
-s No output; just return proper exit codes.

Examples

cmp a.out mailer
Compare **a.out** and **mailer.**

cmp -l mailer1 mailer2
Compare files **mailer1** and **mailer2.** Display each difference.

nm   display namelist

```
nm [options] [file(s)]
```

nm displays the symbol table of each file in the argument list. If no file is specified, **a.out** is used.

Useful Options

-g Display global symbols.

-n Sort output numerically (instead of alphabetically).

-u Display only undefined symbols.

Example

nm -u mailer
Display undefined symbols in object file **mailer.**

od octal, decimal, hexadecimal, or ASCII dump

```
od [option] [file(s)]*
```

od displays **file** (or the standard input if no file is specified) in format indicated in **option.**
Octal is the default format.

Useful Options

-a bytes as ASCII format

-b bytes as unsigned octal

-d words as unsigned decimal

-h words as unsigned hexadecimal

-o words as unsigned octal

-x words as hexadecimal

Examples

od - a .
Display the contents of the current directory in ASCII format.

od scanner
Display contents of file **scanner** in unsigned octal format.

size size of an object file

```
size [object_file(s)]
```

Displays the number of bytes required by the text, data, and BSS portions of an object
file. Displays sum in hexadecimal and decimal. If no **object_file** specified, **size** uses
a.out.

Examples

size
Display size information on **a.out.**

size echo2 gets
Display size information on object files **echo2** and **gets.**

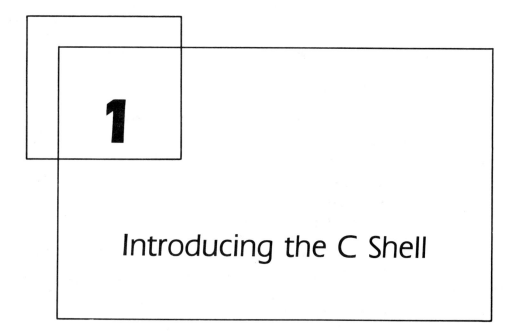

Introducing the C Shell

1.1 WHAT IS THE C SHELL?

One of UNIX's most important components is its user interface, or *shell*. Unlike the situation in many other operating systems, the shell has no special status. It is just another program. Since it can therefore be revised or replaced with relatively little trouble, several alternative shells with different features have become available. One of the most popular is the C shell, developed by Bill Joy at the University of California (Berkeley).

Why is the C shell popular, and why is this entire book dedicated to describing it? The C shell has a wide variety of features aimed at full-time professional users, system administrators, and system analysts. It allows many kinds of shorthand, customization, job control, and access to past commands. It even provides an extensive command language with a syntax similar to the C programming language (hence the name). The C shell can make UNIX much easier to use and can allow rapid development of utilities, special user interfaces and procedure files, and even general-purpose programs. If you use UNIX on a daily basis, administer a UNIX installation, develop UNIX-based applications, or work with users of UNIX systems, you will find many C shell features to be convenient, efficient, and easy to use and explain.

1.2. WHAT ARE THE C SHELL'S FUNCTIONS?

The C shell's main purpose is simply to read and interpret your commands and provide the interface with UNIX. That is, it accepts your command lines, checks the syntax, calls the appropriate built-in or UNIX commands, and takes control when other commands finish. It is interactive because it responds to your instructions and reports errors, status, and results.

But the C shell can do much more than this:

- It can let you customize your system (or environment) to suit the way you work.

- It can allow you to abbreviate long names, commands, and sequences of commands.

- It can save old commands so that you can repeat them, revise them, correct them, or maintain a record of them.

- It can provide job control so that you can create new jobs, execute them either with or without terminal interaction (*foreground* or *background*), and terminate them.

- It can let you write programs at the command level. These can simply execute commands sequentially or use constructs such as loops and decisions. They may even have arguments and allow interaction.

1.3 HOW DO YOU USE THE C SHELL?

You use the C shell in three ways:

1. Interactively, to execute UNIX commands.
2. In customization, to define a working environment.
3. In programming, to create new tools as C shell programs (called *scripts*).

Let's look at each of these in more detail.

Interactive Features

The C shell is handy interactively because of the shorthand it provides. You can assign short names to long pathnames, complex commands with options and arguments, or entire sequences of commands. You can also create a history list and recall commands when you need them again. When you use the history list to recall commands, you do not need to remember the order of the arguments, the options, the names of the files, operator precedence, special notation, restrictions, or unusual forms. The C shell also lets you use special characters and other shorthand to refer to entire groups of files, run one command to provide arguments for another, and connect the output of one command to the input of another.

Customization

The C shell has special files that it uses to define your working environment. There is one for logging in, another for logging out, and a third for initializing the shell and running scripts. By placing commands in these files, you can control terminal characteristics, prompts, pathnames for directory searches, and permissions. You can also make your own special tools available automatically and provide your own logout and other custom procedures. The C shell can make your computer system act the way you want and suit your working style, needs, and applications.

Programming

Shell scripts are a powerful tool for invoking and organizing UNIX commands. They can even substitute for systems programs written in a general-purpose language such as C. At the simplest level, they can invoke one command after another. This is comparable to the batch or procedure files provided in many operating systems (e.g., MS-DOS). This keeps you from having to remember where you are in a sequence, look up commands in a manual, or do a large amount of repetitive typing. In fact, if the entire operation is repetitive (such as printing a set of files or reports, updating an accounting database, or recompiling a set of programs), you may be able to leave the computer completely unattended. The script will provide commands automatically when they are needed.

The C shell's more advanced programming options can handle an even wider range of problems. Decision sequences and loops allow a C shell script to perform almost any programming task. A script can provide interaction, interrupt and error handling, and status reporting just like UNIX commands. Typical applications include file management, format conversions, disk or file housekeeping, searches, cataloging, on-line help, electronic mail, and security management. Here the C shell acts much like the extended job control languages available on large computers.

One key factor is that shell scripts are easy to write. All you need is an editor. You don't need to compile a script, link it, or load it. Debugging is straightforward, since the C shell has options that display intermediate output as a script executes.

1.4 TYPICAL EXAMPLES OF C SHELL USE

Let us describe how typical users might take advantage of the C shell's features.

A C programmer could assign special short names to the programs he or she is currently developing. The programmer could also abbreviate commands that provide extended or printed error output or run the debugger with a special list of options. The record of past commands comes in handy for repeating all or part of the standard edit-compile-link-load-debug sequence. Job control lets the programmer edit one program while a long compilation or linking process executes. The programmer could even write a shell script that compiles a long program in the background (freeing the terminal for other work), saves errors in a special file, loads and links the output if there are no errors, provides a printed listing, and places a copy in a common directory. Other scripts could ensure that all programs throughout the system are current versions, check whether a utility is already available, and determine whether and where a particular function is defined.

A writer could assign special short names to his or her current text files or to standard files (so-called boilerplate) that must be inserted in specific places. The writer could also abbreviate commands that run the word processor, spelling checker, grammar checker, print formatter, and index generator with special sets of options or parameters. The record of past commands is handy for repeating all or part of the edit–spelling check–grammar check–print format–print cycle. Job control lets the writer work on a new document while the system is checking, formatting, or printing an old one. A shell script could first submit a file to the word processor, transfer the output to the spelling checker, and then either return to the word processor or go on to the print formatter, depending on whether any misspellings were found. Other scripts could find and load sets of standard text files, delete obsolete versions of documents, and combine files into complete reports with backups.

A financial analyst could assign special short names to the current accounting files, latest data from a remote or centralized database, or a spreadsheet template. The analyst could also abbreviate standard options for a spreadsheet, graphics program, database, statistical analysis program, or report writer. The record of past commands is useful for a repetitive sequence of loading data, verifying it, analyzing it in a spreadsheet, and testing the results in a statistical program. Job control lets the analyst examine graphs or enter a new spreadsheet while the system is recalculating a large worksheet or financial model, sorting a database, or printing a report. A script could load data from a mainframe, analyze it using a spreadsheet template or financial model, graph the results, place the numeric output and graphs in a report, make backup copies of all key files, and send summaries to all departments. Other scripts could check whether a database is available locally before loading it from a central facility, ensure the protection of files containing sensitive financial data, and insert a financial summary as an appendix to a prospectus or quarterly report.

C shell scripts can be particularly helpful for users who are unfamiliar with UNIX. A script can handle all the details of login, setting up or loading files, calling programs, transferring data between programs, changing formats, backing up files, sending files or messages to other users, and logging out. The user does not have to know anything about UNIX or the shell, nor does the user have to cope with file system notation, command syntax, confusing error messages, or an enormous set of manuals. A standard script can start up automatically and lead the user interactively through each step.

Furthermore, C shell scripts are an easy way to implement extra or custom utilities, perform housekeeping functions, provide on-line help, monitor system status and security, and even handle simple functions such as reminders, telephone list management, and appointment calendars. This book contains many practical example scripts; UNIX installations often maintain a library of common scripts for general use.

1.5 WHAT SYSTEMS DOES THE C SHELL RUN ON?

The C shell runs on most UNIX systems, including Versions 6 and 7, System III, and System V from AT&T. Designed at the University of California at Berkeley, it runs on all systems from the Berkeley Software Distribution (BSD). These include 2.9BSD, 4.1BSD, 4.2BSD, and 4.3BSD. Systems based on any of these versions will usually include the C shell. Note that the C shell is just a program (like other UNIX utilities) written in the C language.

There are two widely distributed versions of the C shell. The one with the most features runs on Berkeley 4.1BSD and later versions. Its unique facilities include enhanced job control and directory stacks for easy switching of directories and return to previous directories. It also has pattern-matching operators and an extended list of predefined variables. The C shell's job control features do not work on UNIX versions 6 and 7, System III, or System V.

The second version of the C shell is included in many proprietary implementations of UNIX, such as Microsoft's XENIX. These systems may be based on Version 7, System III, or System V. They generally lack enhanced job control, pattern-matching operators, and some predefined variables. Systems advertised as having "Berkeley enhancements" usually have this version of the C shell.

If you are not sure whether your system has the C shell, check your UNIX documentation. Section 1 should contain a manual page describing **csh(1)**. If your system lacks the C shell, reading about its use may encourage you to ask your system administrator or manufacturer to implement it.

1.6 WHY THE C SHELL?

All versions of UNIX have a standard shell, called the Bourne shell. It is compact, requires minimal resources, and executes quickly. Developed at AT&T, it has become the most widely used shell.

The Bourne shell and the C shell are not compatible syntactically. Both interactive commands and shell scripts differ.

Bill Joy wrote the C shell as part of the ongoing UNIX updating activity at Berkeley. Among his aims were to allow users to easily substitute custom programs for existing UNIX commands. The extended setup files and the ability to name or rename command sequences (called an *alias* mechanism) are particularly useful in this regard. Joy also made the syntax for shell scripts similar to that of the C language to promote consistency and readability.

The C shell was originally designed on a large machine, where system resources and memory were not at a premium. It executes slowly in many small computer implementations. However, as low-cost computers become more powerful and the cost of memory decreases, this will become less of an issue.

The only way really to appreciate the advantages of the C shell is to see it in action. This book will show you what the C shell can do. Our aim is to encourage you to use the C shell by demonstrating how handy and powerful it is in a wide variety of applications. Let's first take a quick tour of some of its key features.

2

Climbing into Your Shell:
A Tour of the C Shell

This chapter provides a whirlwind tour of the C shell. Like a seven-day tour of six European countries, it concentrates on the highlights rather than on the fine points. Chapters 3 through 10 present more details. The best way to appreciate the brief tour is to log on and run the examples as you read.

Before we begin, a word of caution: UNIX systems vary. Therefore, different versions of the C shell exist on different UNIX systems. Berkeley BSD versions, for example, have features not found in XENIX. Moreover, UNIX commands sometimes have different options. For this tour we have tried to present examples that work in most C shell environments. You should, however, bring along your UNIX user's guide (along with a few travel belongings) to resolve any problems.

Our tour begins at login. You'll see how to set up the C shell as your command interpreter. You will also learn how to display messages at login, specify what kind of terminal you have, and correct typing mistakes. We also introduce the C shell's special files; it uses these when you login, run shell programs (scripts), and logout.

Next we introduce the C shell's history and alias mechanisms. The history list lets you reissue commands or modify old ones. The alias mechanism lets you abbreviate often-used commands or sequences of commands.

Our tour continues with a look at the standard features of a UNIX shell. These provide input and output redirection, pipes, command groups, and background processes. These let you combine commands in many useful ways.

At the next stop we present C shell variables and command substitution. Variables let you save long character strings (such as filenames) and use them to build new commands. Command substitution lets you use one command's output within another.

The UNIX system encourages customization. You can create your own commands by writing C shell programs (*scripts*). All you do is use an editor to create and save a file of UNIX commands. When you make it executable, its name becomes a command. We will show you a typical shell script, starting with a simple version and adding enhancements as we learn new C shell features.

Shell scripts can read input from the keyboard, display output, and have their output piped. This part of the tour describes the C shell's I/O features.

A script can do much more than just execute one command after another. The C shell allows loops and decision sequences, just like a programming language. At this brief stop we introduce the C shell's programming features and demonstrate them by modifying the **.login** setup file.

Some shell scripts will become new utilities. If you intend to use them often, you'll want them to check for errors. A script can report errors and exit with a special status, just like an operating system utility.

The final part of our tour returns us to aliases. Here we learn how to pass arguments and use shell variables to create useful commands.

We end the tour with (as expected) a goodbye. One C shell special file does its work at logout. We show you how to run commands in it before signing off.

That's our tour schedule. Good luck!

2.1 GETTING IN: LOGIN AND SETUP FILES

Let's start at the very beginning; for UNIX users, life begins at login.

Logging In to UNIX

Your first look at UNIX should reveal a message like

```
login:
```

You must respond with your username, RETURN, and your password. If you identify yourself correctly, UNIX should grant you access to the system. What appears next may vary—it may be a greeting, a message of the day, or the date and time of your last login. You may also see the message

```
You have mail.
```

which indicates that an "electronic letter" (hopefully not junk mail) is waiting in your UNIX mailbox. Regardless of what you see, it should end with the command or shell prompt, either **$** (standard shell) or **%** (C shell).

If you see **$,** ask your system administrator to change your account to use the C shell automatically. If you are the system administrator, look in Chapter 9 and Appendix F ("UNIX Database Files") for information on how to do this. For now, just type

```
$ csh
%
```

to execute the C shell.

Setting Up Your Terminal

You may want to customize some terminal settings to coincide with your habits. The **stty** (set terminal) command lets you do this. From the shell prompt, type

```
% stty
```

to see your terminal's current settings. (Remember to end each command line with the RETURN or ENTER Key.) Look for these parameters:

```
erase
kill
intr
```

If you don't see them, try the **-a** option with **stty**. The **erase** parameter is the backspace command, **kill** cancels the current command line, and **intr** is the interrupt key. **kill** and **erase** are only effective before you press RETURN; you may use **intr** at any time. Suppose you see the following settings (yours may be different):

```
intr = ^c; erase = #; kill = @;
```

Here, **#** erases the previous character, **@** cancels the entire command line, and control-c (**^c**) interrupts the current command. Let's change these settings using **stty:**

```
% stty erase ^h
% stty kill ^x
% stty intr DEL
```

This sequence changes **erase** to control-h (**^h**), **kill** to control-x (**^x**), and **intr** to the **DEL** key (not the word *DEL*).

These are the most commonly used terminal settings. You'll also want to set up your terminal for the **vi** editor. To do this, you must set a UNIX environment variable called (you guessed it) **TERM.** Type the command

```
% env
```

(or **printenv,** if you don't have **env**) and look for **TERM.** You'll need to set it to the code for your terminal. For example, suppose you have a VT100 terminal. The command

```
% setenv TERM vt100
```

tells **vi** what you have. Check with your system administrator if you aren't sure what code to use.

The C Shell's Special Files

The C shell has special files you can use to customize your working environment. Type the command

```
% ls -a
```

to display the file names in your current directory. See if the names

```
.cshrc
.login
.logout
```

appear. These are your setup (and shut-down) files. The C shell, as you might expect, reads the **.login** file when you login and the **.logout** file when you logout. The **.cshrc** file defines special C shell characteristics. As you might guess, we'll start with **.login.**

The .login Setup File

Changes such as redefined terminal settings will stay active only during your current login session. You must reset them every time you login. To avoid this nuisance, put them in your **.login** file using any UNIX editor (e.g., **ex, vi,** or **ed**). For example, you could enter the following:

```
stty erase ^h
stty kill ^x
stty intr DEL

echo "Welcome to the C shell."
```

The **stty** commands are the same as before. We add the **echo** command to display a welcoming message. When you login now, the C shell executes these commands automatically, just as if you had typed them at the keyboard.

2.2. SHORTHAND WITH THE C SHELL: HISTORY AND ALIAS MECHANISMS

Most users find themselves issuing many identical or similar commands. It is therefore convenient to be able to reissue, edit, and abbreviate command lines.

The C shell keeps a record of your commands (called a *history list*) and allows you to create command names (called *aliases*). You can even make these options available automatically at login.

History List

When using the history list, you generally want the current command number displayed at the prompt. This makes it easier to refer to previous commands (we call these *events*) by number. To do this, you must change the prompt from its default value % with the command

```
% set prompt = '\!% '
```

A number should now appear before the % (we assume **2%** in the following discussion). Be sure to use single quotation marks and type a space after the % and a backslash before the **!.** The C shell increments the command number automatically from now on.

Now let's initialize the history list. The command

```
2% set history = 13
```

tells the C shell to start saving commands. There's room for 13 (you're not superstitious, are you?); the C shell drops the earliest one to make room when the list is full. Enter the following commands (we show only **history**'s output here):

```
3% ls -a
4% date
5% who
6% history
     2 set history = 13
     3 ls -a
     4 date
     5 who
     6 history
```

The C shell stores the **ls, date,** and **who** commands in your history list with their numbers. The **history** command displays the list. Note that **history** also appears in the list (after all, **history** has a history too, circular as that may sound).

Let's examine some history commands. We invoke most of them with **!.** For example, **!!** repeats the last command (we call this a *redo*), **!4** repeats command **4,** and **!v** repeats the most recent command beginning with the letter **v.**

For example, let's use the **more** command (it pages a file's contents on the terminal) to examine the password file, **/etc/passwd:**

```
7% more /etc/passwd
```

To execute this command again, simply type !!:

```
8% !!
more /etc/passwd
```

The C shell displays the command before executing it. Now let's use the visual editor (**vi**) to examine the system file **/usr/include/stdio.h:**

```
9% vi /usr/include/stdio.h
```

To repeat command 7, we can type

```
10% !7
more /etc/passwd
```

and to edit **stdio.h** again we can type

```
11% !v
vi /usr/include/stdio.h
```

The history mechanism also allows us to build new commands from parts of old ones. To get a long listing of file **/usr/include/stdio.h,** for example, we can type

```
12% ls -l !$
ls -l /usr/include/stdio.h
```

!$ indicates the last word of the previous command. To correct typing mistakes, use the caret symbol (^). For example, if we mistakenly type

```
13% ls /user/include
/user/include not found
```

all we must enter to correct **user** to **usr** is

```
14% ^er^r
ls /usr/include
```

The C shell replaces **er** with **r** in the previous command. Chapter 6 describes the history mechanism in more detail.

Aliases

An alias is an abbreviation for a frequently used command or series of commands. For example, say you want to abbreviate **history** as **h.** The command

```
15% alias h history
```

does this. Similarly, the command

```
16% alias list ls -l
```

makes **list** display a long listing of our directory.

Now let's assign an alias to two commands:

```
17% alias blocks 'pwd; du -s'
```

Alias **blocks** uses **pwd** (print working directory) to display the directory name and **du** (disk usage with the size option) to report how many blocks it contains. Here we put quotation marks around the definition because the semicolon is a special character used to separate commands. When we type the alias, as in

```
18% blocks
/u/sara
10
```

we see the output of **pwd** and **du.** The directory **/u/sara** (denoted by **.**) contains 10 blocks of data.

The **alias** command with no arguments displays all defined aliases:

```
19% alias
blocks    pwd; du -s
h         history
list      (ls -l)
```

We'll see more of aliases later, but let's turn our attention now to making these definitions available automatically at login.

The .cshrc Setup File

Before processing the **.login** file, the C shell reads and executes another setup file—the **.cshrc** file. This is where you should store commands used to initialize the history list, change the prompt, and define aliases. For example, we could place the following statements in **.cshrc:**

```
set prompt = '\!% '
set history = 13
alias h history
alias list ls -l
alias blocks 'pwd; du -s'
```

Now these definitions will be set automatically at login time.

2.3 MAKING THINGS HAPPEN: ISSUING COMMANDS

In this section we'll explore ways to issue commands to the C shell. We'll use simple UNIX commands and special C shell notation to build more complex commands. You will, for example, see how to control a command's input and output and how to connect commands. You'll also learn how to group commands and run background jobs. We'll introduce the file expansion characters, which let you specify groups of files and abbreviate long names.

The UNIX File System

Since most commands operate on files, we must explore the organization of the file system. UNIX's file system is hierarchical—it branches out from a single point (the *root*). It may include many directories that in turn contain subdirectories or files. As a UNIX user, you have your own starting point (a *node*) within the file system. Everything below it belongs to you. This node, your *home directory,* is the starting directory for each UNIX session. By using UNIX commands, you can create files and subdirectories in your private file system. You also have limited access to the rest of the file system. Finally, you can "move around" within the file system by changing your current working directory.

To specify a UNIX file, you simply type its name as long as the file is in the current working directory. If it is somewhere else, you must specify where. You can do this by naming the sequence of directories (called a *path*) that leads to the file. A path can start either at the root or at your current directory.

Simple Commands

We have already used the C shell to issue simple commands such as **stty, set, history,** and **alias.** Now let's examine the file system.

The **pwd** (print working directory) command displays the full pathname of our current working directory:

```
1% pwd
/u/sara
```

Note that slashes separate directory names, and the initial / designates the root. **/u/sara** is our home directory. Now let's copy a file from another directory to it using **cp** (copy):

```
2% cp /usr/include/stdio.h /u/sara
```

This puts a copy of file **stdio.h** in directory **/u/sara.** We can verify that it worked by listing the contents of our working directory:

```
3% ls
stdio.h
```

Are you curious to see what's in **stdio.h?** It is a standard I/O file for C. Try the **cat** (concatenate) command:

```
4% cat stdio.h
```

We omit the output here. Since it scrolls rapidly (even speed readers have problems keeping up with 9600 baud), let's use **more,** a paging utility:

```
5% more !$
more stdio.h
```

Note that we used the history mechanism to refer to the last word of command 4.

Now let's create a new subdirectory using **mkdir** (make directory):

```
6% mkdir system
```

Since we'll be working with files in **system,** let's make it our working directory. We use **cd** (change directory) and **pwd** to verify the change:

```
7% cd system
8% pwd
/u/sara/system
```

Let's copy two files to our new directory: the system password file (**/etc/passwd**) and the system group file (**/etc/group**). We use **cp** again in

```
9% cp /etc/passwd /etc/group .
```

The single dot is shorthand for the current working directory. Again, we verify the contents of this directory:

```
10% ls
passwd group
```

The files are present. Let's rename (using **mv** for move) **passwd** as **password** and remove **group** (using **rm**):

```
11% mv passwd password
12% rm group
```

You may issue several commands to the C shell on one line. To do this, separate them with semicolons. For example, let's return to our home directory and list its contents. We will put the two commands (**cd** and the **list** alias) on a single line:

```
13% cd ..; list
total 6
-rw-r--r-- 1 sara proj1 2046 Feb 15 14:29 stdio.h
drwxr-xr-x 2 sara proj1   80 Feb 15 16:03 system
```

The two dots indicate the directory above the current one (called the *parent*). Note that our home directory now contains two entries: file **stdio.h** and directory **system.**

Input and Output Redirection

You can easily instruct the C shell to use files for command input and output instead of the terminal. We call this *redirection*. Let's consider output redirection first. The command

```
14% ls /usr/bin > comlist
```

stores the list of names in the **/usr/bin** directory in a file called **comlist.** The > symbol redirects output. Note that the C shell creates file **comlist** if it doesn't already exist.

Using output redirection with the **cat** command lets you create short text files without an editor. For example, the command

```
15% cat > memo
Budget meeting at 10:45
control-d
```

tells the C shell to read from the keyboard (until you type **control-d**) and store the input in file **memo.** You can also add lines to the end of an existing file. The command

```
16% echo "Send report via UPS" >> memo
```

makes the C shell add the output of the **echo** command to the existing **memo** file.

Input redirection can, for example, let us use the **mail** command to send ourselves the **memo** file as a reminder of the morning's schedule. The command

```
17% mail sara < memo
```

instructs the C shell to use file **memo** as input instead of the keyboard. The < symbol indicates input redirection.

Connecting Commands with Pipes

The C shell provides another tool to control a command's input and output. You can connect the output of one command to the input of another with a *pipe*. For example, the command

```
18% echo "Send budget report by courier" | mail sara
```

mails updated instructions to **sara.** The **mail** command uses the output of **echo** as its input. Similarly, the command

```
19% list /usr/include | grep "^d"
```

uses the **list** alias and the **grep** command in a pipe. **list** displays a long listing of all files and directories in **/usr/include,** and **grep** searches for a pattern. The pipe results in the selection of only directory names from **/usr/include.** How does this work? Try each command separately. **list** by itself returns all files and directories in **/usr/include:**

```
-rw-r--r--   3 bin   bin   12146 Sep 17 11:04 a.out.h
. . . . .
drwxr-xr-x   3 bin   bin     208 Oct 11 11:59 dos
. . . . .
drwxr-xr-x   2 bin   bin     672 Oct 11 11:57 sys
. . . . .
```

Working from **list**'s output, **grep** selects only lines beginning (^) with **d** (directory names). You'll see the output

```
drwxr-xr-x   3 bin   bin   208 Oct 11 11:59 dos
drwxr-xr-x   2 bin   bin   672 Oct 11 11:57 sys
```

This is a long listing of directory names in **/usr/include.**

Command Groups

We have already seen how to combine commands with a semicolon. To redirect the output of multiple commands, group them by enclosing them in parentheses. For example, the command

```
20% (date;who;pwd) > status
```

redirects the output of **date, who,** and **pwd** to file **status.**
    This is different from

```
21% date;who;pwd > status
```

which redirects only **pwd**'s output.

Background Commands

So far we have issued only *foreground* commands. The C shell cannot accept further input until these finish. We can also execute a command in the *background;* this allows several tasks to run at the same time. Typically, you place commands (or jobs) in the background when they are time-consuming and don't require interactive input or produce terminal output. Examples are sorts, compilations, spreadsheet calculations, equation solutions, text formatting operations, and long printouts.

To make the C shell create a background job, simply put the **&** character at the end of the command. For example,

```
22% du -s /etc > disk_storage&
62
```

runs the disk usage command (**du**) for the /**etc** directory and saves its output in the file **disk_storage.** 62 is a process identification (PID) that UNIX assigns to identify a particular job.

The **ps** (process status) command reports status information on all executing jobs. The **kill** command lets you cancel a background job (nonviolently). For example,

```
23% kill 62
```

cancels the **du** command (process 62).

File Expansion Characters

The C shell lets you apply commands to groups of files and abbreviate filenames. Several characters have special meanings through a mechanism called *file expansion*. Suppose, for example, we have the following files in our current directory:

```
24% ls
main.c main.doc main.s sub1.c sub2.c sub3.c sub4.c
```

We can use file expansion characters to list parts of this directory. The most common is *****, a wildcard meaning "any characters." Study these examples:

```
25% ls sub*
sub1.c sub2.c sub3.c sub4.c
```

sub* specifies all file or directory names that begin with **sub,** including the name **sub** itself.

```
26% ls *.c
main.c sub1.c sub2.c sub3.c sub4.c
```

*.c specifies all file or directory names that end in **.c.**
The expansion characters, **[ ]**, specify a list of characters:

```
27% ls *.[cs]
main.c sub1.c sub2.c sub3.c sub4.c main.s
```

*.[cs] specifies all names ending in **.c** or **.s.** We can also use brackets to specify a range:

```
28% ls sub[2-4].c
sub2.c sub3.c sub4.c
```

Another useful special character is ~, representing your home directory. For example, try the command

```
29% du ~ > disk_storage&
```

This runs the disk usage command on your home directory and sends the output to the file **disk_storage,** all in the background.

You can also use braces {} to save on typing. For example, the command

```
30% ls /usr/include/{signal.h,stdio.h}
/usr/include/signal.h /usr/include/stdio.h
```

selects only the **signal.h** and **stdio.h** files from **/usr/include.**

2.4 TAKING THE LOAD OFF YOUR FINGERS: SHELL VARIABLES AND COMMAND SUBSTITUTION

C shell variables hold strings. You can store pathnames in them and use them in commands. You can also use the output of one command as an argument for another. We call this *command substitution*.

Shell Variables

Shell variables can save time and reduce typing errors. For example, the following sequence sets the name **c** to the string **/usr/include:**

```
1% set c = /usr/include
2% ls $c
3% cp $c/signal.h .
```

The C shell substitutes **/usr/include** for **$c.** This is a convenient way to abbreviate long pathnames.

We can also combine shell variables with braces. For example, the command

```
4% more $c/{signal.h,stdio.h}
```

pages only files **signal.h** and **stdio.h** from **/usr/include.** It's as if you typed

```
5% more /usr/include/signal.h /usr/include/stdio.h
```

Command Substitution

The C shell lets you control the output of commands in several ways. We've seen how to redirect output or pipe it to another command's input. Command substitution lets us put the output of one command inside another. To do this, enclose the embedded command in grave accent marks (` , sometimes called "back quotation marks").

For example, suppose we want to deal with part of the **date** command's output. All we must do is the following:

```
6% set d = `date`
7% echo $d
Sat Feb 2 10:45:22 PST 1985
```

This sets a shell variable **d** to the string output from the **date** command. We call **d** a *wordlist*. Now we can reference individual words as **$d[1], $d[2],** and so on. The command

```
8% echo Today is $d[1]. The time is $d[4]
Today is Sat. The time is 10:45:22
```

demonstrates how this technique lets us control the format of **date**'s output.

2.5 A FIRST STEP TOWARD AUTOMATION: A SIMPLE C SHELL SCRIPT

UNIX lets you extend and tailor your personal system. One way to create new tools is through C shell programs. We call them shell *scripts*. Using an editor such as **vi,** you enter standard UNIX command lines into a file and make it executable. When you run the script, the C shell executes the commands just as if you had typed them from the keyboard. They can involve redirection, pipes, or background commands. Scripts can also have arguments such as filenames.

Let's look at a typical example.

The ppd (Prepend) Script: First Version

Suppose you want to keep a record of your disk usage. You plan to use the command line

```
1% (date; du ~) >> ~/disk_storage&
```

This results in the background execution of **date** followed by **du** (disk usage) applied to your home directory. We add the output to the file ~/**disk_storage.**

Running this command updates ~/**disk_storage.** The only problem is that the latest information goes at the end of the file instead of at the beginning. Let us create a script called **ppd** (for *prepend*) to append at the beginning. Script **ppd** will have a filename as its argument and will read from the standard input. This allows us to use it in a pipe as follows:

```
2% (date; du ~) | ppd ~/disk_storage&
```

Here's the text for **ppd** (the line numbering is for reference only).

```
1   # csh script to prepend standard input to file argument
2   # Version 1
3
4   set tf = /tmp/ppd.$$          # name temp file
5   set dest = $argv[1]           # get argument name
6
7   cat - $dest > $tf             # copy standard input, $dest to $tf
8   mv $tf $dest                  # replace original file
```

File **ppd** contains two UNIX commands plus variable definitions and comments for documentation. The first character in a script must be the symbol **#**. **#** is also the comment symbol; the C shell ignores everything after it on a line.

We use a shell variable to hold the pathname of the temporary file. UNIX provides the **/tmp** directory for general use. The idea here is to make **ppd** a tool anyone can use at any time. Line 4 defines a temporary filename using the current process number (**$$**). Since this number is unique systemwide, two users calling **ppd** at the same time won't try to use the same temporary file.

Line 4 sets variable **tf** to the temporary filename. Line 5 sets **dest** to **$argv[1]**, a C shell variable that lets scripts refer to command line arguments. **$argv[1]** is the first argument, **$argv[2]** the second, and so forth.

Line 7 uses **cat** to combine the standard input and the argument file into a new file called **$tf**. The − option reads the standard input first. Line 8 renames **$tf** to the original filename (**~/disk_storage**). **~/disk_storage** now has the latest information at the beginning.

To make **ppd** executable, we use the **chmod** (change mode) command:

```
3% chmod +x ppd
```

Enter the **ppd** script and run it a few times (use your history list!).

2.6 GIVING INFORMATION AND GETTING RESULTS: INPUT AND OUTPUT

C shell scripts can read character data directly from the keyboard and provide output on the terminal screen. You may, for example, want to prompt for keyboard input or display error messages. We'll approach these subjects inside out and consider output first.

Output

We have already used **echo** to display strings. It writes its arguments to the standard output (by default, your terminal). For example, the following script, called **status,** reports current status information:

```
1    # csh that gives system status
2
3    set d = `date`
4    echo "Today's date: $d[2-3] $d[6]"
5    echo "Current time: $d[4]"
6    echo Number of users: `who | wc -l `
7    echo Current disk storage: ` du -s ~`
```

Line 3 uses command substitution to assign the current date to variable **d.** Lines 4 and 5 print the date and time by accessing different words in **d.** Lines 6 and 7 also use command substitution to print the number of users logged in and the number of blocks in your (home directory) file system. We obtain the number of users by piping the output of **who** to **wc. wc** (with the **-l** option) simply counts the number of lines in the standard input.

Enter the **status** script, make it executable, and run it. Here's some typical output:

```
1% status
Today's date: Feb 09 85
Current time: 11:20:38
Number of users:    3
Current disk storage: 1754  /u/sara
```

Input

A shell script can use interactive input just like any other program. Let's look at an example.

Suppose you don't always login to your UNIX system from the same terminal. You may, for example, use either a TVI920 or a VT100. Each will require its own **TERM** variable as described previously in this tour.

Let's modify the **.login** file to ask what terminal you are using. We'll use **echo** for the prompt and the **gets** command to read from the keyboard. (Use **$<** in place of `gets` on BSD systems.) We'll then use the input string in the **setenv** command.

Include the following statements in your **.login** file:

```
echo -n "Input your terminal type: "
setenv TERM `gets`
```

The **echo** command displays the prompt; the **-n** option leaves the cursor on the same line. In XENIX, you'll need to use **\c** at the end of the prompt string instead of **-n.**

You then type your terminal code, and the C shell uses command substitution to make the input into an argument for **setenv.**

2.7 DECISION TIME: SELECTIVE EXECUTION

The tools presented so far let you combine UNIX commands to manipulate character strings. The C shell also has programming features. For example, it has loop constructs and **if** statements. These features make the C shell into a programming language as well as a simple command interpreter.

As in common high-level programming languages, **if** and **if-else** provide a decision-making capability. We will present examples that handle special cases and validate inputs.

if Statements

Let's modify **.login** for a special situation. Suppose you submit your work time sheets on Fridays. We'll use an **if** statement to check the day of the week; if it's Friday, we'll display a message that time sheets are due (you do want to get paid, don't you?). Here's the code to add to your **.login** file:

```
1    # csh to greet you in your .login file
2
3    set d = `date`                        # get date
4    echo "Today is $d[1]"
5    if ($d[1] == Fri) then
6      echo ================
7      echo Time sheets due!
8      echo ================
9    endif
10   unset d
```

Line 3 stores the date in **d** using command substitution. Line 4 prints the day of the week by accessing the first word in **d.** Lines 5 through 9 contain the **if** statement. Line 5 uses parentheses to create an expression (**$d[1] == Fri**). The **==** is a relational operator meaning "is equal to." If the expression is true, the C shell executes statements 6, 7, and 8. Line 9 marks the end of the **if** statement. Line 10 releases the shell variable **d; unset** is the opposite of **set.**

if-else Statements

We can extend our login reminder message to vary with the time of day. This can be helpful if you work strange hours. Enhance **.login** by including these statements:

```
 1   # csh to greet you in your . login file
 2
 3   set d = `date ' +%H %a' `              # get hour and day of week
 4   if ($d[1] <= 12) then
 5     echo −n Good morning. . .
 6   else if ($d[1] <= 18) then
 7     echo −n Good afternoon. . .
 8   else
 9     echo −n Good evening. . .
10   endif
11   echo Today is $d[2]
12   if ($d[2] == Fri) then
13     echo ================
14     echo Time sheets due!
15     echo ================
16   endif
17   unset d
```

Line 3 now executes the **date** command using **date**'s built-in formatting (not available with all versions of **date**). We quote the formatting string to make it a single argument. The two field descriptors (**%H** and **%a**) store the hour (00–23) and the day of the week in **d.** Since **d** is a wordlist, we refer to its first word as **$d[1]** and its second as **$d[2].** Lines 4 and 5 display "Good morning" if the hour is less than or equal to (<=) 12. Lines 6 and 7 similarly display "Good afternoon" if the hour is less than or equal to 18 (6 P.M.). Otherwise, line 9 prints "Good evening." Note that lines 11 and 12 refer to the day of the week as **$d[2]** instead of **$d[1].**

As an exercise, modify this script even further. How about having it display "Why are you still here?" between 9 P.M. and 8 A.M.?

2.8 SMARTER C SHELL PROGRAMS: CHECKING FOR ERRORS

To make your C shell scripts more robust, you will want to add error checking. For example, a script can verify that you gave it the correct number of arguments. Also, if the arguments are files, it can verify that they exist and are readable or writable. This avoids unexpected side effects (processing the wrong file, creating or destroying the wrong directory, etc.) caused by typing errors, misreadings, and other minor problems.

This section shows how to include error checking in shell scripts. You'll learn how to detect errors and return status to the C shell. You'll also see how the C shell checks file status.

The ppd (Prepend) Script: Second Version

Let's add error checking to the **ppd** script. Remember, **ppd** requires a single file argument. First, we'll use an **if** statement to check that it has one and only one argument. Calling **ppd** with an incorrect number of arguments makes it print an error message and return to the shell (using **exit**) with an error status. Next we will determine if the argument is a writable file. To do this we use another **if** statement with the C shell's built-in file inquiry operator. If the file is not writable, we check to see if it exists. If all is well, we execute the same statements as before. Note that this version forces you to prepend information to an existing file. That is, **ppd** won't create a destination file.

Here's the text:

```
1    # csh to prepend standard input to file argument
2    # Version 2
3
4    if ($#argv !=1) then                  # check for number of args
5      echo "Usage: ppd output_file"
6      exit 1                              #exit on error
7    endif
8
9    set tf = /tmp/ppd. $$                 # name temp file
10   set dest = $argv[1]                   # get argument name
11
12   if (-w $dest) then                    # make sure it's writable
13     cat - $dest > $tf                   # concatenate $tf with target
14     mv $tf $dest                        # replace original file
15     exit 0                              # exit with good status
16   endif
17
18   if (-e $dest) then                    # does it exist?
19     echo "ppd: $dest not writable. "
20   else
21     echo "ppd: $dest does not exist. "
22   endif
23   exit 1                                # exit on error
```

Line 4 checks for the correct number of arguments. The C shell keeps the number of arguments in the special variable **$#argv.** Lines 5 and 6 print an error message and exit if this variable is not 1 (**!=** means "not equal"). A nonzero exit status value indicates an error.

Line 12 uses the C shell's file inquiry operator (**-w**) to see if the file argument is writable. If it is, lines 13 and 14 perform the prepend operation. Line 15 terminates the script with good (0) status.

Lines 18 through 23 handle errors; they determine why the file is not writable. The possibilities are that it doesn't exist (line 21) or that we can't modify it (line 19). Line 18 uses the **-e** file inquiry operator to verify the file argument's existence. Line 23 returns an error status for either condition.

Let's test our enhanced **ppd** script. Suppose we use it in a pipe. The command

```
1% (date; du ~) | ppd
Usage: ppd output_file
```

indicates that the error occurred in **ppd,** not **date** or **du.** We forgot to specify a file argument.

Now suppose we want to put a block of text from file **header** in front of the text of **memo1.** By accident, we type **memo** instead of **memo1:**

```
2% ppd memo < header
ppd: memo does not exist.
```

The script detects the error and reports that file **memo** does not exist.

Finally, let's try to prepend the **header** file to the UNIX password file. The result is

```
3% ppd /etc/passwd < header
ppd: /etc/passwd not writable.
```

2.9 A ROSE BY ANY OTHER NAME: EFFECTIVE USE OF ALIASES

Aliases are more than shorthand for command sequences or different names for UNIX commands. They can have arguments, pipes, and variables. You can define an alias to perform a task and store it in **.cshrc** so that it's always available. Furthermore, aliases execute faster than shell scripts.

For example, suppose we want to generate a long listing of only directory names. Perhaps we want to know the permission bits or the owner's name. Let's define an alias called **ldir** using the **ls** and **grep** commands.

```
1% alias ldir 'ls -l \!* | grep "^d"'
```

Recall that we pipe **ls**'s output to **grep** to display only lines starting with **d** (directory names). The \!* notation allows us to pass arguments to **ldir.** The command

```
2% ldir /usr/include
drwxr-xr-x    3 bin    bin    208 Oct 11 11:59 dos
drwxr-xr-x    2 bin    bin    672 Oct 11 11:57 sys
```

shows the output for the **/usr/include** directory.

We may also want a command to list just directory names. This is useful for examining a directory containing many unknown filenames. We create an alias called **dir** for this purpose:

```
3% alias dir \
'set d = `ls -1F \!* |grep /`; if ($#d) echo "$d:gh";unset d'
```

This definition is tricky. Type a RETURN after the \ and continue through the whole line. Try **dir** on several directories. How does it work?

Let's go through it a step at a time. The **ls** and **grep** commands do most of the work. With the **-1F** options, **ls** lists names in one (**-1**) column, adding a / after directory names (**-F**). Piping **ls**'s output to **grep** lets us select only directory names. For example, the command

```
4% ls -1F /usr/include  |  grep /
dos/
sys/
```

displays the directory names **dos** and **sys.**

If we set a shell variable to this output (using command substitution), we can refer to each name individually. Enter these commands:

```
5% set d = `!!`
set d = `ls -1F /usr/include  |  grep /`
6% echo $d
dos/ sys/
```

Command 5 uses the history redo (**!!**) to repeat command 4 and store its output in **$d** as a wordlist. Command 6 displays the directory names.

Using the C shell's special modifiers, we can eliminate the / from the names. The command

```
7% echo $d:gh
dos sys
```

uses **:h** to extract the header names (only the pathname in front of the final /) for all items (**:g** modifier) in the wordlist. Without the **:g** modifier (using **$d:h**), the C shell extracts the header pathname for only the first item in **$d.**

Now let's return to **dir**'s definition. It consists of three commands, separated by semicolons. The first creates the wordlist and saves the output in **d.** The second uses an **if** statement to determine whether the wordlist is empty. If **$#d** is not zero, **dir** echoes the directory names; otherwise, it displays nothing. The third command unsets **d.**

2.10 GETTING OUT: LOGOUT

Our tour is about to end. The features we have presented should give you a good idea of the C shell's power. Before you logout, we've got a few more things to show you.

We have noted that the C shell executes the **.cshrc** and **.login** files when you login. When you logout, surprisingly enough, it executes a file called **.logout.** You can place commands here that you want to execute before heading home or going out to lunch.

The .logout Special File

Typical **.logout** commands involve recording your logout date, sending reminder messages, and generating summary reports.

For example, suppose you want to run your disk storage usage utility (using **ppd**) when you logout on Friday. Put the following commands in **.logout:**

```
1% cat .logout
nohup                      # continue to run jobs after logout
set d = `date`
if ($d[1]  == Fri) then
     (date; du ~)  |  ppd ~/disk_storage&
endif
```

When you logout, UNIX normally terminates all background processes (this depends on your system administrator). To avoid this (and allow the disk storage utility to run), we use the **nohup** command. It lets background jobs continue to run after logout.

Next we set a shell variable **d** to the date. Using an **if** statement, we run our disk storage utility in the background if it's Friday.

We can extend this approach. Suppose you typically login and logout several times during the day. It makes little sense to update the disk storage file each time. Let's make our **.logout** file ask whether we want an update. Here's the modified text:

```
2% cat .logout
nohup                      # continue to run jobs after logout
set d = `date`
if ($d[1]  == Fri) then
     echo -n "Update disk_storage usage? "
     if (`gets`  == y) then
          (date; du ~)  |  ppd ~/disk_storage&
     endif
endif
```

We include the new statements within the original **if** statement. If it's Friday, an **echo** command prompts us for a response. We use the **-n** option to position the cursor after the prompt message and the **gets** command (see Appendix D) to read the response.

A Final Goodbye

It's time to conclude the tour. The command

```
3% logout
```

terminates your login session.

We hope you found the C shell tour enjoyable. As you continue to explore the C shell, keep in mind the following key features:

- You customize your session using the special files **.cshrc, .login,** and **.logout.**

- You reexecute commands with the history mechanism and rename command sequences with aliases.

- Shell variables allow you to save long strings for reuse in subsequent commands. Input/output redirection, pipes, command groups, and command substitution are the C shell's building blocks for constructing commands.

- The UNIX file system has a hierarchical structure. You can specify files by pathnames leading from the current directory or from the root directory.

- The C shell is a programming language. You can create new tools by writing C shell scripts—text files containing C shell commands, programming constructs, error checking, and input and output directives.

3

Basic Command Forms

In the simplest sense, you use the C shell to issue commands. A command is usually just the name of the file containing the program. You type the name, press the RETURN key, and wait for the program to finish. You have executed a UNIX command!

However, we can do more than this with the C shell. We can build complex commands by combining basic forms. This chapter describes the C shell's basic command forms. Chapter 4 considers more complex structures.

We begin this chapter by describing the UNIX file system. Commands frequently involve both filenames and directory names. We then describe a command's basic format. We build on this by combining commands on a single line. Input and output redirection let you prepare input for submission and save output for later reference. Pipes let you create new tools by connecting the output of one command to the input of another. Finally, conditional execution allows alternative sequences depending on results of previous commands. The chapter contains many examples that build on command forms discussed earlier. You will see how complex commands are really combinations of simple forms.

3.1 WHAT'S IN A NAME? DIRECTORY AND FILE NAMES

We use the file system to keep track of programs and data. The file system defines the organization of data and the files themselves. Understanding UNIX's file system is a key to using the C shell effectively.

UNIX has a hierarchical file system as illustrated in Figure 3-1. We often refer to this as an *inverted tree structure* because the base of the tree is at the top. The base is an overall directory called the *root*, designated by / (slash). The root may contain files

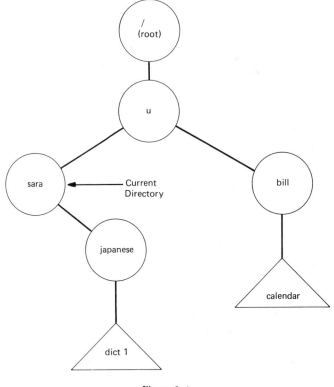

Figure 3–1.

and other directories called *subdirectories*. A subdirectory may in turn contain further subdirectories as well as individual files. Each user has a default working directory, called the *home directory*. This is where you start when you login to UNIX. You may change working directories at any time by using the **cd** command.

A *pathname* identifies a particular file or directory uniquely. An *absolute pathname* starts at the root and names each directory along the way to the destination file (or directory). We separate directory levels with a / (slash). The pathname

```
/u/sara/japanese/dict1
```

specifies a file or directory called **dict1.** Starting at the root (/), we enter subdirectory **u,** go to subdirectory **sara** (in **u**), go to subdirectory **japanese** (in **sara**), and find file **dict1** in subdirectory **japanese.** (From the pathname, we don't know **dict1** is a file; in fact, it could be a subdirectory.)

A *relative pathname* tells how to reach the destination from the current directory. If the current directory is /**u**/**sara,** we can specify the file **dict1** with the relative pathname

```
japanese/dict1
```

Relative pathnames never start with /, whereas absolute pathnames always do.

There are two special directory names: . (dot) and .. (dot-dot). Dot is the current working directory. Dot-dot is its parent (the next directory closer to the root). For example, the pathname

```
../bill/calendar
```

starts at the current working directory (/**u**/**sara**), goes up one level to directory **u** (the parent), descends to directory **bill,** and specifies the file **calendar.** The **..** notation lets us move toward the root of the file hierarchy (remember that we move *up* to the root). Thus, the pathname

```
../..
```

actually refers to the root (/). From our current directory (/**u**/**sara**) we move up one level to /**u** and a second level to /**.** Note that

is a valid pathname (in this case /**u**/**sara**), in the current directory.

You use the **cd** (change directory) command to change your working directory. The **pwd** (print working directory) command prints the name of the current working directory. The following commands illustrate **cd** and **pwd:**

```
% pwd
/u/bill
% cd /u/sara
% pwd
/u/sara
% cd ../bill
% pwd
/u/bill
```

We start at directory /**u**/**bill** and change to directory /**u**/**sara** by specifying the full pathname /**u**/**sara**. We return to directory /**u**/**bill** by specifying the relative pathname **..**/**bill**. **pwd** displays the new working directory.

Filenames and directory names may be up to 14 characters long (Berkeley versions allow up to 255 characters). Capital and lowercase letters are distinct. It is best to avoid using special characters ($, >, <, and | are a few) in filenames and restrict characters to letters, numbers, the underscore, and dot. Here are some example filenames:

```
Compile_err
compile_err
dictionary
dict1
cal.1985
```

(Note that **Compile_err** and **compile_err** are distinct names.)

Because users share the file system, UNIX imposes multilevel security to avoid unwarranted intrusions and to thwart nosy neighbors. Central to this is a concept of ownership of files and directories. You own your own home directory as well as all files and subdirectories you create. This prevents other people from destroying (or even examining, if you want) your files and directories.

Let's examine the security of UNIX files more closely. Each file or directory has an owner, belongs to a user group, and contains permission bits. There are three types of access: read (**r**), write (**w**), and execute/search (**x**). The **ls** (list) command displays these mnemonic triplets in three ordered categories: owner access, group access, and "others" access. Table 3-1 displays the meaning of each possible read, write, and execute triplet.

We use **ls** to display these permission bits by specifying either the −**l** (long listing) or −**ld** (long listing for directories) options. The information displayed (in order) contains the file type, an access permission triplet for each of the three ordered categories, the number of links (for plain files) or the number of subdirectories (for directory names), the owner and group, the file size, the date of last access, and the filename. For example, we can list file **calendar** and subdirectory **japanese** as follows:

```
% ls −l /u/bill/calendar
-rw-r----- 1 bill projw 538 Feb 10 12:53 /u/bill/calendar
% ls -ld /u/sara/japanese
drwxr-xr-x 2 sara proj1 928 Feb 10 13:09 /u/sara/japanese
```

This shows that **calendar** in **bill**'s home directory is readable and writable by **bill** (**rw-**), read-only for anyone in group **projw** (**r--**), and unreadable by anyone else (**---**). The directory **japanese** in **sara**'s home directory is readable and searchable by group **proj1** and everyone else (**r-x**), and writable as well (meaning that new files can be created) by

TABLE 3-1 FILE AND DIRECTORY PERMISSIONS

rwx	read, write, execute/search
rw−	read, write
r−x	read, execute/search
r−−	read only
−wx	write, execute/search
−w−	write only
−−x	execute/search only
−−−	no access

sara (**rwx**). Note the use of the first character position to denote a directory (**d**) or a plain file (**-**).

3.2 TAKING CHARGE: ISSUING COMMANDS

The C shell is ready to accept a command when it displays the prompt (**%**). We specify a command by typing its name followed by its arguments. We end the line with a RETURN, although we can continue a long command on a second line by typing \ (backslash) first. The C shell reads the command line and calls the command. The prompt returns when the command finishes executing.

How does the C shell find UNIX commands? Most are just user programs. They are not built into the operating system or the shell. The C shell looks in the directories named in the C shell path variable, **$path**. By default, these directories are **.** (the current directory), /**bin** (common binary files), /**usr**/**bin** (other binary files), and possibly /**usr**/**ucb** (commands from Berkeley). Adding UNIX commands is simply a matter of placing programs in one of these directories.

Single Commands

The general format for a single command is

```
command-name [arguments] ⟨RETURN⟩
```

command-name is a simple name (or any valid pathname); it may optionally have one or more **arguments.** These may be flags, which indicate specific options for the command (like "sort in reverse order" or "display an extended listing of a file"). Each flag is usually a single character preceded by a $-$. Arguments may also be filenames, pathnames, directories, or special options. The exact format varies. Spaces always separate arguments. Let's look at some examples:

1. The command

   % **pwd**

   prints the full pathname of the current working directory. It has no arguments.

2. The command

   % **wc** $-$**c** **chap6**

   displays the number of characters in file **chap6**. The $-$**c** flag is an option to **wc** (word count), and **chap6** is a filename argument.

3. The command

```
% mkdir japanese utils
```

creates two subdirectories, **japanese** and **utils.** It has two arguments (**japanese** and **utils**) separated by a space.

4. The command

```
% find . −name gets.c −print
```

searches the file system starting at the current directory for a file named **gets.c** and prints its full pathname. Remember, the format of individual commands vary. The arguments −**name** and −**print** are options specific to the **find** command. The pathname (**.**) is position-dependent (it must be the first argument), and **gets.c** qualifies the −**name** parameter.

Multiple Commands

You can issue several commands on a single line by putting semicolons between them. The format is

```
command1; command2; . . . commandn
```

The C shell executes the commands sequentially. The shell prompt returns when the last one finishes. Each command may have arguments.

Using multiple commands is appropriate when a set of commands forms a logical group. You can then type the whole set at one time without waiting for each to finish. For example,

```
% mkdir proposal; cd proposal
```

creates a new directory called **proposal** and changes the current working directory to it. You can begin creating files and working from within your new directory when the C shell is ready for another command. The sequence

```
% cd utils; cc −o gets gets.c; cd ..
```

specifies three commands: change directory to **utils,** compile the program **gets.c,** and return to the parent directory. The compile command depends on the first **cd** command since it obtains its source file from the current directory. The last **cd** command returns to the original directory.

Command Groups

We can make commands execute without affecting the current *environment,* the set of characteristics describing a user's work area. (These characteristics include the working directory, user ID, and other conditions.) To do this, simply enclose the commands (called a *command group*) in parentheses. We refer to this as creating a *subshell* within its own environment. You may compare it to constructing a temporary climate-controlled room inside a building. That room has its own environment, and changing its controls has no effect on the outside world.

In the previous example, we altered the environment by changing the working directory to **utils**. We used the command

```
cd ..
```

to return to the original working directory. Defining a command group makes the last **cd** unnecessary. Using parentheses to create a subshell results in the following structure:

```
% (cd utils; cc -o gets gets.c)
```

The shell prompt returns when the compile command finishes. We have not altered the current directory since **cd** applies only in the subshell's temporary environment. The subshell disappears when the command group finishes. This is a useful approach whenever you want to retain the current environment for subsequent commands. Furthermore, you can use a command group anywhere in place of a single command.

3.3 SENDING RESULTS WHERE YOU WANT THEM: OUTPUT REDIRECTION

Many UNIX commands, such as **who, ls** and **date,** normally display their output on the terminal. Once it is overwritten or scrolls off the screen, you must execute the command again to view it. Output redirection lets you save output in a file for later reference or for use as the input to another program.

Standard Output

We refer to the output that normally appears on the screen (excluding error messages) as *standard output.* We may send standard output to a file by using the notation

```
command > file
```

We say that > diverts or *redirects* the standard output. Here **command** is a single command (or command group) and **file** is any valid file pathname. The spaces surrounding

$>$ are optional. If the file does not exist, the C shell creates it. If it does exist, its previous contents are destroyed. For example,

```
% du > status
```

calls the disk usage command for the current directory and redirects the output to a file called **status.** To place the time and date in front of the disk usage command, type

```
% (date; du) > status
```

You must use command groups (parentheses) to combine the output of multiple commands. Omitting the grouping, as in

```
% date; du > status
```

causes the output of **date** to appear on the terminal and the output of the **du** command to go to **status.** Because redirection destroys the previous contents of a file, the command

```
% date > status; du > status
```

causes the output of the **du** command to overwrite the date information.

We use output redirection to save a command's results for later reference.

```
% od -x scan > scan_dump
```

Here we use the octal dump command with the $-$**x** option to display the file **scan** in hexadecimal notation. We redirect the output to the file **scan_dump.** We may then examine file **scan_dump** with an editor.

We can also use redirection to avoid cluttering the terminal. You can later use an editor to look at the parts of interest. For example, the following command lists all files in the directories /**bin** and /**usr**/**bin.** It collects these names in the file **unix_commands.**

```
% ls /bin /usr/bin > unix_commands
```

Finally, we use redirection to build text files for permanent reference. For example, the UNIX password file contains all users in the order they were added to the system. To create a file of users sorted by username, we type the following **sort** command:

```
% sort -t: /etc/passwd > users
```

Since the password file separates data fields with a colon, we change **sort**'s field separator to a colon with the $-$**t** option. We store the result in file **users.**

Appending Output

What if we don't want to destroy a file's previous contents? We can append the new standard output, that is, place it at the end of a file. If the file does not exist, the C shell creates it. The format

```
command >> file
```

places the standard output of **command** (or command group) at the end of **file.** For example, the commands

```
% date >> status
% ls -l >> status
% du -s >> status
```

build the file **status** from the output of the **date, ls,** and **du** commands. Each time you execute this sequence, the file **status** will accumulate the output. Changing the first command to

```
% date > status
```

will destroy the previous contents of **status.**

Diagnostic Output

Sometimes a command has special output to inform you of problems. We call this the *diagnostic* or *error output*. It normally appears on the terminal but is distinct from the standard output. It may, for example, contain the command messages reporting the failure to find a file, incorrect parameters, or a violation of security status. Note that redirecting standard output does not affect diagnostic output. For example, consider the following sequence in which we redirect the output of a compilation:

```
% cc gets.c > compile_out
"gets.c":7: newline in string or char constant
"gets.c":8: syntax error
Error in file gets.c: Error. No assembly.
```

(Your compiler may display a different error message.) The C compiler detected errors in compiling the program **gets.c.** The diagnostic messages appear on the terminal even though we redirected the standard output.

You can redirect diagnostic output along with standard output by using the notation

```
command >& file
```

for redirection and

```
command >>& file
```

for appending. This redirection allows us to save diagnostic messages from **command** in **file.** For example, the following commands illustrate redirection of the error output to the file **compile_out:**

```
% cc gets.c >& compile_out
% cat compile_out
"gets.c":7: newline in string or char constant
"gets.c":8: syntax error
Error in file gets.c: Error. No assembly.
```

The command

```
% (date; cc gets.c -o gets) >>& compile_log
```

adds to the file **compile_log** a running record (with the date and time) of the compilation of file **gets.c.** We use command grouping to redirect all output. This line appends both standard and diagnostic output to **compile_log.**

Separating Standard Output and Diagnostic Output

Sometimes you may want to save diagnostic output in one file and standard output in another. The command

```
% cat calendar logfile >& save
```

saves both types of output in file **save.** Let's look at the contents of the file **save:**

```
% cat save
Oct 14 Planning meeting
Oct 21 Budget meeting
cat: can't open logfile
```

We see that the C shell stored the contents of **calendar** in **save** as well as the error message. We can use command grouping with redirection to separate diagnostic and standard output. The command

```
% (cat calendar logfile > save) >& errfile
```

redirects standard output to **save** and diagnostic output to **errfile.** Note that the redirection order here is important. You must place > within the command grouping and >& outside.

The C shell opens **errfile** *first* for diagnostic and output redirection. Because we use command grouping, it then opens **save** for output redirection only. Note that **errfile** does not pick up the standard output because that has already been redirected. Now let's examine both **save** and **errfile**:

```
% cat save
Oct 14 Planning meeting
Oct 21 Budget meeting

% cat errfile
cat: can't open logfile
```

The **cat** command copied **calendar** to file **save** and placed the diagnostic message in **errfile.**

Safer Redirection and Appending

Redirection can easily destroy a valuable file accidentally. The command

```
% who > current_users
```

will destroy the contents of **current_users** without checking with you. Similarly, the command

```
% date >> statis
```

will create file **statis** if it does not exist. Thus mistyping **statis** for **status** sends the date information to the wrong file. To avoid such problems, the C shell provides a protective version of redirection and appending. This works as follows:

1. It does not allow redirection if the file already exists.
2. It does not allow appending if the file does not already exist.

This keeps you from accidentally destroying a valuable file or creating a new file just because of absent-mindedness or typing errors. The command

```
% set noclobber
```

activates this additional protection. Now you will see the message

```
% who > current_users
current_users: File exists
```

if **current_users** exists (even if it is empty) and

```
% date >> statis
statis: No such file or directory
```

if **statis** does not exist.

You can override the extra protection (if you really want to erase the old file or create a new one) by simply adding **!** ("Do what I mean!") to the redirection command. Thus

```
% who >! current_users
```

will allow the redirection even if **current_users** exists. Also

```
% (date; cd utils; cc -o gets gets.c) >>&! compile_log
```

will go ahead and create **compile_log** if it does not already exist. You must put a space between **!** and the destination file.

To remove the protection, use the command

```
% unset noclobber
```

We suggest setting **noclobber** because of the extra protection it provides. You must then specify **!** when the C shell should destroy (or create) a file.

3.4 GETTING THE INPUT YOU NEED: INPUT REDIRECTION

You can redirect input as well as output. For example, the **mail** command normally reads from the terminal. If you type

```
% mail bruce
We need to schedule a meeting to discuss
the new project goals.
^D
```

mail sends the letter you typed at the terminal. **^D** (control-D) simply terminates the input. In practice, you normally want to create letters with an editor that allows you to revise them, reformat them, correct the spelling, and remove caustic remarks and other things you probably shouldn't have included anyway. The command

```
% mail bruce < proj.memo.1
```

mails the contents of file **proj.memo.1** to **bruce.** In general, we may redirect terminal or standard input by using the format

```
command < file
```

command will then read from **file** instead of from the terminal. As in output redirection, the spaces around < are optional.

You can also use input redirection to submit the same input (such as a meeting notice) at a later time. Furthermore, you can keep a record of input stored in a file.

Input redirection is particularly convenient with commands such as **mail** and **tr** (translate) that only read from the standard input. For example, suppose we have a file called **report** that contains all uppercase characters. This file may have been created on a non-UNIX system, and we wish to create a version in lowercase. The command

```
% tr "[A-Z]" "[a-z]" < report > report.low
```

converts all uppercase letters to lowercase in file **report** and (using output redirection) stores the result in file **report.low.** File **report** is unchanged. Similarly, the command

```
% ex - target < com.list
```

invokes the **ex** editor using input from the file **com.list. target** is the text file we are editing. File **com.list** contains a set of **ex** commands. The − option (you need the surrounding spaces here) turns off interactive prompts and messages from **ex.** This allows you to specify an entire standard sequence of editing commands at once.

3.5 MAKING THE RIGHT CONNECTIONS: PIPES

Sequences of commands often require temporary files to hold intermediate results. For example, the command

```
% who > temp; wc −1 < temp; rm temp
      22
```

returns the number of people signed on UNIX (22 in this case); **who** displays information on each person, one per line; **wc** counts the number of lines; and **temp** is just a temporary file that we must delete afterwards.

We can eliminate the need for a temporary file by using a *pipe* to connect the output of **who** to the input of **wc.**The command

```
% who | wc −1
      22
```

accomplishes the same task.

The general format of a pipe is

```
command1 | command2 . . . | commandn
```

The pipes connect the standard output of **command1** to the standard input of **command2**, and so forth. You can connect any reasonable number of commands this way; typically you will not need to connect more than three or four.

What commands can be connected with pipes? Remember the following rule:

The command on the left side of a pipe must write to the standard output and the command on the right side must read from the standard input.

Let's look at an example. Suppose you want to locate a file called **tester** beneath your current directory and remove it. You may be tempted to try

```
% find . −name tester −print | rm
```

The system comes back with

```
Broken pipe.
```

Don't call a plumber. The problem is that **rm** takes its arguments from the command line, not the standard input. The C shell reports the error message "Broken pipe" because it cannot connect the output of **find** to the input of **rm.**

You may wonder if the only way to solve this problem is to wait for the **find** command to display the pathname, then issue the **rm** command. The **find** command, it turns out, has options to execute commands for you. The command

```
% find . −name tester −exec rm "{}" \;
```

locates the full pathname of the **tester** file and passes it to the **rm** command via the option − **exec** (execute the following command). The {} argument means "substitute the pathname here," and the \; argument terminates the − **exec** option.

You can use pipes for many purposes. For example, the command

```
% ps | grep −c −v PID
```

returns the number of processes you have running. The **ps** command displays information on all your processes with a heading that includes the word **PID**. We use **grep** to ignore the header by searching for all lines that do not contain (− v) **PID**. The − **c** flag counts the lines. Still another example is

```
% awk −F:'{print $1}' /etc/passwd | pr −4 > users
```

It records the usernames in your system password file. The **awk** command displays the first field (the username) of the UNIX password file, /**etc**/**passwd**. The **pr** command formats it into four columns. Output redirection saves the result in file **users.** You must use single quotation marks around the argument **'{print \$1}'** because **\$1**, {, and } are C shell special characters.

The command

```
% cat dict1 dict2 dict3  |  sort +1  |  pr  |  lpr
```

concatenates files **dict1**, **dict2**, and **dict3**, sorts the single (big) file by the second field (**+1** means skip one field), formats it using **pr**, and prints it using the line printer command, **lpr**. Here we pipe both the input and the output of **sort** and **pr**. We refer to these intermediate steps as *filters*. A filter is a program that reads data from standard input, performs transformations on it, and writes the transformed data to standard output. You can combine filters conveniently using pipes. As you might imagine, pipes are particularly useful with text processing, searching, and sorting commands.

We can also allow diagnostic output to pass through a pipe as well as standard output with the notation

```
command1  | & command2
```

where **command2** reads its standard input from all output of **command1**. For example, suppose we have a large C program with many compile errors. The following command compiles file **pcman.c**, sending standard and diagnostic output to **more** for convenient viewing.

```
% cc pcman.c  | & more
```

Alternatively, to produce a hard copy of the messages, we use the command

```
% cc pcman.c  | & pr  |  lpr
```

We need to connect **cc** with **pr** (or **more**) using **| &** since **cc** writes its error messages to the standard error.

3.6 ONLY ON CONDITION: CONDITIONAL
COMMAND EXECUTION

Conditional command execution makes one command execute only if a previous one succeeds (or if it fails). For example, we might want the output of a **grep** command printed only if it finds what we want. To do this, use the logical operator **&&** (then) as follows:

```
% grep Aug.84 transac > costs && lpr costs
```

TABLE 3-2 CONDITIONAL COMMAND EXECUTION

First command succeeds	Operator	Second Command Executes
yes	||	no
no	||	yes
yes	&&	yes
no	&&	no

This command searches a transaction file for August 1984 entries to create a file called **costs** and prints it using **lpr**. Read this command as "*If* **grep** succeeds, *then* execute **lpr**." Note that although this is sequential command execution, it is conditional on the result of **grep**. If the **grep** command finds no **Aug.84** entries, we avoid sending an empty file to the printer.

Similarly, we can use the logical operator \|\| (else) to make the second command execute only if the first command fails. The following command mails user **marty** a list of errors from the compilation of a file called **tester.c.**

```
% cc tester.c >& err || mail marty < err
```

Read this command as "*If* the compile succeeds, do nothing; *else* send mail to **marty**." If there are no errors, nothing is sent to **marty**. In this case, the C shell creates an empty file, **err**, in the process.*

Table 3-2 summarizes conditional command execution.

3.7 PUTTING IT ALL TOGETHER

As an explorer of the UNIX file system, you may need to know the full pathname of a file. Berkeley versions of UNIX include the **whereis** command, which displays the full pathname of a command and its manual page location. Suppose you wish to locate the **vi** editor. The command

```
% whereis vi
vi: /usr/bin/vi /usr/man/man1/vi.1
```

displays this information. The **whereis** command is fast, but it searches only a few standard directories that contain commands.

All versions of UNIX include the **find** command, your ticket to finding any file's pathname in the file system. To locate **vi**, for example, we type

---

*Non-BSD versions (XENIX, System III) use conditional command operators opposite to the way just described. You'll need to use **&&** for \|\| and vice versa.

```
% find / -name vi -print
find: cannot open /usr/mail/spool
find: cannot open /mnt/src
/bin/vi
```

We start at the root for our search and, unfortunately, travel to "forbidden areas" of the file system (directories **/usr/mail/spool** and **/mnt/src** are unreadable). Eventually, the **find** command locates **vi** in the **/bin** directory. How can we discard these error messages (some systems may produce pages of them) and still get our desired output?

We'll discuss this later, but first we must learn about a special directory called /**dev**. All of the UNIX special device files (terminals, tape drives, disks) reside here. This organization provides *file and device independence* in UNIX. That is, a filename and a device name are the same to the C shell. If you list the contents of the /**dev** directory, you will see a **tty** entry. The full pathname /**dev**/**tty** is the device pathname for your terminal. You can use this name as the destination of output redirection in the same way as a filename.

Similarly, there is another entry in /**dev** called **null**, which is the famous *bit bucket*. Redirecting output to the full pathname /**dev**/**null** effectively "throws away" the character stream. Let's look at some examples.

Suppose we want to copy all files from our current directory to another directory. We don't want to type all the filenames, but we may have some directories there (say **proj** and **doc**). The command

```
% cp * ../backup
cp: proj directory
cp: doc directory
```

copies all the files (denoted by the argument *) to the direcory **backup** above it. The **cp** command displays error messages for the directories **proj** and **doc** since directory names can be used only as destinations for the copy. We can discard these messages (no copy operation is performed anyway) with the command

```
% cp * ../backup >& /dev/null
```

The symbol >**&** redirects both standard and diagnostic output to file **/dev/null**. Note that **cp** does not produce any standard output, so we are really just throwing away the error messages.

We can also use /**dev**/**null** to reduce the length of a file to zero. The command

```
% cp /dev/null blockf
```

truncates the file **blockf**. Subsequent commands can append, sort, or merge to it.

Let's return now to our **find** command example to put these concepts to work. Since **find** sends error messages to the diagnostic output, we use >**&** to redirect it to the bit bucket, /**dev**/**null**. When **find** locates the file, it writes the full pathname to the standard output. Since >**&** also redirects the standard output, we somehow need to redirect it to the terminal. We can do this by using the filename /**dev**/**tty**, a generic name for "our terminal." We use the command

```
% (find / -name vi -print '> /dev/tty) >& /dev/null
/bin/vi
```

Note that we separate standard and diagnostic output in the usual way, except that we throw away the error messages to /**dev**/**null** and send the standard output to our terminal. Also note that **find** does not stop searching once it has found a filename. Use the interrupt key (DEL or RUBOUT) to stop the search and return to the prompt.

3.8 HINTS AND CAUTIONS

■ Don't use the same filename as an argument to a command and the destination of an output redirection. Suppose, for example, you want to put two files in front of a third. You may cleverly type

```
% cat rept.1 rept.2 rept.3 > rept.3
```

thinking that the "old" version of **rept.3** is now changed to include the files **rept.1** and **rept.2** in front. What happens, in fact, is that file **rept.3** disappears! That is, the "new" version of **rept.3** now only contains **rept.1** followed by **rept.2**, and the original **rept.3** is lost.

This happens because the C shell opens the file specified for output redirection (and truncates it!) before it executes the command. That is, the **cat** command processes an empty file. You can avoid this problem by setting **noclobber**. To prepend files **rept.1** and **rept.2** to **rept.3**, use the commands

```
% cat rept.1 rept.2 rept.3 > temp; mv temp rept.3
```

■ Remember that redirection applies only to one command or command group. If you want it to apply to several consecutive commands, put parentheses around them to make them into a command group.

■ Leave the **noclobber** variable set. It will keep you from accidentally overwriting important files or creating extra ones. Remember to use **!** to deactivate this protection temporarily.

■ When using pipes, be sure that the connected commands use the standard input or output. For example,

```
% ls | cp ../backup
Usage: cp f1 f2; or cp f1...fn d2
```

is an error, since **cp** (copy) does not read from the standard input. It expects all arguments on the command line.

■ Before typing multiple commands, determine any dependencies that could occur, and use conditional command execution to account for them. For example,

```
% cp ap.A ap.B ap.V ap.D appendix; tar c appendix
cp: ap.V: no such file or directory
```

is two commands. One copies several files to a directory named **appendix**; the other archives the **appendix** directory to tape. If one of the files is not found (because we typed **ap.V** instead of **ap.C**), our appendix is incomplete, and we write the tape needlessly.

Since the second command is useful only if the first one succeeds, we could type **&&** instead of **;** to create one command line using conditional execution:

```
% cp ap.A ap.B ap.V ap.D appendix && tar c appendix
```

This command line will not write on the tape unless **cp** is successful in copying all the files to the **appendix** directory.

3.9 KEY POINT SUMMARY

UNIX has a hierarchical file structure. It starts with a root directory (/) and continues through a tree structure of files and directories. You can identify a particular file or directory either by an absolute pathname starting from the root directory or by a relative pathname starting from the current directory. The notation / indicates a directory level along the path, **.** specifies the current directory, and **..** specifies the parent directory (the next one up in the hierarchy).

Each user has a default working directory called the *home directory*. You can change directories with the **cd** command.

Commands consist of program names followed by flags (indicating options) or arguments (see Table 3-3 for a summary). A command line may contain several related commands separated by semicolons; these commands execute sequentially. You can also

TABLE 3-3 SUMMARY OF COMMAND FORMS

% **command-name [arguments]**	single command
% **command; command**	multiple command
% **(command; command)**	command group
% **command | command**	command pipe
% **command |& command**	command pipe with diagnostic output
% **command && command**	conditional command (then)
% **command || command**	conditional command (else)

TABLE 3-4 SUMMARY OF REDIRECTION FORMS

<	standard input redirect
>	standard output redirect
>&	standard and diagnostic output redirect
>!	standard qutput redirect—override noclobber if set
>&!	standard and diagnostic output redirect—override noclobber if set
>>	append standard output
>>&	append standard and diagnostic output
>>!	append standard output—override noclobber if set
>>&!	append standard and diagnostic output—override noclobber if set

form command groups with their own environments by enclosing sequences of commands in parentheses. Pipes direct the output of one command to the input of another, thus allowing them to cooperate. Commands connected by **&&** or $\|$ execute conditionally.

Redirection allows you to use files as the source of standard input and the destination of standard and diagnostic output (see Table 3-4 for a summary). You can either have the output overwrite the old file contents or be appended to them. The **noclobber** option protects files from being overwritten accidentally or created because of forgetfulness or typing errors.

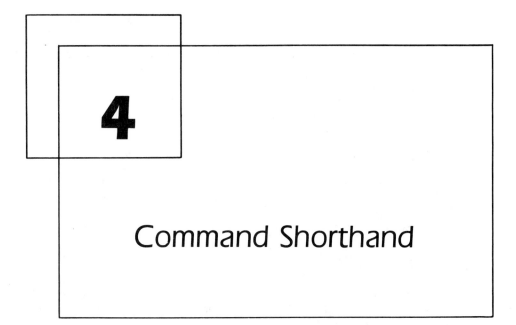

4

Command Shorthand

As we have noted, UNIX allows long, descriptive file and directory names. Its hierarchical file structure often results in long pathnames, and some commands have many arguments and can operate on many files at once. While these features make UNIX powerful, they can also lead to a lot of typing. Fortunately, the C shell provides the following shorthand features that save time and help avoid errors.

- *Filename expansion* lets you abbreviate filenames and specify entire groups of files at one time.

- *Shell variables* let you save strings such as long pathnames for repeated use.

- *Command substitution* lets you use the output of one command within a second command.

4.1 PLAYING YOUR WILDCARD: FILENAME EXPANSION

The C shell allows these wildcard characters in filenames:

?	matches any single character
[list]	matches any character in **list**
[lower-upper]	matches any character in the range between **lower** and **upper** (inclusive)
*	matches any pattern (including null)

These wildcard characters allow us to handle entire groups of files at once, refer to long names with abbreviations, and use parts of names when we are uncertain about the complete versions. Here are some examples:

1. We can combine files **dict1, dict2,** and **dict3** into a single file called **newdict** with

```
% cat dict[1-3] > newdict
```

Note that the C shell sorts matched files alphabetically and then passes them as individual arguments to the command. Thus the order of concatenation is **dict1** first, then **dict2,** then **dict3.**

2. We can list all files starting with a **t** in directory **/bin** with

```
% ls /bin/t*
```

The C shell will match any filename that begins with **t**. This is clearly handy if we know part of a name but not all of it or don't want to type all of it. The expanded command might look like

```
% ls /bin/tail /bin/tar /bin/tee /bin/touch
```

depending on the files in **/bin** on your system.

3. We can list all files or directories in the current directory that begin with **gets** (such as **gets.c** and **gets.backup**) with

```
% ls gets*
```

4. Suppose we have the files **test.c, test.o,** and **test.s** in our current directory. We can remove all three with

```
% rm test.?
```

5. Finally, we can change permission of all our C and assembler source files (all files ending in **.c** and **.s**) to read-only with

```
% chmod a=r *.[cs]
```

The argument **a=r** means "assign read-only permission for all."

You should note the following features of file matching:

1. It does not include file or directory names beginning with . (dot) unless you name them explicitly. Suppose our current directory includes the files **.login** and **.logout**. The command

```
% chmod +x *
```

will not make these files executable (**+x**). Use the command

```
% chmod +x .1*
```

to make **.login** and **.logout** executable.

2. The shell reports an error if there is no matching file. For example, if no files or subdirectory names start with **z** in directory **/bin,** the shell reports "No match" in the following command:

```
% ls −1 /bin/z*
No match.
```

3. The shell reports an error if there is more than one match in a position requiring a single name. Say, for example, we try to save on typing in changing over to directory **japanese** by entering

```
% cd ja*
```

This will work if no other directories start with **ja.** If, however, there is a directory **jazz,** file expansion produces

```
% cd japanese jazz
```

This gives an error message since it does not make sense to change to more than one directory at a time.

Ambiguity sometimes produces unexpected results even without an error message. For example, the command

```
% cp invoices bus*
```

will copy file **invoices** to directory **busplanning** as long as there is no ambiguity. If, however, the current directory contains files **busacctg** and **busrecords,** the C shell will sort the matching file or directory names alphabetically. File expansion results in

```
% cp invoices busacctg busplanning busrecords
```

cp will use them all as source filenames except the last, which it uses as a destination directory. Since **busrecords** is not a directory, the **cp** command will fail. Obviously, you must be careful to avoid ambiguity when using file expansion.

If you are unsure of how the C shell will perform file expansion, prefix the command's arguments with **echo. echo** simply displays the arguments after file expansion. For example,

```
% echo invoices bus*
```

displays

```
invoices busacctg busplanning busrecords
```

which reveals our error.

The C shell also allows the simple abbreviations ~ and { }.

~ stands for the home directory (for example, ~**pam** for Pam's home directory). ~ alone means your own home directory. For example, the command

```
% ls ~
```

lists the files in your home directory. The command

```
% cp ~pam/report ~
```

copies the file **report** from Pam's home directory to your home directory.

{ and } around different parts of common names saves the trouble of typing full filenames. For example, we can type

```
% pr accntg.{jan,feb,mar} | lpr
```

to format and print accounting files for the first three months without typing their full filenames. Similarly, the command

```
% cp /usr/include/{stdio.h,tty.h,math.h} hdrfiles
```

copies only the files **stdio.h, tty.h,** and **math.h** from the **/usr/include** directory to the **hdrfiles** directory.

You can also use this abbreviated form to create new hierarchies. The command

```
% mkdir projm; mkdir projm/us{1,2,3}
```

expands to

```
mkdir projm; mkdir projm/us1 projm/us2 projm/us3
```

creating a **projm** directory and three subdirectories, **us1, us2,** and **us3,** under it. This abbreviation is especially useful for specifying new pathnames (as in a **mkdir** command) because the C shell does not attempt to match the pattern with existing names.

4.2 MARK MY WORDS: C SHELL VARIABLES

The C shell provides *variables* that can hold strings or sets of strings. The main reason for using these variables is to save long strings such as pathnames. We can also use variables to format strings for output reporting or to build new commands.

Defining Shell Variables

We define a C shell variable with the **set** command. Use the following format:

```
set varname = string
```

This creates a shell variable called **varname** and initializes it to a string of characters. If the string includes spaces, you must put quotation marks around it to include them. A *wordlist* variable contains a list of strings divided into separate words. Surround the list with parentheses to define a wordlist. Here are some examples:

```
% set cf = /u/sam/common/gets
```

We assign the name **cf** (current file) to the filename **/u/sam/common/gets.**

```
% set title = "Disk Usage Summary Report"
```

Here we use quotation marks to preserve the spaces in the variable **title.** If you omit the quotation marks, the C shell ignores all the words following the first space. Thus the command

```
% set title = Disk Usage Summary Report
```

assigns only the word **Disk** to variable **title.**

```
% set ml = (marty ann bruce cal sara bill)
```

This command creates the wordlist variable **ml** (mailing list) consisting of six usernames: **marty, ann, bruce, cal, sara,** and **bill.**

Using C Shell Variables

We can use C shell variables in commands by preceding their names with **$.** The shell performs *variable expansion*—it uses the assigned string in place of the variable name. For example, to get a long listing of the file **/u/sam/common/gets,** all we must type is

```
% ls −l $cf
```

To include the text of our report title in the output file **disk.sum,** we can type

```
% echo $title > disk.sum
```

Finally, to mail file **urgent.memo** to each user on our mailing list, we use the command

```
% mail $ml < urgent.memo
```

We can also refer to words in a wordlist variable using brackets around the index:

```
$varname[index]
```

where **varname** is the variable's name, and **index** is a number indicating the word's position (starting with 1). **index** may also indicate a range of numbers. So, to mail the file **meeting.status** to user **bruce** and file **meeting.sched** to all users except **bill,** we can type

```
% mail $ml[3] < meeting.status
% mail $ml[1-5] < meeting.sched
```

To determine the number of words in the wordlist variable, use

```
$#varname
```

The command

```
% echo There are $#ml people on the project.
```

produces

```
There are 6 people on the project.
```

Sometimes you may want to know whether a shell variable is **set.** The notation

```
$?varname
```

yields true (1) when **set** and false (0) otherwise. For example, the command

```
% echo $?ml
```

returns 1 if the shell variable **ml** is set, 0 otherwise. The command

```
% test $?ml && mail $ml < memo
```

uses the **test** command to see if **$ml** is **set** (that is, if a mailing list exists). If so, the C shell mails the **memo** file to the users in the list.

You must put braces { } around variable names to insulate them from other strings that begin with a letter or number. Suppose we have two files called **gets** and **gets2** in directory **/u/sam/common**. We want to refer to the file **gets2** using our shell variable **$cf** (set to **/u/sam/common/gets**). If we type

```
% ls −l $cf2
```

the C shell responds with

```
cf2: Undefined variable.
```

Instead, use

```
% ls −l ${cf}2
```

and the C shell returns the long listing of file **/u/sam/common/gets2.** These braces aren't necessary if the string begins with a character other than a letter or number; for example,

```
% ls −l $cf.old
```

will display the long listing of file **/u/sam/common/gets.old.**

We can release a variable when we no longer need it with the **unset** command. Use the format

```
unset varname
```

For example, to release the shell variable **cf,** type

```
% unset cf
```

Accessing Pathname Variables

Because variables often hold pathnames, the C shell provides specific notation for handling them. We can specify four different pathname parts: **r** for the root, **h** for the header, **t** for the tail, and **e** for the extension. The *root* is the pathname excluding the extension. The *header* is the pathname excluding the final filename. The *tail* is the final file or directory name in a pathname. The *extension* follows the dot (**.**) in the final file or directory name. We use a colon to separate the pathname specifier from the variable name. Table 4-1 illustrates the pathname specifiers for variable **$cf,** which has the value **/u/sam/common/gets.c.**

TABLE 4-1   PATHNAME SPECIFIERS FOR VARIABLES

	Command	Output
no specifier	echo $cf	/u/sam/common/gets.c
root	echo $cf:r	/u/sam/common/gets
header	echo $cf:h	/u/sam/common
tail	echo $cf:t	gets.c
extension	echo $cf:e	c (BSD only)

We can use the modifier **g** (global) to make the pathname specifiers apply to each entry in a wordlist. For example, suppose only the users' home directories are in directory **/u.** We can generate the wordlist variable **hd** (home directories) using file expansion with

```
% set hd = (/u/*)
```

The * matches all entries in **/u,** the users' home directories. Now the command

```
% echo $hd
```

might produce

```
/u/ann /u/bill /u/bruce /u/cal /u/marty /u/sara
```

Then the command

```
% echo $hd:gt
```

produces the pathname tail for each word:

```
ann bill bruce cal marty sara
```

This is a handy way of creating a mailing list variable. To define the shell variable **ml,** type

```
% set ml = ($hd:gt)
```

Of course, you may also refer to a single word in variable **hd,** as in

```
% echo $hd[2]:t
```

which produces

```
bill
```

The following terminal session illustrates the use of C shell variables. (The numbers on the left are for reference only.)

```
1   % set wf = ~sam/jobw/driver.c
2   % set j = ~/japanese
3   % ls -l $wf
    -rw-r--r-- sam projw 4300 Jun 25 12:02 /u/sam/jobw/driver.c
4   % cp $wf $wf.bk
5   % chmod a=r $wf.bk
6   % ls -l $wf.bk
    -r--r--r-- sam projw 4300 Jun 25 14:02 /u/sam/jobw/driver.c.bk
7   % cd $j; pwd
    /u/sara/japanese
8   % cat dict? | sort | pr | lpr
9   % cd $wf:h; pwd
    /u/sam/jobw
```

Lines 1 and 2 define shell variables **wf** (working file) and **j.** Line 3 does a long listing of file **/u/sam/jobw/driver.c.** Line 4 copies file **driver.c** in directory **/u/sam/jobw** to **driver.c.bk** in the same directory. Line 5 changes the permission of **/u/sam/jobw/driver.c.bk** to read-only. Line 6 does a long listing of this file to show the changed permission.

Line 7 changes directories to subdirectory **japanese** under the home (~) directory (stored in variable **$j**) and displays the current working directory. Line 8 concatenates all files that start with **dict** followed by a single character. It sorts the concatenated files alphabetically by the first word in each line, formats the result with **pr,** and then sends it to the line printer spooler. Line 9 changes directories to **/u/sam/jobw.**

4.3 BUILDING STRINGS FROM COMMAND OUTPUT: COMMAND SUBSTITUTION

Many UNIX commands display information only. We can replace a command with its output by using *command substitution:* substituting the output of the command for the command itself. We use the grave accent character (`) to do this. For example, the command

```
% set d = `date`
```

assigns the current date to the variable **d,** breaking it into separate words at spaces, tabs, and newlines. Note that these marks are different from the single quotation marks. This command is equivalent to creating a wordlist, as in

```
% set d = (Tue Jun 18 14:22:11 PDT 1985)
```

This is useful because you can now reference each item from the wordlist individually. Let's explore ways in which we can obtain current information about our system (using the **date, ps,** and **who** commands), manage our files (**ls**), and maintain a mail list (**mail**).

This sequence manipulates the **date** command's output:

```
% set d = `date`
% echo $d
Tue Jun 18 14:22:18 PDT 1985
% echo Today is $d[1]
Today is Tue
% echo The time is $d[4]
The time is 14:22:18
```

Another example uses the **who** command and the predefined variable **user** (set to your username).

```
% echo $user
sara
% set w = `who | grep $user`
% echo $w
sara tty05 Jun 18 09:22
% echo You have been logged on since $w[5]
You have been logged on since 09:22
```

This time we create the wordlist using command substitution with two commands that are joined by a pipe. Note that the C shell expands **$user** within command substitution.

Command substitution can be embedded in strings:

```
% echo "there are ` who|wc -l` users logged on"
there are 6 users logged on
```

Here's an example that reports the size of a file:

```
% set wf = /u/sara/japanese/dict1
% set fs = `ls -l $wf`
% echo $fs
-rw-r--r-- sara lang 3212 Feb 14 12:02 /u/sara/japanese/dict1
% echo File $wf is $fs[4] bytes long
File /u/sara/japanese/dict is 3212 bytes long
```

This assigns the output of the **ls -l** command to the variable **$fs.**

Earlier in this chapter we introduced the idea of keeping a short local mailing list in a shell variable. Larger lists, of course, require a disk file. Let's assume we keep our mailing list in a file called **mlist** in our home directory as follows:

```
% cat ~/mlist
ann
marty
bill
sara
george
anthony
karen
pat
 .   .   .
```

When you use command substitution, newlines convert to spaces. Using this, we can now send a memo to each individual on our list with

```
% mail `cat ~/mlist` < memo
```

The command substitution produces an argument list (separated by spaces) containing each person's name.

There are many other ways to use command substitution. For example, suppose you want to edit all files in your current directory that contain a particular pattern (for example, **XENIX**). You simply type

```
% vi `grep -l XENIX *`
```

How does this work? First, the **vi** (visual) editor accepts multiple filenames from the command line. Furthermore, **grep** has a −l option, which returns the names of the files containing the requested pattern (**XENIX** in this case). Executing the **grep** command by itself might produce

```
% grep -l XENIX *
ch11
ch13
ch2
ch5
ch8
preface
```

Instead of typing each filename, we feed the output directly to **vi** using command substitution. You can use this technique to edit all files that reference a particular pattern.

4.4 DON'T LOSE ANYTHING IN TRANSLATION: QUOTING

One problem with assigning special meanings to characters such as **!**, *****, and **:** is that we occasionally want to use them literally, that is, just as themselves. For example, we may want to print them in a prompt, search for them in a file, add them to user-supplied input, or use them with their literal meanings in documents, graphs, and charts. We may also need to use them literally in definitions, thus allowing the C shell to assign their special meaning only when we apply the definitions.

This raises the problem of how to tell the C shell that we want characters to have their normal meanings, not their special meanings. We refer to the process as *quoting* or *escaping*. It works like a manual override on an automated system such as a conveyor belt, traffic light, or electric door. Obviously, quoting is a complex business that can create a lot of confusion and make commands difficult to understand. You should understand how quoting works, since many command shorthand techniques use special C shell characters. Let's begin by showing you the set of special characters, methods of escaping them, and examples of their uses.

Table 4-2 lists the characters you may want to use both literally and with their special meanings. Note that some characters have special meaning in certain contexts only. For example, the dash ($-$) specifies a range when used within file expansion brackets. Others have different meanings. !, for example, has a special meaning (history) when used in conjunction with other characters (as in !3 or !ls). It also is used with redirection (as in >&!).

We can use the following methods to escape characters: \ to escape a single character such as $, *, or a carriage return and " or ' (double or single quotation marks) around strings to treat most of their characters as literals (the exceptions are !, $, \, and grave accent within double quotation marks and ! and \ within single quotation marks).

Variable names present a special problem. Here the C shell provides the following features:

- Variable names within double quotation marks are expanded (replaced with their meanings), while ones within single quotation marks are not (they are treated as literals).

TABLE 4-2 C SHELL METACHARACTERS THAT MUST BE ESCAPED

Symbol	Meaning
SPACE, TAB	command argument separator
RETURN	command line terminator
$	variable identifier
* [ ] ? { } ~ $-$	file expansion
> < & !	redirection
! ^	history (Chapter 6)
|	pipe
;	command delimiter
( )	command group
\ ' "	quoting
`	command substitution
&	background tasks (Chapter 5)

- The modifier **:x** quotes the variable's contents and expands it to a wordlist; the modifier **:q** quotes a wordlist.

Let's look at some examples.

Escaping Characters

You can escape any single character by preceding it with \\. For example, we can use \\ ahead of a carriage return to escape the newline character in the following command line:

```
% cp master.text /u/sam/utils/doc; cp master.text \
/u/bill/backup
```

The \\ at the end of the first line keeps the carriage return from terminating the command (its normal function). This allows us to continue a long command line to the next line. We must break a command line at a word boundary (that is, the C shell forces a word break at the \\).

Here are some other examples.

1. The following commands print the **$wf** variable's value and name:

```
% echo $wf
/u/sam/utils/doc
% echo $wf is stored in the \$wf variable.
/u/sam/utils/doc is stored in the $wf variable.
```

The \\ in front of the final **$wf** prevents the C shell from treating it as a variable (that is, \\ escapes the **$**).

2. The following command prints an asterisk:

```
% echo \*
*
```

Without the \\, the C shell would take * to mean "all filenames in the current directory." For example,

```
% echo *
```

displays the filenames in the current directory.

Escaping Strings

While \\ is a convenient way to escape a single character, we still need a way to handle strings. These may contain several special characters, and backslashes would clutter them and make them hard to read. The alternatives are as follows:

1. Surrounding a string with double quotation marks makes most characters into literals but allows variable expansion and command substitution. That is, the C shell still replaces variables with their current values or commands with their output, as in the following examples:

```
% echo "***** directory $wf:h *****"
***** directory /u/sam/utils *****
% echo "***** `date` *****"
***** Wed May 15 14:13:54 PDT 1985 *****
```

Here the C shell expands **$wf:h** (**/u/sam/utils**) and `date` but does not expand *.

2. Surrounding a string with single quotation marks has the same effect except that it does not allow variable expansion or command substitution. That is, the C shell treats variables such as **$wf** and commands such as `date` as literal strings. For example, in

```
% echo 'use the var name $wf in your script' | mail sam
```

Sam receives the mail message

```
use the var name $wf in your script
```

because the C shell does not expand the shell variable **$wf** inside single quotation marks. Similarly, the command

```
% echo 'use vi `grep −l MAX *.c` to change your files' \
| mail marty
```

sends Marty the message

```
use vi `grep −l MAX *.c` to change your files
```

(We used \ to quote the newline.) There are a few peculiarities here:

- Neither set of quotation marks will escape ! when used in a history command (discussed in Chapter 6), so you must still put \ in front of it.

- Neither set of quotation marks will escape \, so you must use \\ to have \ taken literally. Consequently, this allows you to use \ to continue a long line onto a new line within quotation marks, preserving the newline within the string. You must precede the \ with a space. For example,

```
% echo "Please change the permission setting on your \
file $wf to read only- -Thanks " | mail sam
```

mails the two-line message contained in double quotation marks to user **sam.**
The shell expands variable **$wf,** and \ allows the command to continue to the
next line.

3. The C shell treats strings within quotation marks as a single unit, including any
embedded spaces. This becomes important when using a command such as **grep,** whose
format is

```
grep pattern file1 . . . filen
```

Here **pattern** is a search pattern, and all other arguments are **grep**'s input files. To search
for a pattern containing a space, put quotation marks (single or double) around it. Otherwise, the C shell interprets the first word as the pattern and everything else as filenames.
The command

```
% grep February 21 feb.status
```

searches files **21** and **feb.status** for the pattern "**February**", whereas the command

```
% grep "February 21" feb.status
```

searches file **feb.status** for the pattern "**February 21**" (with the embedded space).

You usually choose between single quotation marks and double quotation marks
based on whether or not you want the shell to expand variables or apply command
substitution. If you want to quote **$** or **`**, use single quotation marks. Let's look at several
examples.

1. The following command looks for the pattern **dict[1-4]** in all files that start with
ch and end in **.doc.** Argument **dict[1-4]** contains pattern expansion characters recognized
by **grep** that are the same as C shell file expansion characters. We must quote this pattern
to prevent expansion by the C shell.

```
% grep "dict[1-4]" ch*.doc
```

We can use either single or double quotation marks here. If we did not put any quotation marks around the pattern, the C shell would perform file expansion and create up to
four arguments in place of one. By using quotation marks, we pass the single argument
dict[1-4] to the **grep** command.

2. Suppose we have a file called **phone.numbers** in our home directory. The format
of the file is

```
lastname firstname prefix number
```

with spaces separating each field.

An example listing of this file might be

```
% cat phone.numbers
Andrews Bill 201 5347689
Hill Art 805 4445620
Johnson Bill 415 5283941
Johnson Mary 303 8583911
Smith Bill 619 5836322
Waller Henry 805 7873004
Zeller Louis 408 3239939
```

We decide to use the UNIX **awk** utility to print a list of people and their telephone numbers for the 805 prefix (entries for which field 3 is "805"). We use the pattern **$3 == "805"** (field 3 equals "805") and the action **{print $2, $1, $4}** (print fields 2, 1, and 4). Since **awk** and the C shell share many special characters, we must quote the pattern and the action.

```
% awk '$3 == "805"'  '{print $2, $1, $4}' phone.numbers
Art Hill 4445620
Henry Waller 7873004
```

Here we must use single quotation marks because **awk** uses $ as a field specifier. We also need quotation marks to embed spaces in both the pattern and the action. To appreciate the value of quotation marks, try issuing this command using \ to quote.

3. Now suppose we create a shell variable with

```
% set bill = "Johnson Bill"
```

We use quotation marks to embed the space. To display Bill Johnson's telephone number (using both first and last names in the search because we don't want Bill Smith's or Mary Johnson's number), we can type

```
% grep "$bill" phone.numbers
```

Here we must use double quotation marks around **$bill;** the C shell won't expand **$bill** in single quotation marks; unquoted, it expands **$bill** into two words, losing the embedded space.

Quoting Variables: :x and :q

Suppose we create a shell variable containing several words:

```
% set pat = "rev.1 rev.2 seminar"
```

These could be filenames or character patterns for use in a **grep** command. To preserve the spaces between words, we use double quotation marks. The C shell considers this string to be a single item. The command

```
% echo $#pat
1
```

verifies this. But we want to create a wordlist that allows references to each word. One
way to do this is with the command

```
% set pw = ($pat)
% echo $pw
rev.1 rev.2 seminar
% echo $#pw
3
```

We can now reference each word in the new shell variable **$pw** individually. For example,
the command

```
% cat $pw[1-2]
```

concatenates the **rev.1** and **rev.2** files. And the command

```
% grep $pw[3] *.doc
```

searches for the word **seminar** in all our ***.doc** files.

So far, so good. Now suppose we want to include special characters in our pattern
list. Let's use * and [ ] and examine the ways to quote these special characters in variables.
For example, we define **$pat** with

```
% set pat = "dict[1-4] *.doc"
```

What if we want to create a wordlist from this pattern list? We have a problem! When
we try

```
% set pz = ($pat)
```

the C shell performs file expansion. In other words, the command

```
% echo $pz
dict3 a.doc b.doc
```

lists the files in our current directory that match the patterns **dict[1-4]** and ***.doc** (in this
case the files **dict3, a.doc,** and **b.doc**). Moreover, the command

```
% echo $#pz
3
```

shows that we now have three items in the wordlist, as a result of the file expansion.
But we want to reference the two items in the list literally, as **dict[1-4]** and ***.doc.**

What if we try double quotation marks? The commands

```
% set pz = ("$pat")
% echo "$pz"
dict[1-4] *.doc
% echo $#pz
1
```

illustrate several points. First, we quoted **$pz** in the **echo** command to show what the C shell stored. Second, variable **$pz** is not a wordlist but only a single item (**$#pz** is 1). Therefore, we can't reference the individual words in **$pz**. In fact, variables **$pz** and **$pat** are the same. This is clearly not what we want. We need another quoting mechanism to help us create a wordlist.

Quoting with :x. The **:x** variable modifier allows us to quote the pattern list but expand it into separate words at spaces and tabs. The following commands verify this:

```
% set pz = ($pat:x)
% echo $#pz
2
```

Now we can reference each pattern individually and still prevent file expansion. For example,

```
% grep "$pz[1]" ch*
```

is the same as typing

```
% grep "dict[1-4]" ch*
```

Note that we need to quote **$pz[1]** to prevent file expansion before the C shell executes the **grep** command.

Quoting with :q. The **:q** modifier has two applications. First, we can use it as an alternative to double quotation marks for single-word shell variables. For example, we can quote variable **$bill** (a single string that includes a space) with

```
% grep $bill:q phone.numbers
```

and obtain the same effect as with double quotation marks.

The second use of the **:q** modifier is to quote a wordlist variable. This preserves the wordlist. For example,

```
% set new = ($pw $pz:q)
% echo $new:q
rev.1 rev.2 seminar dict[1-4] *.doc
% echo $#new
5
```

verifies that the new pattern list (variable **$new**) contains five items and that no file expansion occurs. Note that we only need to quote the **$pz** variable; variable **$pw** contains no file expansion characters.

Double quotation marks will not work here because they do not preserve the **$pz** wordlist. And **$pz:x** will not work either, since using **:x** with a wordlist variable is the same as using no quoting mechanism at all.

We can summarize **:x** and **:q** as follows:

- If the variable is *not* a wordlist, use **:x** to quote the variable and create a wordlist.

- If the variable *is* a wordlist, use **:q** to quote the variable and preserve the wordlist.

Double quotation marks do not work in either case.

4.5 PUTTING IT ALL TOGETHER

Let us now illustrate the use of both basic command forms and command shorthand in a practical task.

User Marty asks us to check the differences between his version of a C program and the versions used by Ann and Cal (users **ann** and **cal**). Perhaps he wants to determine whether he has the latest release. We do not know where Ann and Cal keep their versions of the program; we only know that the filename is **scanx.c** (where **x** represents a version number). Marty's version is **scan31484.c.** How do we accomplish this task?

We first define some shell variables. We use the **find** command with command substitution to determine the full pathnames of the **scan** modules.

```
% set m = `find ~marty -name scan31484.c -print`
% set a = `find ~ann -name scan\*.c -print`
% set c = `find ~cal -name scan\*.c -print`
```

The notation ~**marty** specifies user Marty's home directory—**find**'s starting point. In the first command we specify the filename completely, but in the second and third commands we rely on **find**'s file expansion mechanism (which, fortunately, uses the same notation as the C shell) to find the correct filename. Note that we must quote the * with \ so that the C shell does not apply file expansion.

Now if we type

```
% echo $m; echo $a; echo $c
```

the C shell displays the pathnames

```
/u/marty/ms/tks/scan31484.c
/u/ann/projw/tools/scan32284.c
/u/cal/bkup/scan31884.c
```

Marty, Ann, and Cal have different programming styles, and we do not want indenting, tabs, and the like to show up as coding differences. So we use the C beautifier program (**cb**) to eliminate as many style discrepancies as possible (**cb** standardizes spacing and indentation). We store the output of **cb** in the temporary files **mc** (Marty's code), **ac** (Ann's code), and **cc** (Cal's code). Of course, we use the shell variables already defined to save on typing. Here is the command:

```
% cb < $m > mc; cb < $a > ac; cb < $c > cc
```

Now let's generate the program differences. First we place a label in an output file called **chgs:**

```
% echo "***** ann's ($a) changes *****" > chgs
```

We use double quotation marks to expand the variable and escape the * and the apostrophe (same as the single quotation mark). Better go over that twice! Then we use the **diff** command with the **-b** option to ignore trailing spaces and tab characters. **diff** displays the differences between its two file arguments.

```
% diff -b mc ac >> chgs
```

We append the output to the file **chgs.** Now we issue the same two commands for Cal's changes, appending the output each time:

```
% echo "***** cal's ($c) changes *****" >> chgs
% diff -b mc cc >> chgs
```

To complete the task, we mail the results to Marty along with a notice that explains the contents of **chgs.**

```
% echo "This mail message contains the differences \
between your $m:t module and ann's ($a:t) and \
cal's ($c:t) " | cat - chgs | mail marty
```

echo lets us use variable expansion. We pipe our message to the **cat** command. The − option tells **cat** to read from the standard input first. This prepends the help message to the text in **chgs.** Again, we use double quotation marks with the **echo** command to expand the variables and escape the apostrophe and the parentheses. We specify the **:t** modifier to extract the filenames (for example, **scan32284.c** for Ann's module name) from the pathname variables. Furthermore, \ escapes the newlines (but they are retained in the text, making the mail message easy to read).

Finally, we can remove the temporary files with

```
% rm mc ac cc chgs
```

4.6 KEY POINT SUMMARY

Filename expansion allows you to specify entire groups of files at once. It also lets you refer to files by abbreviated names or by as much of the names as you know. The main problem is that the expanded filename could be ambiguous (there might be more than one match in a situation requiring a single name).

C shell variables are particularly useful for holding long strings such as pathnames. You can also use them to format strings and to build new commands. The **set** command defines a string variable; the **unset** command releases one. The C shell provides special notation for extracting parts of pathnames.

Command substitution allows you to use the output of one command within another command. If you create a wordlist, you can reference each word individually. Frequently you can combine one or more operations within a single command, eliminating the need for temporary files, shell variables, or intermediate steps.

Sometimes you need to use special characters and variable names with their literal or ordinary meanings. This requires that you mark them as literals through a process called quoting or escaping. You can use \ to escape a single character and quotation marks (either single or double) to quote entire strings. Shell variables and command substitution marks expand within strings surrounded by double quotation marks.

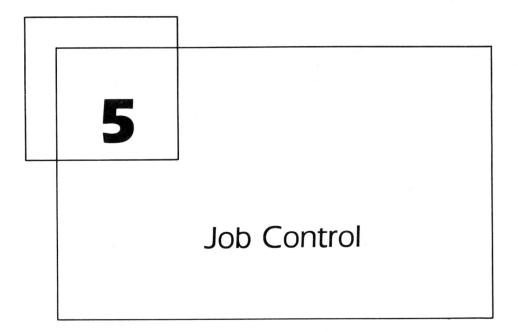

5

Job Control

UNIX lets users run more than one program at a time. You can thus keep working on the system (submit additional programs, check status, or organize or document files), even while long jobs such as compilations, sorts, merging of files, or recalculation of large models are still incomplete. We refer to the job that has our immediate attention (and control over the terminal) as the *foreground* job. We call other jobs for which the C shell does not wait *background jobs.*

Two implementations of job control are available. All versions of the C shell allow users to make jobs execute in the background, determine their status, and terminate them. You can even make background jobs continue after you logout. C shell versions running under 4BSD and later versions provide even more features (called *full job control*); this includes the ability to stop jobs temporarily (*suspend* them), restart them, and move them between foreground and background.

Note that we define a *job* as consisting of the commands specified in a single command line. This may involve several *processes,* each consisting of an executable program along with its data, files, and directory. Each process has a set of open files (at least standard input, standard output, and diagnostic output), a working directory, and a unique process identification **(PID).**

5.1 IN THE MAIN RING: FOREGROUND JOBS

So far, we have considered only foreground jobs. These have our immediate attention and control over terminal input and output. Such a job may consist of one process, as in

```
% who
```

It may also consist of several sequential processes, as in

```
% who; date; ls
```

A job may even have processes that depend on each other, as in

```
% who  |  wc  -l
```

With a foreground job, we simply wait until it finishes. The C shell displays its prompt when it is ready for our next command line.

This works fine for short jobs. If the waiting time is excessive, we can simply interrupt the job (usually with the DEL or RUBOUT key), and the C shell will terminate it prematurely.

But what if the job is a long one? If we run it in the foreground, we have lost the use of the system. All we can do is watch it work at recalculating a huge set of equations, compiling a long program, backing up a hard disk, adding the current month's accounting records to the overall company database, or examining a large document for spelling or punctuation errors. Any of these tasks could take minutes or even hours. On many computer systems, all you can do is take your lunch break, peruse the day's junk mail (nonelectronic, that is), or catch up on your magazine reading.

5.2 OVER AT THE SIDESHOW: BACKGROUND JOBS

The C shell lets you assign the long job to the background while you proceed with other tasks. Now you have the use of the system, even while it is doing jobs you have already submitted. Of course, this is most useful when the background jobs require little or no attention—that is, when they seldom request operator input or rarely produce intermediate output that you must examine.

To make a command execute in the background, put an ampersand (**&**) after it. For example, we might type

```
% (date; cd utils; cc -o gets gets.c) >>& compile_log &
[1] 26432
%
```

(The space before **&** is optional.) We used this command line in Section 3.3 to illustrate redirection of standard and diagnostic output. (*Note:* Don't confuse the first **&,** which redirects diagnostic output, with the ending **&,** which assigns the entire command to the background.)

If we run this as a foreground job, we must wait for it to finish (signified by the C shell displaying the command prompt). But this is simply a waste of time. After all, the command does not require any input, and its output is redirected to a file.

When we make the command run in the background, the C shell responds with a job number (inside brackets) and the process identification (**26432** in this case). It then immediately displays the prompt, and we can enter more commands. Some versions of the C shell return only the process ID.

We can initiate more than one background job. The following sequence initiates three (note the **&** at the end of each command line):

```
% du > storage_info &
[1] 26435
% cc -o gets gets.c >& errfile &
[2] 26441
% ls -l /bin /usr/bin > dir_list &
[3] 26448
```

The **du** command records disk usage of all subdirectories under the current directory. The **cc** command compiles file **gets.c**; **gets** is the object file, and **errfile** contains any compile-time errors. We redirect both the standard and diagnostic output to **errfile** using **>&**. The **ls** command produces a long listing of all files in directories **/bin** and **/usr/bin**. File **dir_list** contains the listing. Note that after each command line, the C shell displays the job number followed by the process ID. The job number is unique within our C shell process; the process ID is unique systemwide.

How do we decide which jobs to place in the background? Normally, a background job should not require user input, and you should redirect its output to a file. Good candidates are jobs that run noninteractively, such as formatting a large document, searching the file system for particular kinds of files, solving complex equations, or compiling long programs.

Setting CPU Limits

Normally, the C shell lets all jobs (including background jobs) execute as long as necessary. Some UNIX systems impose account funding limits. This prevents "runaway" programs from using up someone's entire account. For example, we may restrict processes to a maximum of 600 seconds of CPU time (time used by the central processing unit) with the command

```
% limit cputime 600
```

If a process exceeds this limit, the C shell terminates that process and prints the error message

```
Cputime limit exceeded
```

You may, however, remove or increase the limit on individual jobs. Suppose, for example, you want to run a program **calc,** which performs time-consuming calculations on a data file (here named **exper.data**). The **unlimit** command removes the CPU time limit for this job as follows:

```
%  (unlimit cputime; calc exper.data > data.summary) &
```

Because we created a command group using parentheses, the CPU time limit remains at 600 seconds for other jobs.

    You may also increase the limit for an individual job. For example,

```
%  (limit cputime 3600; find / -atime +90 -print > old.files) &
```

increases the limit to 3600 seconds (long time!) for a **find** command. We expect this search to take a while, because the argument / instructs **find** to search for files starting at the root (i.e., the entire file system) that have not been accessed in at least 90 days (**-atime +90**). Subsequent jobs still have the 600-second CPU limit in force.

5.3 MANAGING YOUR RESOURCES: JOB CONTROL

To control and monitor background execution, we need commands that operate on jobs and processes. Two important commands, **jobs** and **ps,** give us status information on background jobs. The **ps** command displays a table of all your currently executing processes. Let's look at sample output from a **ps** command for the three background jobs we submitted (**du, cc,** and **ls**).

```
% ps
  PID   TTY STAT       TIME COMMAND
 26435 i22 R          0:01 du
 26441 i22 S          0:00 cc -o gets gets.c
 26442 i22 R          0:00 ccom /tmp/ctm264414 gets.c
 26448 i22 R          0:00 ls -l /bin /usr/bin
 26572 i22 R          0:00 ps
```

Since the exact format of this display may vary, you should refer to your UNIX reference manual for a description. Here, **ps** displays the process ID (**PID**), terminal identification (**TTY**), process status (**STAT**), current CPU usage (**TIME**), and command name (**COMAND**). What does this tell us? Underneath **COMMAND,** we see our three background jobs, **du, cc,** and **ls.** All of them are running (**R**), except for **cc.** We also see a process called **ccom.** This new process is part of the **cc** job. (Remember, jobs may consist of more than one process.) **cc** generated process **ccom** to perform part of the compilation procedure. Meanwhile, **cc** is sleeping (**S**), waiting for **ccom** to finish. The **ps** command shown is the one that generated the display; it is in the foreground. This display is a window into the execution status of your processes (foreground or background, running or not).

The **jobs** command, available on the C shell running under BSD versions, is another command that provides a "snapshot" of your processes. It reports the status of background jobs. Let's try it for the same three background jobs:

```
% jobs
  [1]  + Running                    du > storage_info
  [2]  - Running                    cc -o gets gets.c >& errfile
  [3]    Running                    ls -l /bin /usr/bin > dir_list
```

A background job may be Running, Stopped, Terminated, or Done, or have Exit status. Although similarly named, Stopped, Terminated, Done, and Exit all represent different status conditions. We will discuss these shortly.

The **jobs** command labels each job by number (in brackets). A plus sign indicates the current background job. It is generally the first job placed in the background. A minus sign indicates the next job in line. All other jobs are unmarked. For our three processes, **du** is the current job, **cc** is next, followed by **ls.** All are running at the same priority level. If the **du** job finishes before the **cc** job, **cc** becomes the current job. The only significance of the current job is that you can use shorthand notation to refer to it in job control commands.

Terminating Processes

Up to now most of your C shell commands have been foreground jobs. If you aren't happy with the results, you stop the command with the interrupt signal (DEL or RUBOUT). What about background jobs? If an interrupt terminated them, you would stop them all every time you stopped a foreground job. Instead we must use the **kill** command to terminate background jobs.

For example, to terminate the **du** process (the current job), type

```
% kill %
```

or, by process ID number (PID),

```
% kill 26435
```

If your version of the C shell has the **jobs** command, you'll receive the message

```
  [1]  + Terminated                du > storage_info
```

Otherwise, the C shell will refer to **du** by its process ID number. The **kill** command accepts either a process ID or a job number. To cancel the **cc** job, we type

```
% kill %2
```

TABLE 5-1 FORMATS FOR THE
KILL COMMAND

Background job: % **du** > **storage_info &**

% **kill 26435**	(process ID)
% **kill %**	(current job)
% **kill %1**	(job number)
% **kill %du**	(initial string)
% **kill %?storage**	(string matching)

Use the process ID if your version of the C shell lacks job numbers and the **jobs** command. Table 5-1 shows different ways of terminating the **du** process with the **kill** command.

The C shell notifies you when a background job changes status. Assuming we "killed" our **du** process and let the **cc** and **ls** jobs run to completion, the C shell would display these messages.

```
[1]  + Terminated                       du > storage_info
%
[2]  + Done                             cc -o gets gets.c >& errfile
%
[3]  + Done                             ls -l /bin /usr/bin > dir_list
%
```

Terminated indicates abnormal termination, resulting from the **kill** command. *Done* indicates that a job completed normally, whereas *Exit* would indicate that it terminated from a nonzero exit status.

Note that when we terminated job 1, job 2 became the current job. Similarly, when job 2 finished, job 3 became the current job.

Detached Jobs

A *detached job* is a background job that continues to run after you logout. Some systems allow any background job to run after logout. On other systems, logging out sends a **hangup** signal that terminates all your processes. To prevent this, precede your background command with the word **nohup.** For example, the command

```
% nohup cc -o num num.c >>& compile_log &
```

lets your **cc** command run detached. If you logout before it completes, the background process continues to execute. **nohup** is just shorthand for "no hangup."

Full Job Control

Most versions of the C shell include simple job control (background execution using **&** and the **kill, ps,** and **nohup** commands). Versions of the C shell running under 4BSD or later versions implement full job control (the ability to suspend jobs, restart them, and transfer them from foreground to background). Full job control allows us to interrupt long jobs at any time and respond to their occasional requirements for input and output. Let's look at some common scenarios.

Suppose we decide to do some file housekeeping. We want to locate all zero-length files using the **find** command and save their pathnames. (Later we can send mail to users asking them to clean up.) We type

```
% (find / -size 0 -print > zero.files) >& /dev/null
```

We search the file system starting at the root (/), looking for zero-length files (**-size 0**). We discard error messages (to **/dev/null**) and store the pathnames in the file **zero.files.** Having no other work in mind (slow day!), we issue the command in the foreground.

Suddenly, a message appears on the screen:

```
message from bill tty3 . . .
We're meeting in 5 minutes. Can you please bring the
newest accounting data from your files?
```

We can (heaven forbid!) use a traditional communication device (such as a telephone) to answer Bill, but we still need access to our UNIX files to retrieve the accounting data. If we interrupt the **find** command, we will have to start it over from the beginning. We want to stop it temporarily, print the accounting data, and restart it.

Can the C shell accommodate us? The answer is yes; all we must do is type ˆ**Z** (**control-Z**). This suspends the **find** command, our foreground job. The C shell displays the message

```
Stopped
%
```

indicating that it has suspended (not terminated) the **find** process. Now we can print the accounting data for Bill:

```
% pr accntg.summary | lpr
```

We've got just a minute or two left to make that meeting. How do we restart the **find** command? Just use the **fg** (foreground) command:

```
% fg
(find / -size 0 -print > zero.files) > & /dev/null
```

Note that the C shell displays the command that it activates. We leave our terminal, stop by the printer, and proceed to the meeting with report in hand. The **find** command continues in the foreground—no problem, since the meeting will probably last forever.

Until now we have described two job states, foreground and background. We just illustrated a third state: *suspended*. The **fg** command restarts a suspended job in the foreground. This command takes a job number as its argument. For example,

```
% fg %2
```

brings job 2 into the foreground, starting it if it is stopped. In fact, you may suspend any job, stopping execution temporarily to do other work, prepare new input, or examine output.

Let's consider another scenario. Suppose we have the following background job running to format a proposal:

```
% jobs
[1] + Running    nroff -ms proposal.[1-3] > proposal.out
```

We suddenly remember that we intended to make some minor changes to file **proposal.3.** We want to suspend the job and check the **proposal.3** file. We use the **stop** command since it is a background job:

```
% stop %
```

This suspends the current job (**%**), our **nroff** process. The **stop** command takes the same arguments as **kill** (see Table 5-1). For example,

```
% stop %2
```

stops background job 2.

We need to know if **nroff** has processed file **proposal.3** yet. The following **tail** command will display the last 10 lines of **proposal.out,** showing us how far the job progressed.

```
% tail proposal.out
```

Taking into account that **nroff** buffers its output, we conclude that it did not get to **proposal.3.** We can then edit that file and resume the current job in the background. To do this, use the **bg** (background) command:

```
% bg
```

Like **fg, bg** can take a job number as an argument. For example,

```
% bg %3
```

resumes job 3 in the background.

Note that to move a foreground job into the background, you must suspend it first using **^Z.** Then use **bg** to restart it in the background.

For example, we might start a similar text formatting job in the foreground. We format files **policy.1, policy.2,** and **policy.3** using the **ms** macro format set with the **nroff** command:

```
% nroff -ms policy.[1-3] > company.policy
```

If we then decide to edit a letter or do other brief tasks, we can type ˆ**Z.** to suspend the **nroff** job. The C shell again responds with

```
Stopped
%
```

(*Note:* A suspended foreground job always becomes the current job.) Now we type

```
% bg
```

and the current job resumes in the background. The C shell displays the prompt, and we begin our other work.

By the way, the C shell alerts you if you try to logout with any stopped jobs. You'll see the message

```
There are stopped jobs.
```

You then have a chance to remain logged on. When you logout a second time, the C shell terminates your stopped jobs.

Terminal Input for Background Jobs

C shell versions with full job control do not allow background jobs to read from the terminal. Otherwise, a background job could intercept keystrokes for the foreground job. If a background job requests terminal input (for instance, a text formatter wants the user to select a title, page length, or font interactively), the C shell suspends it automatically and notifies you.

Suppose we have a utility **backup** that backs up files to floppy disk or tape. We run it as follows:

```
% backup /u/sara /dev/rx01&
[1] 2404
```

backup has two parameters, the directory to archive and the device name. As long as all the files fit on one floppy (or tape), all is well. If not, the utility displays the message

```
DISK FULL - INSERT NEW DISK AND PRESS RETURN
```

and waits for the user to press the RETURN key when it needs a new disk. How can we run **backup** in the background for large directories, ones that will require several floppies?

Job control provides the answer. When **backup** needs a new disk, it reports this and attempts to read from the terminal. The C shell intercepts the attempt and notifies us with

```
[1] + Stopped (tty input)    backup /u/sara /dev/rx01
%
```

We install the new disk and type **fg** to bring the suspended utility to the foreground. Now we can type the required input (e.g., RETURN), and the program will continue to execute. To return it to the background, type ˆZ. (to suspend it), then **bg.** The **backup** program now continues until it finishes or needs another disk. Obviously this technique makes sense only for jobs that require very infrequent input.

Terminal Output for Background Jobs

Normally, a background job writes to the terminal unless we redirect its output. We can explicitly restrict this writing with the command

```
% stty tostop
```

This is shorthand for "terminal output stop." When **tostop** is in force, the C shell suspends any background job that attempts to write to the terminal. This also helps us control background jobs. For example, the following command searches the subtree **/source** for all files named **usage.c** and displays their pathnames.

```
% find /source -name usage.c -print &
[1] 26900
```

The C shell will notify us when the **find** command is ready to write to the terminal (with the information we want):

```
[1] + Stopped (tty output)    find /source -name usage.c -print
%
```

We can bring it to the foreground with

```
% fg
/source/import/sec4/usage.c
```

Note that the **find** command now displays its output, the full pathname of the file. We suspend this job with ˆZ and resume it in the background with **bg.** When it has more information to report, the C shell will stop it again and notify us. This continues until the **find** command finishes.

You can remove the terminal output restriction with

```
% stty -tostop
```

Notification of Changes in Background Jobs

The C shell notifies you when background jobs change status. When a background job finishes, for example, the C shell displays "Done". Notification normally occurs before the next shell prompt. This could mean a considerable delay if you are running a long foreground task, such as the **vi** editor.

Suppose we want to format and print a document. We first run the files through the **spell** program. Let's do this in the background:

```
% spell NHS.grant* > grant.out &
[1] 1603
```

Although we have other work to do, this task has high priority. We want to correct any spelling errors before formatting and printing. To force immediate notification of a change in its status, we type the command

```
% notify
```

No argument is necessary because the **spell** job is the current job. The **notify** command can, however, apply to a particular job. The command

```
% notify %5
```

for example, sends us notification only for job 5.

Now we can enter the **vi** editor to work on another task:

```
% vi feb.minutes
```

In the middle of our editing session, the C shell reports

```
[1]  + Done        spell NHS.grant* > grant.out
```

(Don't worry—this message is not stored in the **vi** buffer.) We suspend the **vi** job with **^Z** to check the output of the **spell** command. If there are no errors, we submit a formatting job in the background and pipe it to the line printer:

```
% nroff -ms NHS.grant* | lpr &
[2] 1622
```

Note that the C shell labels the **nroff** job 2, because the suspended **vi** job is 1. We return to our editing with the foreground command:

```
% fg
vi feb.minutes
```

You can force the C shell to provide immediate notification for all background tasks. Set the predefined shell variable **notify** (different from the **notify** command). For example,

```
% set notify
```

provides immediate notification when any background job changes status.

Implied Directory Changes

Suppose you submit a background job, change directories, and then bring the job back into the foreground. What is the current directory? Bringing a background job into the foreground causes an implied change directory (**cd**) command if the job has a different working directory. The C shell warns you when this happens. For example, suppose we are working in our **japanese** directory, and the **pwd** and **jobs** commands produce the following output:

```
% pwd
/u/sara/japanese
% jobs
[1]  +  Running   cc -o gets gets.c
[2]  -  Running   du > storage_info
```

Both jobs are running in the background. We decide to bring the compile job to the foreground (since it is the current job, we don't need to specify an argument) and type

```
% fg
cc -o gets gets.c (wd: ~/utils)
```

The C shell warns us that our working directory is now **/u/sara/utils.** Why did this change occur? When we originally issued the **cc** command, we typed

```
% cd utils
% cc -o gets gets.c &
% cd ../japanese
```

We changed to directory **utils,** issued the **cc** command, and then changed to another working directory (**../japanese**). Bringing the **cc** job to the foreground forces the change directory back to **utils.**

Some versions of the C shell even politely return to the original directory when the foreground job finishes. The implied directory change is only in effect temporarily. In this case the C shell reports the new current working directory before issuing the prompt. To bring the above **cc** job to the foreground, we type

```
% fg
cc -o gets gets.c (wd: ~/utils)
```

When the foreground job (**cc**) finishes, the C shell displays the new working directory:

```
(wd now: ~/japanese)
%
```

5.4 HINTS AND CAUTIONS

■ Don't spend a lot of time checking the status of background jobs. This defeats the purpose of putting them in the background in the first place. It's like setting an automatic timer and then standing and watching it count down. Rely on notification from the C shell.

■ If your version of the C shell doesn't have job control, use an audio reminder, as in

```
% (nroff -ms annual.rept > doc85; echo -n 'ˆG') &
```

This command line formats a large document using **nroff** and redirects the output. When **nroff** finishes, the C shell sends a beep to the terminal. We use the **-n** option with **echo** to suppress the usual newline character. The beep is thus the only indication that something has happened.

We can even receive background job notification while working in the **vi** editor. The only problem is that **vi** beeps when you enter an incorrect command. To distinguish a **vi** beep from a background job beep, use this form:

```
% (nroff -ms annual.rept > doc85; \
  echo -n 'ˆG'; sleep 1; echo -n 'ˆG') &
```

Now the C shell notification becomes two beeps, one second apart (**sleep 1**).

If you are out of the room (or if the radio is too loud), use your mail service. The command

```
% (date > err; cc system.c -o system >>& err; mail pa < err) &
```

compiles a lengthy C program and saves the errors, if any, in a file called **err.** When the **cc** process finishes, you receive the message

```
You have new mail.
```

at your terminal. If the compile resulted in errors, you have a list in your mailbox; otherwise **err** just contains the date.

■ Be careful when stopping sequential foreground jobs. Suppose we want to compile a program **tester.c,** then run it, all in a directory named **projw.**

```
% cd projw; cc tester.c -o tester; tester
```

If we type ˆ **Z** during compilation, the C shell suspends **cc.** If we then resume execution with **fg,** the C shell doesn't execute **tester.** To avoid this problem, use parentheses to make the compilation and execution into a single job:

```
% (cd projw; cc tester.c -o tester; tester)
```

Now typing ˆ **Z** stops the entire procedure. Typing **fg** will execute **tester** following the **cc** command.

■ You cannot stop built-in commands (such as **cd** in the last example). This should not present a problem since they typically finish executing before you could type ˆ**Z** anyway.

■ When bringing a background job to the foreground, watch carefully for implied directory changes. Your working directory may change without an explicit **cd** command.

5.5 KEY POINT SUMMARY

You can run jobs either in the foreground or in the background. Background jobs cannot read from the terminal without user intervention. This allows the computer to run long noninteractive jobs while you do other work. UNIX versions with full job control let you suspend and restart jobs and transfer them from foreground to background or vice versa.

TABLE 5-2 JOB CONTROL COMMANDS

command &	Create background job.
ps	Display process status information.
jobs	Display background job numbers, status.
nohup command &	Allow command to execute after logout.
fg	Bring current job into foreground.
fg %n	Bring job **n** into foreground.
bg	Put current job into background.
bg %n	Put job **n** into background.
ˆZ	Suspend foreground job.
stop %	Suspend current background job.
stop %n	Suspend background job **n**.
stty tostop	Suspend background jobs that write to terminal.
stty -tostop	Allow background jobs to write to terminal.
notify	Notify when current job changes status.
notify %n	Notify when job **n** changes status.
set notify	Notify when any job changes status.

Background jobs should require little or no user input. Remember to redirect their output to files (or be prepared to decipher intertwined output).

Under full job control, the C shell suspends background jobs requiring input from the terminal. When output redirection is inappropriate, use the **stty tostop** command to suspend a background job that attempts to write to your terminal.

Table 5-2 summarizes the job control commands.

6

History and Alias Mechanisms

The C shell's history and alias mechanisms further simplify the issuing of commands. The *history* mechanism lets us refer to previous commands, while the *alias* mechanism lets us name commands or sequences. These unique features of the C shell are the reasons why many people choose it as their UNIX interface.

The first half of this chapter describes the history list. You will learn how to set it up, recall previous commands, and edit them. If your C shell has the "save history" capability, you can even preserve a history list between sessions.

The remaining sections describe how to assign shorthand names (*aliases*) to common commands or operations. You will learn how to set up aliases and pass arguments to them. Examples demonstrate the value of aliases and show how the C shell executes them.

6.1 THE PAST IS ALWAYS PRESENT: THE HISTORY LIST

The history mechanism saves your commands in a list, thus allowing you to avoid repetitive typing. You can use the list to correct a spelling error in a long command, recall a filename, or even repeat an entire command (we call this a *redo*). You can also build new commands from old ones.

After login, the C shell numbers your commands sequentially, starting at 1. You determine how many commands it remembers by setting the predefined variable **history**. The default value is 1 (forget everything except the last command), but you can extend the historical record with the **set** command. For example,

```
% set history = 10
```

makes the C shell remember the last 10 commands. You can use the **set** command with
no arguments to display the **history** variable. If **history** is not set, it will not appear in
the list. If you type more commands than you have told the C shell to remember, the
earliest one drops off the list to make room for the latest one. Like shell variables, the
history list disappears when you logout.

Displaying the History List

To display the history list, type

```
% history
```

For example, you might see:

```
 2 who
 3 cd proposal.257
 4 date
 5 ls -l cvrletter
 6 cat cvrletter
 7 cd chapter.5
 8 ls -l
 9 tail -20 section.4
10 vi section.4
11 pr section* | lpr
12 history
```

This is a snapshot of your last 11 commands. Note that the C shell stores every command
you type—even ones with errors. For example, say you want to examine the file **cvrletter**
with the **cat** command. If you accidentally type

```
% cay cvrletter
cay: Command not found
```

the C shell stores the erroneous command as number 13 and reports that it cannot find
the **cay** command. Note also that the C shell stores commands before performing file
expansion. For example, command 11 in the list contains the file expansion character ***,**
not the actual filenames used.

   You can display just part of the history list. For example, the command

```
% history 5
```

displays the last five commands. To put the most recent command first, use the **-r** flag,
as in

```
% history -r 5
```

Be careful—only BSD versions of the C shell allow the history command to have arguments. On all other versions, pipe the history command to the **tail** command, as in

```
% history | tail -5
```

Choosing the Size of the History List

Most users make the history list reasonably long (say, 20 entries) but usually not more than a screen's worth. In fact, you may want a short list (say, 10 entries) if you are working on a slow terminal or a dial-up line.

If you manage files for other users, you may want a very long history list (say, 100 entries). The historical record is, after all, crucial to verify sequences of commands. (Did I really delete all those files?) Of course, in normal use you will want to display only part of the list (as with **history 20**).

History Repeats Itself: Reissuing Past Commands

The C shell refers to past commands as *events*. Since the history list lets you refer to events by number, you may want the current command number displayed with the prompt. Putting an exclamation point in the prompt string does this. The command

```
% set prompt = '\!% '
```

changes the prompt to the command number followed by the percent sign. Remember, you must escape the exclamation point with \ because the C shell expands it even inside quotation marks. We use quotation marks to include a space after the **%** to increase readability. The following three commands show the new prompt. Note that the C shell adds 1 to the event number with each command.

```
16% pwd
/u/sam/jobw/projecta
17% ls *.c
debug.c echo2.c gets.c
18% date
Wed February 15 13:58:30 PST 1984
```

Most history commands begin with **!**. For example, typing **!!** redoes the previous command. To reexecute other commands, type **!** and the event number. For example, typing

```
19% !17
```

makes the C shell expand and display event 17, store it in the history list as event 19 (in this case), and execute it. You will get an error if event 17 is not in the list.

Suppose we have been at the terminal for a while (long day!) and our history list looks like this:

```
99% history
    90 date
    91 vi letter.1
    92 nroff -ms letter.1
    93 nroff -ms letter.1 | lpr
    94 vi letter.2
    95 nroff -ms letter.2
    96 vi letter.2
    97 nroff -ms letter.2
    98 nroff -ms letter.2 | lpr
    99 history
```

We have used the **vi** (visual) editor to modify text files **letter.1** and **letter.2**. **nroff** is a text formatter and **lpr** a line printer utility. At this point we discover a typing error in **letter.2.** We want to edit it again, display it on the terminal for proofing, and finally print it. We do not have to reenter commands 96 through 98, since they are still on the history list. To repeat command 96, we can access the history list by relative command ("four commands ago") and type

```
100% !-4
```

Since the C shell adds each command to the history list, we can continue through formatting and printing by just repeating **!-4.** Accessing events by relative command number makes it easy to reexecute a series of commands.

Executing Past Commands by Matching Strings

The C shell also allows us to find an event by matching the initial string. For example, typing

```
103% !vi
```

finds the most recent command starting with **vi.** In this case it is **vi letter.2.** This kind of context searching is convenient for alternating between editing and formatting a file. Frequently, you need only type a single character to match the event. Here we can type **!v** and **!n** to alternate between the **vi** and **nroff** commands.

Similarly, a programmer debugging a C program can type **!vi** and **!cc** to recall previous **vi** and **cc** commands. For example, the sequence

```
% vi gets.c
% cc gets.c
```

```
% !vi
% !cc
```

shows a programmer alternating between correcting file **gets.c** and compiling it.

Context searching keeps recent commands from interfering with references to past commands. For example, issuing an **ls** command does not keep us from later using **!v** and **!n** to edit and format.

We can also search for events by matching a string anywhere in the past command line. All we must do is put question marks around the target string. For example, the command

```
104% !?letter.1?
```

searches for and executes the most recent command containing the string **letter.1.** It finds command 93, **nroff -ms letter.1 | lpr.**

If the C shell cannot find an event or match a string on the history list, it reports an error. For example, say we request a command beginning with **cat:**

```
105% !cat
cat: Event not found
105%
```

The C shell does not store this attempted command in the history list (note that the command number remains 105).

Changing the Course of History: Building New Commands

You can build new commands by selecting words from previous commands. **!$** refers to the last word of the last command. For example, suppose we type the command

```
105% ls -l phone.numbers
```

If we decide to make the file **phone.numbers** unreadable by others, we can type

```
106% chmod o-r !$
```

!$ refers to **phone.numbers.** Also, the command

```
107% pr -t -l15 !$ | more
```

formats and paginates the **phone.numbers** file.

We can use any word from any event on the history list. The C shell numbers the words in each command, starting at 0. For example, it numbers the words in command 107 as follows:

0	1	2	3	4	5
pr	**-t**	**-115**	**phone.numbers**	|	**more**

You can easily identify "words" since spaces separate them. Exceptions include the C shell's special symbols such as | , <, >, and **&;** these are always words by themselves. You can refer to individual words with **:n** (where **n** is the word number) following the event identification. **:n** is a history command modifier. For example,

```
108% cp !!:3 backup
```

copies **phone.numbers** to the **backup** directory. **!!** refers to the previous command (107), and **:3** refers to word 3 (**phone.numbers**).

We can also specify a range of words. If the command we are referencing is

0	1	2	3	4
ls	**-l**	**proposal.23**	**proposal.16**	**proposal.5**

then typing the command

```
109% chmod -w !ls:2-$
```

removes write permission on files **proposal.23, proposal.16,** and **proposal.5.** In this case we identified the event by searching for the latest **ls** command. Modifier **2-$** refers to all words starting with word 2. Finally,

```
110% ls -l !ls:$
```

lists **proposal.5.**

The modifier * refers to words 1 through the last (that is, everything except the command itself). So **!3:*** refers to words 1 through the last of event 3. Furthermore, **2*** refers to words 2 through the last. So for command 109 we can substitute **2*** for **2-$. !*** alone refers to words 1 through the last of the previous command. We can use this to check file expansion arguments. For example, we might type the following as a test before deleting some files:

```
111% echo unit* zone*
unit1 unit3 unit7 zone.a zone.m zone.s
```

If the list is what we expect, we can simply type

```
112% rm !*
rm unit* zone*
```

to remove the files. Since **!*** refers to words 1 through the last of the previous command, it matches the arguments of the **echo** command.

Editing Previous Commands

You can also build new commands by editing previous ones. This is particularly useful for correcting typing errors or changing a single word. Use the ^ (caret) symbol to correct mistakes in the previous command. Say you type **tooc** instead of **toc** in

```
113% nroff pref tooc ch.1 ch.2 ch.3 index
tooc: not found
```

You may correct the error with

```
114% ^too^to
nroff pref toc ch.1 ch.2 ch.3 index
```

The C shell displays and executes the corrected command line.

If the changes are not in the previous event, use the more general **:s** modifier. To substitute the file **ch.2a** for **ch.2** in command 114, type

```
115% !114:s/ch.2/ch.2a/
```

This results in

```
nroff pref toc ch.1 ch.2a ch.3 index
```

In this example the final / is not necessary since a carriage return follows immediately. However, the command

```
116% !114:s/ch.2/ch.2a/ > bk.csh
nroff pref toc ch.1 ch.2a ch.3 index > bk.csh
```

requires the final / because of the > **bk.csh** after the substitution.

You do not have to use the / character as the delimiter. In fact, you may use any nonalphanumeric character as long as you use the same one within a single command and make sure it does not conflict with characters in the substitution. (*Hint:* Use a delimiter other than / when the search or replace strings contain pathnames.)

We can also change all occurrences of a string by using the global indicator **g.** The command

```
117% !114:gs/ch/chp
```

changes command 114 to

```
nroff pref toc chp.1 chp.2 chp.3 index
```

Unfortunately, you cannot edit across words with either form (ˆ or **:s**) of command modifier. The C shell does not store spaces; it only stores command line arguments as separate words.

Look Before You Leap

The **:p** modifier prints a command derived from the history list without executing it. The C shell stores it in the history list as if it had been executed (excluding the **:p**). This allows you to check the command. If it is correct, you can then just type **!!** to execute it.

For example, the history command

```
118%  pr  !114:1-4:p
```

displays

```
pr pref toc ch.1 ch.2
```

If this is what you intended, simply type **!!** to execute it.

Pathname Qualifiers

You can use the pathname qualifiers **:t** (tail), **:e** (extension), **:h** (head), and **:r** (root) with history words. (These are the same qualifiers we use to modify variables.) In particular, the **:h** and **:t** qualifiers are handy for accessing directories or filenames from previous commands. For example, suppose you wanted to edit the file **/u/sam/utils/ttydriver.c.** Your first command might be **ls -l** to examine the permission bits.

```
% ls -l /u/sam/utils/ttydriver.c
```

After you learn that you have permission to edit the file, you decide to change directories. Using the **:h** qualifier, you need only type

```
% cd !$:h
cd /u/sam/utils
```

to change to the **/u/sam/utils** directory. The **!$** fetches the last word from the previous command, and the **:h** qualifier extracts the head pathname.
The command

```
% vi !ls:$:t
vi ttydriver.c
```

calls the visual editor to edit the file **ttydriver.c** Here we use a pattern search for the previous **ls** command, applying the **:t** qualifier to its last word to extract the filename.

Metacharacters in Pattern Searching

We can also search for patterns using the special characters **&**, **{}**, **%**, and the null string. We call these *metacharacters* because they have special meaning in history substitution commands. Let's look at each individually along with examples of their use.

The C shell uses **&** as a *remembered pattern* metacharacter. You can use it in a substitution command on the right-hand side of the delimiter to repeat the search text specified on the left-hand side. The commands

```
1% cp kwords /u/sara/japanese/dictionary
2% ^japanese^&.old^
cp kwords /u/sara/japanese.old/dictionary
```

copy the file **kwords** to two different directories: directory **dictionary** under **japanese** and directory **dictionary** under **japanese.old.** Using **&** saves us from having to type **japanese** twice in the substitution command. We can also use **&** in a general substitution (**:s**) command. For example, the command

```
3% !1:s/kwords/&.old
cp kwords.old /u/sara/japanese/dictionary
```

substitutes the word **kwords.old** for **kwords** in command 1.

We can use the null string on the left-hand side of the delimiter to repeat the search pattern from the latest substitution command. If that pattern is **kwords,** the command

```
4% !1:s//awords
cp awords /u/sara/japanese/dictionary
```

copies file **awords** to **/u/sara/japanese/dictionary.** We did not have to type the search pattern **kwords** or the destination directory. If the remembered pattern does not exist in the referenced command, the C shell reports

```
Modifier failed.
```

If the C shell has no previous left-hand side pattern, it reports

```
No previous lhs.
```

Use the **{}** metacharacters to insulate a history substitution from the characters that immediately follow it. Suppose your history list contains the command

```
% cat sec6.[1-3] > ch6
```

To repeat this command but send the output to file **ch6.bkup,** type

```
% !{cat}.bkup
cat sec6.[1-3] > ch6.bkup
```

This searches the history list for the pattern **cat** and appends the string **.bkup** at the end of the command. The braces keep the shell from taking **cat.bkup** as the matching pattern. The result without braces would be

```
% !cat.bkup
cat.bkup: Event not found.
```

We can append the **%** metacharacter to a pattern search command to extract the argument containing the pattern. If, for example, we have the command

```
% ls -l /u/sam/jobw/smdsav /u/sara/jobw
```

in our history list, we can change to directory **/u/sam/jobw/smdsav** by typing

```
% cd !?smd?%
cd /u/sam/jobw/smdsav
```

Here the C shell searches the history list for the pattern **smd** and extracts the argument **/u/sam/jobw/smdsav.** (*Hint:* This approach is useful when you know a pattern in an argument rather than the argument number.)

Saving the History List

The command

```
% history -h 15 > logfile
```

saves the last 15 commands in file **logfile.** The **-h** option tells the C shell to omit the command numbers. You may then later execute all commands in **logfile** with

```
% csh logfile
```

This works the same as if you had typed the commands. You can thus store a series of commands you might need later.

You can use the **-h** option with the **source** command to initialize a history list when you login. The command

```
% source -h logfile
```

causes the C shell to place all of **logfile**'s commands on the active history list without executing them. You can thus preserve your history list across login sessions.

You may want to set up this feature automatically. The C shell will save and restore part of the history list if you set the predefined variable **savehist.** The following command tells the C shell to save the last 10 commands when you logout.

```
% set savehist = 10
```

The C shell will save the commands in the file ~/.**history.** At login, it executes the equivalent of

```
% source -h ~/.history
```

and returns the command to the history list. You should set **savehist** in your **.login** file (see Chapter 9). (*Note:* Only BSD versions of the C shell allow the **-h** option with the **history** and **source** commands and maintain the **savehist** variable.)

Common Mistakes with the History List

Here are a few common errors in using the history list.

- Failing to set the **history** variable or save the history list between sessions.

- Forgetting that each new command (even an erroneous one) changes the list. The exception is an erroneous event identification.

- Ignoring the fact that the C shell stores commands in the history list before expanding aliases, variable names, and file expansion characters and before performing command substitution.

- Forgetting that the C shell numbers words in an event starting from 0 (not 1) and always counts special symbols as separate words.

- Ignoring changes in the environment since previous commands were executed.

Let's examine each of these separately and show examples of common pitfalls.

Setting Up. The C shell will not save any commands (except the most recent one) in the history list if you forget to set the **history** variable. Note that you can make the C shell **set history** automatically by putting the **set history** command in your ~/.**cshrc** file.

If you logout and back in, don't forget that the commands you just typed are no longer on the list. History starts over at login unless you use **savehist.**

History Marches On. It's easy to forget that history is always changing. Consider the following commands:

```
10% ls -l cshell
11% cd $!
Variable syntax.
12% cd !$
cd $!
Variable syntax.
```

Commands 11 and 12 both result in a "variable syntax" error. We typed **$!** instead of **!$** in command 11. The C shell interprets words beginning with **$** as variables. In command 12, we corrected the typing mistake. Unfortunately, we are now referencing the last word of the last command (**$!**) instead of **cshell** from command 10. Thus we just repeat the old mistake. We should refer to command 10 by typing

```
12% cd !10:$
```

or

```
12% cd !ls:$
```

History Has a History, Too. The C shell stores the history command like any other. Using **history** to examine the last command makes **history** the new last command. **!!** will now reference the history command, not your previous command.

Order of Expansion. What we type and what programs see as arguments are sometimes different. The C shell expands a history command and stores it in the list before expanding aliases, variable names, and filename expansion characters and before performing command substitution. For example, the command

```
13% ls tty*
```

lists the names of all files or directories that begin with **tty.** Suppose we then cleverly type

```
14% cd !$
```

expecting **!$** to reference the last argument passed to the **ls** command. If there is more than one directory that has a name beginning with **tty,** however, **cd** prints the following message:

```
tty*: Ambiguous.
```

(Your C shell may print a different error message.) What's the problem here? Remember, the C shell stores commands unexpanded in the history list. The **cd** command fails because the C shell attempts to execute

```
% cd tty*
```

and more than one directory or file has a name starting with **tty.**

Numbering Words. When accessing words from events, remember that the first word is 0, not 1. Also, the C shell considers special symbols as words by themselves even if they do not have spaces around them. The following examples illustrate this:

```
 0   1   2
date;who
 0    1 2  34    5
ls -l | tee>lsfile
```

The special symbols **;**, **|** , and **>** are separate words.

Changing Circumstances. Repeating a command may not make sense if the environment has changed. Consider the sequence

```
10% cp utils/setup.c ../backup
11% cd busrpts
```

The first command copies file **setup.c** to a backup directory. The second changes directories. If we now attempt to reexecute command 10, it will fail. The problem is that both of its pathnames are relative to the current directory, which we changed in command 11.

TABLE 6-1 ACCESSING WORDS FROM PREVIOUS COMMANDS

The expansions assume that all commands reference the following command in the history list:

	0	1	2	3	4	5	6
15%	**nroff**	**pref**	**toc**	**ch.1**	**ch.2**	**ch.3**	**index**

History Command	Expanded Command
cat !15:*	cat pref toc ch.1 ch.2 ch.3 index
	word(s): 1 through last
cat !15:1	cat pref
	word(s):1
cat !15:^	cat pref
	word(s):1
cat !15:3–5	cat ch.1 ch.2 ch.3
	word(s): 3 through 5
cat !15:2 −	cat toc ch.1 ch.2 ch.3
	word(s): 2 through next to last
cat !15:2*	cat toc ch.1 ch.2 ch.3 index
	word(s): 2 through last
!15:−2	nroff pref toc
	word(s): 0 through 2
cat !15:$	cat index
	word(s): last

TABLE 6-2 HISTORY COMMAND SUMMARY

N, m, n are integers; **str, s1, s2** are strings.	
set history = n	Initialize history variable to **n.**
history	Display the history list.
!N	Invoke event **N.**
!str	Invoke most recent event beginning with **str.**
!-N	Invoke **N** events in the past.
!?str?	Invoke most recent event containing **str.**
!!	Reissue the last command.
!$	last word of last command.
!N:$	last word of event **N.**
!N:ˆ	word 1 of event **N.**
!N:n	nth word of event **N.**
!N:n-m	nth through **m**th words of event **N**
!N:-n	0 through **n**th words of event **N**
!N:*	1 through the last word of event **N**
!N:n*	**n** through the last word of event **N.**
!N:n-	**n** through the next to last word of event **N.**
!N:n:h	pathname head of word **n** of event **N**
!N:n:t	pathname tail of word **n** of event **N**
!N:n:r	pathname root of word **n** of event **N**
!N:n:e	pathname extension of word **n** of event **N** (BSD)
!N:p or **!N:n:p**	Print the expanded history command; no execute.
ˆs1ˆs2ˆ	Substitute **s2** for **s1** in the previous command.
!N:s/s1/s2/	Substitute **s2** for **s1** in event **N.**
!N:gs/s1/s2/	Globally substitute **s2** for **s1** in event **N.**
!N:s/s1/& s2/	Substitute **s1 s2** for **s1** in event **N.**
!N:s//s2/	Substitute **s2** for remembered pattern in event **N.**
!?str?:s//s2	Substitute **s2** for remembered pattern in event containing **str.**
!{s1}s2	Search history for **s1**; append **s2** to command.
!?s1?%	Search history for **s1**; produce argument containing **s1.**

History Command Summary

Table 6-1 summarizes the syntax for accessing words from previous commands. Table
6-2 summarizes the syntax of history commands. The history mechanism can save on
typing as well as provide a historical record. Use it!

6.2 USING YOUR OWN PET NAMES: ALIASES

An important feature of the C shell is its ability to let you assign a name, or *alias,* to a
command or sequence of commands. You can use an alias just like any other command.
Its definition can include a sequence of commands, combined in any way you like; it can
use pipes, redirection, and even background execution. Your alias can rename existing

commands and name commands with specific option flags. Furthermore, an alias can create and reference shell variables, include command substitution, and use other aliases. For increased generality, you can even pass arguments.

Alias Command Format

Use the following format to create an alias:

```
alias name definition
```

You define an alias by giving its name followed by a definition. This is usually one or more commands or, possibly, a previously defined alias. If the definition contains special symbols, put single quotation marks around it. For example, the command

```
% alias h history
```

defines the alias **h** to be the **history** command. Typing **h** thereafter invokes **history.** The command

```
% alias cx chmod +x
```

allows you to type **cx** instead of **chmod + x.** Now typing

```
% cx search cpdir
```

makes the files **search** and **cpdir** executable. Note that this alias allows you to specify any number of file arguments. That's because the C shell substitutes **chmod + x** wherever you use it. We refer to this as *alias substitution*.

To display a definition, just type **alias** and the name. For example, to display what **cx** means, type

```
% alias cx
chmod +x
```

alias with no arguments lists all aliases and their definitions:

```
% alias
cx      chmod +x
h       history
```

To release an alias, use the **unalias** command. For example,

```
% unalias cx
```

releases **cx** as an alias.

Referencing Other Aliases

An alias definition may refer to another alias. The definition

```
% alias ah 'h | head -15'
```

assumes that alias **h** exists for the **history** command. The command **ah** (ancient history) displays the first 15 lines of the history list. (Note that here we use quotation marks to define alias **ah** because it contains the pipe symbol, | .)

Can aliases refer to themselves? Let's investigate. Suppose you want to create a revised **who** command that reports the date as well as the usual information. You try the following:

```
% alias who 'date; who'
% who
Alias loop.
```

What's wrong here? The C shell has the following rule:

Aliases may refer to themselves as long as the command name appears first in the definition.

This allows you to alias a command to the same command name but include an option. For example,

```
% alias ls ls -l
```

displays a long listing of your files when you type **ls.**

How can we correct our alias loop example? First, remove the alias with the unalias command:

```
% unalias who
```

Second, either make **who** the first command in the definition or use the absolute pathname for **who.** Either

```
% alias who 'who; date'
```

or

```
% alias who 'date; /bin/who'
```

will solve the looping problem.

Arguments in Aliases

Unless you specify otherwise, the C shell assumes that all arguments come at the end of the alias definition. For example, you can use arguments with the **cx** alias defined earlier. The command

```
% cx *
```

makes all files in the current directory executable. The command expands to

```
% chmod +x *
```

What if we want arguments placed somewhere besides at the end of the definition? For example, let's look at the **find** command. To locate the file **ttydoc.77** starting from our home directory, we type

```
% find ~ -name ttydoc.77 -print
/u/sam/jobs/man/ttydoc.77
```

We want to create an alias called **loc** that takes a filename as an argument to the **find** command. Instead of typing the verbose form of the **find** command, we want to type

```
% loc ttydoc.77
```

The alias should use the **find** command to locate the file. How can we pass the **ttydoc.77** argument so that it will appear in the proper position?

Two common argument designations let us pass parameters to aliases:

!*   words 1 through the last of the current command´
!^   word 1 of the current command

For this example we use **!^**, since the **find** command requires a single filename argument. The alias definition is as follows:

```
% alias loc 'find ~ -name \!^ -print'
```

Note that we must escape the **!** character. This keeps the C shell from interpreting it as a history list reference when we define alias **loc**. Now the argument (word 1 of the current command) will end up between **-name** and **-print** when we use **loc**.

As a second example, let's create an alias **ldir** that displays long listings of only directory names (i.e., not ordinary files). Our approach is the following:

```
% alias ldir 'ls -l | grep "^d"'
```

This takes the long listing of the current directory and pipes it to the **grep** command. The **grep** command displays only lines that begin with the letter **d** (directories). The following commands show a sample output:

```
% ldir
drwxr-xr-x 8 sara other 64 Jun 20 17:12 doc
drwxr-xr-x 5 sara other 96 Apr 12 22:09 drivers
drwxr-xr-x 2 sara other 32 Aug 30 11:32 src
```

If you attempt to apply **ldir** to the directory **../utils** with the command

```
% ldir ../utils
```

you will get the error message

```
Broken pipe.
```

What's wrong here? The problem is that we want the argument to apply to **ls,** not to **grep.** After alias substitution, the C shell tries to execute

```
% ls -l | grep "^d" ../utils
```

We can place the argument correctly by using the !* symbols in the definition, that is,

```
% alias ldir 'ls -l \!* | grep "^d"'
```

Note that we need \ to escape the ! in the definition again.

   With this definition we can now pass any number of arguments to the alias. The command

```
% ldir ../utils /usr/bin ~
```

expands to

```
ls -l ../utils /usr/bin /u/pa | grep "^d"
```

The result is long listings (of directories only) of the three directory names: **../utils, /usr/bin,** and ~ (your home directory).

   The similarity in syntax between alias argument passing and history list processing is no accident. In fact, when the C shell is passing arguments to the alias, it treats the current command as if it were the previous command. So if the alias definition includes the notation !^, the C shell substitutes word 1 of the current command. (Remember, the C shell starts numbering history words at 0.) Similarly, if the alias definition includes !*, the C shell substitutes everything except word 0.

   Note the order here. The C shell first checks word 0 to see if it is an alias. If so, it examines the alias to see if it contains history commands. These apply as if the command were already in the history list. Thus **!*** picks up words 1 through the last of the command itself. While an alias definition may include any history command, practical situations rarely call for anything besides **!*** or **!ˆ**. (For an exception see the alias definition for **usage** in Section 11.3.)

Aliases Come First

We have shown examples of aliases that combine commands, reference other aliases, and even cause standard commands to "act differently." How does the C shell execute aliases and in what order? Are there any items that we cannot alias? Understanding how the C shell executes aliases and commands provides insight into its power and uses.

Let's first examine what happens when you issue a command to the C shell. After history substitution, the C shell examines each word that could be a command, according to the following order:

1. Alias substitution
2. Built-in commands
3. Commands in your search path (**$path**)

Note the distinction between built-in commands (they are inside the C shell) and commands that are in the file system. The C shell executes commands such as **cd** and **kill** directly, whereas **who** and **pwd** are programs in the file system (/**bin/who** and /**bin/pwd,** respectively). See Appendix C for a list of the C shell's built-in commands.

It is significant that alias substitution occurs first. You can, for example, assign the alias **cancel** to **kill** with

```
% alias cancel kill
```

if **kill** is too violent for your tastes. BSD versions of the C shell include the **$cwd** (current working directory) shell variable. You can use it to alias the **pwd** command. The alias **pwd,** given by

```
% alias pwd 'echo $cwd'
```

executes faster than the program /**bin/pwd. echo** is a built-in command, and **$cwd** is a built-in shell variable.

Alias Examples

There is an art to creating useful aliases. What is essential to one user may be annoying to another. Let's look at some examples of aliases.

Example 1. You may want to minimize typing or make commands more meaningful. The aliases

```
% alias env printenv
% alias bye logout
```

allow you to type **env** to display your current environment variables (**$HOME, $PATH,** etc.; see Section 9.3). The new command **bye** replaces the built-in command **logout,** when you decide to call it a day.

 Example 2. The **rm** command can be quite unforgiving at times. Even experienced users sometimes make the classic error

```
% rm file1 file2 chap *
```

instead of

```
% rm file1 file2 chap*
```

The first command, of course, removes all files from your directory. To avoid errors like this, you could use the alias

```
% alias rm 'rm -i'
```

This makes the **-i** (interactive) option automatic with **rm,** so it asks for confirmation before removing a file. A typical sequence is

```
% rm secretmail
rm: remove secretmail?
```

This will remove the **secretmail** file only if you type **y.**

 To avoid the alias, use the full pathname for the remove command, **/bin/rm.** Another possibility is to use the alias

```
% alias rm 'mv \!* ~/tomb'
```

which moves (instead of removes) each file to a special "tomb" directory. You can clean **tomb** at a later time with

```
% cd ~/tomb; /bin/rm *
```

 Example 3. You may want an alias that gives you the time:

```
% alias tm '(set d = `date` ; echo $d[4])'
% tm
08:58:48
```

Here we use a subshell with command substitution and a local variable. Shell variable **$d** disappears when the subshell exits. The single quotation marks are necessary to avoid the following error:

```
% alias tm "(set d = `date` ; echo $d[4])"
d: Undefined variable.
```

This occurs because the C shell tries to expand the shell variable **$d[4]** before it is set.

Example 4. UNIX allows other users to write to your terminal. The following command (**mesg**) and its output

```
% mesg
is y
```

indicate that other users can send you messages via the **write** or **talk** command. This may be fine at the shell level, but you may want to "lock out" discussions while you are using the **vi** editor. The alias

```
% alias vi '(mesg n; /bin/vi \!*; mesg y)'
```

turns off messages automatically before calling the **vi** editor. The final **mesg y** turns them back on. The specification **!*** allows you to edit any number of files. There are two notes here: (1) You need to specify the full pathname for **vi, /bin/vi,** to avoid an alias loop error. The pathname may be different on your system. (2) If you suspend (**control-Z**) from **vi,** messages will remain turned off. After returning to **vi,** the parentheses (forming a subshell) enables the C shell to execute **mesg y** when you finally exit **vi.**

Example 5. For you lost souls who are constantly typing **pwd** to see where you are in the file system, here is an alias that gives the current directory names at the prompt:

```
% alias cd 'cd \!*; set prompt = "<$cwd> "'
```

The built-in command **cd** now dynamically displays the current working directory. Let's see how this works.

```
% pwd
/u/pa
% cd tools
</u/pa/tools> cd proms
</u/pa/tools/proms> cd ..
</u/pa/tools> cd
</u/pa>
```

Here the **cd** command changes the prompt as well as the directory. In defining the alias for **cd,** we use the **!*** form to allow zero or more arguments (**cd** by itself returns you to your home directory). We use double quotation marks to insulate the redirection characters < and > and still expand the built-in shell variable **$cwd.** We include the space before the second double quotation mark for a good reason: It keeps the prompt and the next command line from running into each other. For non-BSD versions, substitute `pwd` (command substitution) for **$cwd** in the alias definition.

Example 6. You may want to create aliases to compensate for frequent typing mistakes. The alias

```
% alias ls-l 'ls -l'
```

automatically corrects a common typing error (forgetting the space between **ls** and **-l**). You may even want to make the **ls** command default to the **-l** option:

```
% alias ls 'ls -l'
```

Then, to retain **ls** with no options, set up a separate alias for it:

```
% alias L /bin/ls
```

Here we must again specify the full pathname. If we just type **ls,** the C shell will expand the alias.

Example 7. On UNIX systems that bill for login time, you may want an alias that tells you when you logged in. The following alias and its invocation show this.

```
% alias since 'set t = `who | grep $user` ; echo $t[5]; unset t'
% since
11:13
```

We use the predefined variable **$user** instead of our own name to make the alias more general.

Example 8. You may want to create a large history list to log commands. Suppose you initialize your history list to 60 with the command

```
% set history = 60
```

The following alias definitions (for BSD versions) divided this long list into three parts— **ah** (ancient history), **ma** (middle ages), and **rh** (recent history).

```
% alias ah 'history | head -21'
% alias ma 'history 41 | head -21'
% alias rh 'history 21'
```

The **head** utility simply picks off the specified number of elements from the front of the list. For non-BSD versions, just pipe **history**'s output to the **tail** utility as follows:

```
% alias ma 'history | tail -41 | head -21'
% alias rh 'history | tail -21'
```

When Not to Use Aliases

Aliases take time to expand, and they use memory as well. Therefore, you should not create aliases for infrequently used commands or sequences of commands. This is just as well, since it will probably be harder to remember the alias than to type the original command. You should also not use aliases for commands that must check the validity of arguments or perform looping or other programming functions. You should define shell scripts instead (see Chapters 7 and 8).

Common Mistakes with Aliases

Common mistakes with aliases include using the wrong quotation marks, misplacing arguments, and forgetting to escape an **!**. For example,

```
% alias print 'pr !* | lpr&'
```

attempts to define an alias to format any number of files and send them to the line printer as a background job. The alias fails, however, because we must escape the **!**. The correct alias is

```
% alias print 'pr \!* | lpr&'
```

6.3 PUTTING IT ALL TOGETHER

It is common to define separate directories for each project. Furthermore, it is easier to work "in" the directory we are currently accessing. This means that while working in the UNIX file system, we often want to change directories briefly and then return to where we were (or go somewhere else).

BSD versions include the built-in commands **pushd, popd,** and **dirs,** which let us switch back and forth easily. For C shell versions that lack these commands, refer to Section 11.10. For now, let's see how we can use aliases.

The alias must remember the name of the directory we left. This helps avoid the need to type long pathnames. Consider the following:

```
% pwd
/u/pa/jobw/source
% cd /usr/include/sys
.... stay here awhile ....
% cd /u/pa/jobw/source
% pwd
/u/pa/jobw/source
```

From our current directory we change to **/usr/include/sys** for a while, then return to where we were. Using **cd** involves a lot of typing. Let's introduce two aliases called **gt** (go to a directory) and **gb** (go back or return to the previous directory). These aliases allow us to type the following for our original scenario:

```
% pwd
/u/pa/jobw/source
% gt /usr/include/sys
.... stay here awhile ....
% gb
/u/pa/jobw/source
% gb
/usr/include/sys
```

Note that we can go back and forth between the two directories by typing successive **gb**'s. Let's examine the alias definitions now.

```
% alias gt 'set d1 = $cwd; cd \!^'
% alias gb 'set d2 = $cwd; cd $d1; set d1 = $d2; echo $cwd'
```

The **gt** alias saves the current directory in a shell variable **$d1** before changing directories. You type the same number of characters as in a **cd** command, but the C shell will remember your previous directory.

The **gb** alias is a little more complicated. It saves the current directory in a second shell variable, **$d2.** It then changes the current directory back to **$d1,** moves the old current directory from **$d2** to **$d1** (thus allowing the back-and-forth feature), and finally displays the new directory using **echo $cwd.**

Remember, for non-BSD versions, use these alias definitions:

```
% alias gt 'set d1 = `pwd` ; cd \!^'
% alias gb 'set d2 = `pwd` ; cd $d1; set d1 = $d2; pwd'
```

We can extend this even further. By introducing a third alias, **alt,** we can display the *alternate* directory if we are not sure of its name. For example,

```
% alias alt 'echo $d1'
% alt
/u/pa/jobw/source
```

shows us that the alternate directory is **/u/pa/jobw/source.**

6.4 KEY POINT SUMMARY

The *history* mechanism saves past commands in a list. The history variable determines how long this list is. You can display the list with the **history** command.

You can refer to command (*events*) on the history list by absolute or relative number or by matching strings. This allows you to repeat past commands, make corrections, and reuse filenames. The most recent command is particularly easy to reference.

You can reference individual words within past commands. This allows you to reuse arguments and test file specifications before actually issuing commands. You can even print a command derived from the history list before executing it.

While the history list normally disappears when you logout, the C shell will save and restore part of it automatically if you set the predefined variable **savehist.**

Aliases allow you to abbreviate common commands or sequences of commands. You must define aliases each time you login unless you save them in your **.cshrc** file.

The C shell normally assumes that all arguments come at the end of an alias definition. If you want to put arguments elsewhere, you must use the history mechanism to make the C shell place them properly. The C shell interprets history commands within an alias as if the current command were already on the history list.

7

C Shell Programming

Common tasks often involve repetitive sequences of C shell commands. We may, for example, frequently use sequences that produce new working copies of files and save the old versions, compile and link programs, merge files, and make backup files. Rather than entering the commands each time, we can make them into a program or (if we have literary leanings) a *script*. All we must then do is make the C shell execute the script. This both saves typing and ensures an error-free procedure.

Scripts can even be general-purpose tools that many people use. One example would be a script that checks text files to make sure they do not contain lines too long for an 80-column printer. Another example would be a script that simply beeps the terminal twice. Calling **beep** at the end of a command line provides an audio notification that a background job is finished.

Scripts can also help us define and formalize tools that we might use only once or twice. Suppose we want to convert text files created with a non-UNIX word processor to UNIX. After transferring the files, we must remove any special formatting characters. We can write a script that will process all the files with one command. (Who wants to do it by hand?)

This chapter contains many examples of C shell scripts. Some are useful as is, while others will require customizing to meet your needs. You can use these scripts as models to build your own collection.

128

7.1 WHY IMPROVISE WHEN YOU CAN HAVE A SCRIPT?
C SHELL SCRIPTS

To create a C shell script, you must use an editor to place a sequence of commands in a text file. The first line must contain the number (**#**) symbol in the first column, indicating a C shell script. The syntax is then the same as in an interactive session. You place single commands one per line, separate multiple commands with semicolons, use the pipe symbol | to connect commands, and use the symbols >, <, and >> for redirection. You can also group commands with parentheses and make them execute in the background with **&.**

To make the program executable, use the UNIX command **chmod.** The format is

```
% chmod +x prog_file
```

The argument **+x** makes **prog_file** executable by anyone. To execute it, simply type its name.

For example, let's write a short C shell script that beeps twice at our terminal. This is a general-purpose tool we can use to indicate the termination of a background job. The text file is

```
% cat beep
#
echo -n '^G'
sleep 1
echo -n '^G'
```

When you hold down the CONTROL key and type **g,** the **vi** editor displays the sequence **^G.** The command

```
% echo -n '^G'
```

sounds your terminal's bell. The **-n** option to **echo** prevents a line feed. The second command pauses for one second. The third command just repeats the first.

We can now make this script executable with **chmod** and run it as follows:

```
% chmod +x beep
% (cc -o taxmod taxmod.c >& errs; beep) &
[1] 2602
```

Here we place **beep** after a compile (**cc**) command. The C shell displays the job number and process ID. When **cc** finishes (remember, we placed it in the background), we will hear two beeps, one second apart. We can then check file **errs** to see if the compilation was successful.

What C shell constructs can we use in scripts? The C shell has what amounts to a programming language. It includes constructs for making decisions, looping, handling program arguments, performing arithmetic operations, and evaluating expressions. You may use pipes, redirection, background processing, command groups, shell variables, aliases, C shell commands (**cd, set**), UNIX programs (**who, ls**), and other shell scripts. Let's begin with a simple example that we will expand as we learn more programming constructs.

The script **longlines** detects lines in text files that are longer than a specified number of characters. Initially, we'll assume that the number is 80. How do we approach such a task?

Obviously, we want to use UNIX commands whenever possible in scripts. The one that is handy here is the text processing program **awk**. It will print every line that satisfies a specified condition or contains a given pattern. All we must do is make the condition a length exceeding 80 characters (**length > 80**). Our initial version of **longlines** is as follows.

```
       % num longlines
   1   #
   2   awk "length > 80"
```

Line 1 is just the **#** symbol. Line 2 is the **awk** command, which prints text lines containing more than 80 characters. Rather than using the **cat** command to list the **longlines** script, we have used a special shell script called **num** to display the lines with their numbers. This is simply a convenience for reference purposes. The text for **num** appears below. (You may also use the command

```
       % pr -t -n longlines
```

or

```
       % cat -n longlines
```

if your version of **pr** or **cat** includes the **-n** option.)

THE NUM SCRIPT

Throughout this chapter we use **num** to list the lines in the script examples. Here is the text for **num**:

```
       % num num
   1   # csh to number the files in argument list or the
   2   # standard input if no arguments.
   3
   4   if ($#argv == 0) then                    # arguments?
   5       awk '{printf "%4d    %s\n", NR, $0 }'# use standard input
   6       exit 0
   7   endif
   8
   9   foreach file ($argv[*])                  # argument expansion
```

```
10      if (-f $file) then                              # plain file?
11          awk '{printf "%4d    %s\n", NR, $0 }' $file
12          echo ""
13      else
14          echo2 $0\: No file $file
15      endif
16  end
```

How does **longlines** know what file to process? Since we did not specify an input file for **awk,** it reads from the standard input. This means we can use **longlines** just like a standard UNIX command (such as **mail** or **sort**), as in

```
% longlines < document
% cat dict[1-5]  |  longlines
% grep "business expense" tax84.*  |  longlines  |  \
sort -n +2  |  lpr
```

The first example uses input redirection (<) to make **longlines** read from file **document.** The second example concatenates files **dict1** through **dict5.** We pipe the result to the input of **longlines.** The output, if any, appears on our terminal. The third example searches all **tax84** records in our current directory for lines containing the string "business expense." We use **longlines** afterward since only lines longer than 80 characters contain the summary information we want. We then sort the output numerically (**-n**) by the third field (**+2** means skip two fields). We print this output on a 132-column printer with **lpr.** Note that **longlines** reads from the standard input and writes its standard output to a pipe in this example.

7.2 INCLUDING YOUR OWN THOUGHTS: COMMENT LINES

Even the simplest shell script should contain comments. As in programming languages, comments are for documentation only; the C shell ignores them. They tell what all or part of a script does, how it is used, or how it works. They help you remember what your thoughts were. That way, when you must revise an old script, you won't feel like an archaeologist examining the remains of a lost civilization.

The symbol **#** marks the start of a comment. It can appear either after a command or at the beginning of a line. Here is **longlines** with comments:

```
% num longlines
1   # C shell script to print lines from standard input
2   # that are longer than 80 characters
3   # Usage: longlines < file
4
5   awk "length > 80"              # quotes necessary
```

Note that line 1 contains an introductory comment as well as identifying the file as a script. The other comments describe what **longlines** does and how to use it. We recommend that you include a "Usage:" comment (line 3) in all scripts. It reminds you (and others) how to use it and provides documentation. Blank lines make the script easier to read. Line 5 contains a comment on the same line as the command. Here we warn the reader that the quotation marks in the **awk** command are necessary.

7.3 YOUR PROGRAM TALKS: echo

The **echo** command lets a shell script describe its output. **echo** simply writes its arguments to the standard output. We can, for example, use it to generate titles for tables or prompt the user for an input filename. We can also annotate the output from UNIX commands that may report just numbers or character strings. For commands that take a long time, we can use **echo** to inform the user what the script is doing. For example, a script that sorts records may contain the following statements:

```
echo "sorting transaction records"
sort *.tr >> master
echo "sort done"
```

The following script, called **numfiles**, uses the commands **ls** and **wc -l** to count the number of files and directories in the current directory. Without **echo,** it would display just a number. Here's an initial version using **echo:**

```
% num numfiles
1    # csh script to count number of files and directories
2    # in the current directory
3    # Usage: numfiles
4
5    echo -n "files and directories: "
6    ls | wc -l
```

The **-n** option in line 5 supresses the newline output from the **echo** command. This makes the string "files and directories: " and the number (returned from the C shell) appear on the same line. A typical result is

```
% numfiles
files and directories: 12
```

Note that most general-purpose tools use **echo** sparingly, if at all. This approach allows users to pipe them without worrying about incidental output. Furthermore, the tools do not interfere unnecessarily with the screen display. Commands such as **cat, sort, wc, grep,** and our **longlines** script work well in combinations partly because they omit titles and other incidental information.

7.4 FLEXING YOUR PROGRAM'S MUSCLES: USING ARGUMENTS

The **numfiles** script works only on our current directory. To apply it to an arbitrary directory, we would have to issue a **cd** command first. Let's enhance it to accept a directory name as an argument. We can then use **numfiles** as follows:

```
% numfiles ~/tools
% numfiles ..
% numfiles japanese
```

How does the C shell pass the command line argument (~/**tools**, **..**, **japanese**) to a shell script? It stores them in a special shell variable called **argv**. The first argument is **$argv[1]**, the second **$argv[2]**, and so on. If we call our **numfiles** script with

```
% numfiles japanese
```

the shell stores the string **japanese** in **$argv[1]**. The number of arguments on the command line is **$#argv.**

The following version of **numfiles** allows an argument:

```
  % num numfiles
1 # csh to count number of files and
2 # directories in argument 1
3 # Usage: numfiles directory
4
5 echo -n Number of files/directories in $argv[1]\.
6 ls $argv[1] | wc -l
```

Line 5 reports the directory name using **$argv[1]** with the **echo** command. We use the backslash to quote the colon so that the C shell doesn't expect one of the variable modifiers to follow (e.g., **:h** or **:t**). Line 6 uses the name as an argument to the **ls** command. A typical result is

```
% numfiles japanese
Number of files/directories in japanese: 16
```

Table 7-1 summarizes the notation for referring to command line arguments. The C shell allows **$1** through **$9** for **$argv[1]** through **$argv[9]**. Note that **$0** (not **$argv[0]**) is the script's name. We will use the **$argv** notation since it forces the C shell to check whether enough arguments exist (so-called *range checking*). Furthermore, the **$argv** notation also allows you to specify a range of arguments such as

```
$argv[3-$#argv]
```

for all arguments from 3 to the last.

TABLE 7-1 METHODS FOR ACCESSING C SHELL ARGUMENTS

Symbol	Meaning
$#argv	number of arguments
$argv [*]	all arguments
$argv	same as $argv [*]
$*	same as $argv [*]
$argv [1-n]	arguments 1 through **n**
$0	name of the program
$argv [0]	illegal; must use $0
$argv [n]	argument **n** (**1 <= n <= $#argv**)
$1 $2 ... $9	arguments 1, 2 ... 9; same as **$argv [1]** through **$argv [9]**
$argv [$#argv]	last argument

Let's put these new concepts to work. Suppose we want to change a globally defined constant, **MAXPROP,** used in many C program modules in a real estate package. We want to display the line number and text of each line that uses this constant. We also format and print the results for reference.

We create a shell script **searcher** to automate this task. It displays all lines in a group of files that contain a specified pattern. Its arguments are the directory containing the files to be searched, the pattern, and the files themselves. For example, the command

```
% searcher ~/realestate MAXPROP "*.c"
```

searches all files ending in **.c** in directory ~/**realestate** for the pattern **MAXPROP.** Note that we quote argument 3 (***.c**) so that the C shell will not expand it until the script uses it. Here is the script **searcher:**

```
% num searcher
1    # csh to search directory for pattern
2    # in all files (argument 3 - last)
3    # Usage: searcher directory pattern file(s)
4
5    cd $argv[1]              # change directory to argument 1
6    grep -n "$argv[2]" $argv[3-$#argv] | pr | lpr
```

Line 5 uses **cd** to change to the directory named in argument 1. Line 6 executes **grep,** specifying the pattern as argument 2. We include the **-n** option to output the line number as well as the text. We use double quotation marks around **$argv[2]** in case it contains file expansion or other special characters. (Remember, the C shell expands variables even in double quotation marks.) The notation **$argv[3-$#argv]** refers to the third through last arguments. Note that this technique allows us to use **searcher** with a varying number of file arguments. For example,

```
% searcher ~/realestate MAXPROP build.c menu.c
```

specifies four arguments (two files), and

```
% searcher ~/realestate MAXPROP build.c menu.c sales.c
```

specifies five arguments (three files).

As another example, let's modify the **longlines** script to accept a filename instead of reading from the standard input.

```
      % num longlines
   1  # script to display lines in a file longer than
   2  # 80 characters
   3  # Usage: longlines file
   4
   5  echo $argv[1]\:                 # display filename
   6  awk "length > 80" $argv[1]      # call awk with argument 1
```

Line 5 displays the filename. Again, we use the backslash to quote the colon following variable **$argv[1].** Line 6 calls **awk** with a file argument (**$argv[1]**).

To use this version of **longlines,** type the command followed by the filename, as in

```
% longlines dict1
dict1:
[All lines longer than 80 characters displayed here]
```

Later we will develop a version of **longlines** that can read from either the standard input or a file.

7.5 A QUICK RETURN: exit

How can we stop a script and return control to the C shell? You can use the **exit** statement to terminate execution anywhere in a script. Commonly one uses it to respond to abnormal conditions, such as illegal options or nonexistent files. It's a good idea to check the validity of arguments at the beginning of a script and exit if they are specified incorrectly.

The format of the **exit** statement is

```
exit
```

or

```
exit (expression)
```

exit with no parameter returns the status of the last executed command. Otherwise it returns the value of **expression.** (You may omit the parentheses if **expression** is just an integer.) You can access the status from the C shell in the predefined shell variable **$status.** The UNIX convention is to use 0 for normal (succcessful) exit status and nonzero values for abnormal status.

Note that many UNIX commands return status information. For example, **grep** returns 0 if it finds a match and 1 if it does not. The **test** command returns 0 if the test is successful and 1 if it is not. Let's look at an example of a shell script that returns exit status.

Suppose we have some C programs that use hexadecimal constants to identify I/O hardware devices, such as a joystick or an analog-to-digital converter. We want to find all lines in the programs that contain such constants for checking with current schematics. We represent hexadecimal constants in C using "0x" or "0X" followed by at least one digit that can be 0–9 or A–F (or a–f, for that matter). How can we search for these patterns?

We use the **grep** command with the following expression:

```
"0[xX][0-9a-fA-F][0-9a-fA-F]*"
```

This is tricky. First of all, don't confuse the * with the C shell's file expansion character—they are different! **grep** uses an asterisk to match the previous pattern (in this case 0–9,a–f, or A–F) zero or more times. So this entire expression matches hexadecimal constants with at least one digit. **0[xX]** says the pattern begins with either **0x** or **0X.** Since this expression is difficult to type more than once, we put it in a shell script.

```
  % num hexnum
1   # csh to list lines in a C program that contain hex numbers
2   # Usage: hexnum file
3
4   grep "0[xX][0-9a-fA-F][0-9a-fA-F]*" $argv[1]
```

To list all lines with hexadecimal constants in file **tester.c,** we type

```
% hexnum tester.c > hexlist
```

What if we accidentally specify an unreadable or nonexistent filename? We don't want to pass it to the **grep** command, since it will fail. Instead we use the UNIX **test** command with the **-r** option to check that the file exists and is readable. (Alternatively, Section 7.9 discusses file inquiry operators to do the same thing.) By combining the **test** and **exit** commands using conditional command execution, we can terminate the script if the **test** command fails, as follows:

```
  % num hexnum
1   # csh to list lines in a C program that contain hex numbers
2   # Usage: hexnum file
```

```
3
4    test -r $argv[1]  ||  exit 2
5    grep "0[xX][0-9a-fA-F][0-9a-fA-F]*" $argv[1]
```

Since **grep** returns 1 if it cannot match the pattern, we return 2 if **test** finds an invalid name. We can now examine the **$status** variable to determine what happened. If the **test** command succeeds, the script will return **grep**'s status (either 0 or 1).

Let's test our new script. Suppose our directory contains the files **tester.c,** which has hexadecimal constants, and **filler.c,** which does not. We type

```
% hexnum tester.c >> hexlist
% echo $status
0
```

The 0 indicates that **hexnum** succeeded (hence **grep** succeeded). Now we type

```
% hexnum filer.c >> hexlist
% echo $status
2
```

The status is 2 because we mistyped the filename (**filer.c** instead of **filler.c**), hence the **test** command failed. We try again:

```
% hexnum filler.c >> hexlist
% echo $status
1
```

Status is 1 because **grep** did not find any lines containing hexadecimal constants.

Note that we do not need to display **$status;** we can use conditional command execution based on its value. For example, if we type

```
% hexnum filler.c >> hexlist && lpr hexlist
```

the **lpr** command will execute only if the **hexnum** command succeeds.

7.6 SPEAK AND YE SHALL BE HEARD: REPORTING DIAGNOSTIC OUTPUT

Sometimes we may want a shell script to check for errors. For example, if a script expects a filename as its only argument, it should check both the number of arguments and their validity. We used this technique in our **hexnum** script. We used the **test** command to check for a valid filename and **exit** to return to the C shell if it was erroneous.

Let's include an **echo** statement now to report the error:

```
      % num hexnum
1     # csh to list lines in a C program that contain hex numbers
2     # Usage: hexnum file
3
4     test -r $argv[1] || (echo "Can't read $argv[1].";exit 2)
5     grep "0[xX][0-9a-fA-F][0-9a-fA-F]*" $argv[1]
```

Note that the command grouping on line 4 makes it execute both **echo** and **exit** if the
file is unreadable. Let's try **hexnum** now for a nonexistent file (**filer.c**):

```
% hexnum filer.c >> hexlist
% echo $status
2
```

What happened to the error message? Let's try it without output redirection:

```
% hexnum filer.c
Can't read filer.c.
% echo $status
2
```

In the first example, we expected the error message to appear on our terminal. We
only saw it when we eliminated output redirection (in the second example). This is
because redirection affected **echo**'s output as well as **grep**'s.

Unfortunately, the C shell does not provide a variation of **echo** that writes to
diagnostic output. However, a short C program **echo2** (see Appendix D for its source)
does the job. We will use **echo2** for diagnostic messages in all subsequent scripts. (*Note:*
XENIX provides option **-e** with program **/bin/echo** to write to diagnostic output.)

The following version of **hexnum** uses **echo2:**

```
      % num hexnum
1     # csh to list lines in a C program that contain hex numbers
2     # Usage: hexnum file
3
4     test -r $argv[1] || (echo2 "Can't read $argv[1].";exit 2)
5     grep "0[xX][0-9a-fA-F][0-9a-fA-F]*" $argv[1]

% hexnum filer.c >> hexlist
Can't read filer.c.
% echo $status
2
```

Note that you can redirect **echo2**'s output by using the methods described in Chapter 3
for diagnostic output. For example, the command

```
% hexnum filer.c >>& hexlist
```

redirects the error message to **hexlist.** Similarly, the command

```
% (hexnum filer.c > hexlist) >& /dev/null
```

discards error messages.

7.7 IN THE VALLEY OF DECISION: CONDITIONAL STATEMENTS

The C shell provides **if** constructs (summarized in Table 7-2) that let a script make decisions. Let's look at the different forms as we develop a shell script called **wmail.** We use **wmail** as follows:

```
% wmail user
```

where **user** is a login name on your system. **wmail** determines if **user** is currently logged in and calls the **write** command to initiate a conversation. (Berkeley users may prefer the **talk** command.) If **user** is not logged in, **wmail** calls the **mail** program so you can send a mail message.

The simplest form of the **if** statement is

```
if (expression) command
```

TABLE 7-2 FORMS OF THE C SHELL **if** CONSTRUCT

```
1.    if (expression) command

2.    if (expression) then
          command(s)
      endif

3.    if (expression) then
          command(s)
      else
          command(s)
      endif

4.    if (expression) then
          command(s)
      [else if (expression) then
          command(s) ]
      . . . . .
      [else
          command(s) ]
      endif
```

where the C shell executes the single **command** if **expression** is true. We can use the same operators as in the C language. For example, we can use the following relational operators to compare numeric (integer) values:

>	greater than
<	less than
>=	greater than or equal to
<=	less than or equal to
==	equal to
!=	not equal to

(Table 7-5 in Section 7.8 includes a complete list of the comparison operators.) Let's apply one of these in an initial version of the **wmail** script.

```
      % num wmail
1     # csh script to send mail or converse with a user
2     # Usage: wmail username
3
4     set w = (`who | grep $argv[1]` )
5     if ($#w == 0) echo "$argv[1] is not logged in"
```

Here we set a shell variable **$w** to a wordlist by using **who** and **grep** to search for **user.** If **user** is not logged in, the wordlist will contain nothing. Hence the expression

```
if ($#w == 0)
```

is true. If we tried to talk to user **marty** at this point, we would see the following:

```
% wmail marty
marty is not logged in
```

Marty is probably on one of his extended coffee breaks. Let's add the capability to send mail now. For this, we use the second form of the **if** command

```
if (expression) then
     command(s)
endif
```

You must follow this format precisely. **then** must be on the same line as **if,** and **endif** must be on its own line. Unlike the first form, which executes only a single command line, this form allows more than one line. **endif** marks the end of the **if** construct. Here's the next version of **wmail:**

```
      % num wmail
1     # csh script to send mail or converse with a user
```

```
2    # Usage: wmail username
3
4    set w = (`who | grep $argv[1]` )
5    if ($#w == 0)  then
6         echo "$argv[1] is not logged in...send mail"
7         mail $argv[1]
8    endif
```

Now **wmail** notifies us if **user** is not logged in and calls the **mail** command. (We can then type a mail message, terminating it with **control-D**.) Note that we indent lines 6 and 7 to improve readability.

Now let's add the ability to talk to **user.** We use an **if-else** construct of the form

```
if (expression) then
     command(s)
else
     command(s)
endif
```

You must put **else** and **endif** on their own lines. You may have any number of commands between **then** and **else** and between **else** and **endif.**

```
     % num wmail
1    # csh script to send mail or converse with a user
2    # Usage: wmail username
3
4    set w = (`who | grep $argv[1]` )
5    if ($#w == 0)  then
6         echo "$argv[1] is not logged in...send mail"
7         mail $argv[1]
8    else
9         echo "$argv[1] logged in...let's talk"
10        write $argv[1]
11   endif
```

Lines 9 and 10 acknowledge that the user is logged in and initiate conversation using the **write** command. Note that the shell will execute either lines 6 and 7 or lines 9 and 10— never both!

Now let's add the ability to detect when the user is logged in to UNIX at more than one terminal. To do this we will use an **if-else-if** construct of the form

```
if (expression 1) then
     command(s)
else if (expression 2) then
     command(s)
endif
```

When the shell executes the **else** clause of the first **if** statement, it performs another test (**expression 2**). If **expression 2** is true, it executes the commands following the **then.** You may use additional **else-if** clauses as needed. We use the **if** construct in **wmail** to examine the length of the wordlist **$w.** Here is the final version of **wmail:**

```
    % num wmail
1   # csh script to send mail or converse with a user
2   # Usage: wmail username
3
4   set w = (`who | grep $argv[1]` )
5   if ($#w == 0) then
6       echo "$argv[1] is not logged in...send mail"
7       mail $argv[1]
8   else if ($#w == 5) then
9       echo "$argv[1] logged in...let's talk"
10      write $argv[1]
11  else
12      echo "$argv[1] logged in on ports $w[2] and $w[7]"
13  endif
```

If the user is logged in only once, the length of the wordlist (**$#w**) is 5, and we call the **write** command as before. Rather than have the script call the **write** command when the user is logged in twice, however, we simply display the terminal names.

Let's apply **if-then-else** constructs to the **searcher, longlines,** and **numfiles** scripts. First we combine the **if** construct with command argument notation to check the number of arguments passed to **searcher:**

```
    % num searcher
1   # csh to search named files in directory for
2   # pattern
3   # Usage: searcher directory pattern file(s)
4
5   if ($#argv < 3) then              # less than 3 args?
6       echo2 "Usage: searcher directory pattern file(s)"
7       exit 1
8   endif
9   cd $argv[1]                       # change directory to argument 1
10  grep "$argv[2]" $argv[3-$#argv] | pr | lpr # search for
11                                    # pattern in all files
```

Line 5 uses the **$#argv** notation (see Table 7-1) to reference the number of arguments passed to **searcher.** We use the second form of the **if** construct to execute two commands (lines 6 and 7) when the **if** expression is true. We don't need an **else** clause since **exit** returns control to the C shell if the number of arguments is less than three. We use **echo2** to write the error message to the diagnostic output.

Next let's use an **if** statement to make **longlines** work on either a file (one argument) or the standard input (no arguments). The ability to read from the standard input lets us use **longlines** in conjunction with other commands in a pipe.

```
% num longlines
1    # report lines over 80 chars long
2    # Usage: longlines [file]
3
4    if ($#argv == 0) then          # no arguments
5        awk "length > 80"          # read from standard input
6    else
7        echo $argv[1]\:
8        awk "length > 80" $argv[1]     # use filename passed in
9    endif                          # $argv[1]
```

Line 2 introduces a new notation; words enclosed in brackets are optional. Note the **else** clause on line 6. The C shell executes line 5 if the **if** expression is true (no arguments), lines 7 and 8 if it is false (filename argument).

This enhancement lets us use the **longlines** script as follows:

```
% cat dict[1–5]  |  longlines
% longlines dict1
```

The first example pipes the output of the **cat** command into the input of **longlines. longlines** reads the standard input in this case. The second command forces **longlines** to read from file **dict1.**

Note that many UNIX commands work this way—they read from the standard input unless you follow them with a filename. The commands **pr, sort, cat, awk,** and **grep** are examples. A general-purpose tool that deals with filenames should do this to make it easy to combine with other commands. For example, the command

```
% cat dict[1-5]  |  sort  |  longlines
```

concatenates files **dict1** through **dict5,** sorts them, and displays all lines greater than 80 characters. We could not do this if **longlines** required a filename.

Now let's make **numfiles** operate on the current directory (.) if it has no arguments. Otherwise, the directory name is argument 1.

```
% num numfiles
1    # csh to count number of files or
2    # directories in current directory or first argument
3    # Usage: numfiles [directory]
4
5    if ($#argv == 0) then          # no arguments
6        set dir = "."              # look at current directory
7    else
8        set dir = $argv[1]         # use argument 1 as directory
```

```
9    endif
10   echo -n Number of files/directories in $dir\:
11   ls $dir | wc -l
```

Lines 6 and 8 set a shell variable **dir** to the proper directory name. Line 11 calls the **ls** command using the directory name in **$dir**. As before, we quote the : in line 10 to prevent the C shell from applying a variable modifier to **$dir**.

We can use this version of **numfiles** in the following formats:

```
% numfiles
Number of files/directories in .: 12
% numfiles ~/bin
Number of files/directories in /u/pa/bin: 19
```

Since the first example has no argument, it operates on the current directory. The second command operates on directory **bin** under our home directory.

7.8 EXPRESS YOURSELF: EXPRESSIONS AND OPERATORS

The C shell can perform arithmetic, string comparison, bitwise, and logical operations. The operators have the same syntax and precedence rules as in the C programming language. In this section we describe the operators as well as the evaluation of expressions.

Suppose you are developing programs that communicate with a timer device. This device increments a counter once per second and resets itself every eight hours. We call a C program, called **uptime,** from the C shell to report its status. The command

```
% uptime
/dev/ad1 08:12:13 1895
```

returns the device name (**/dev/ad1**), the time it was last reset (**08:12:13**), and the counter value in seconds (**1895**). We want to write a shell script that displays the counter value in more conventional units: hours, minutes, and seconds.

Assignment Operators

Where do we begin? First, since we must handle decimal numbers, we need to learn the C shell's notation for integer arithmetic. Use the following form to initialize a shell variable with numeric (as opposed to character) data.

```
@ var_name operator expression
```

You must put a space between @ and **var_name. var_name** is a C shell variable, and **expression** is a numeric expression. **operator** is an assignment operator (see Table

TABLE 7-3 ASSIGNMENT OPERATORS

Symbol	Meaning	Example	@ count = 6 echo $count
=	Store value of **expr** in **varname**.	@ count = 0	0
+ =	Add value of **expr** to value in **varname**.	@ count + = 2	8
− =	Subtract value of **expr** from **varname**.	@ count − = 5	1
∗=	Multiply value of **expr** by **varname**.	@ count ∗= 8	48
/=	Divide **expr** by **varname**.	@ count /= 4	1
++	Add 1 to **varname**.	@ count++	7
--	Subtract 1 from **varname**.	@ count--	5

The number on the right is the output of
echo $count if **count** was 6 originally.

7-3). Let's consider a simple example that initializes a shell variable and then adds 1 to its value.

```
% @ counter = 0
% @ counter = $counter + 1
% echo $counter
1
```

Note that you must put a space before and after the **+.** A more compact form uses the assignment operator **+ =** to update a variable. That is, we can initialize and update **counter** as follows. The second line adds 5 to **counter**'s old value.

```
% @ counter = 1
% @ counter += 5
% echo $counter
6
```

You must include spaces around these assignment operators. The C shell also provides a shorthand notation (**++**) for incrementing by 1 (we call this the *auto-increment operator*). Its form is

```
% echo $counter
6
% @ counter + +
% echo $counter
7
```

In this case, do not put a space before the **++.**
    There is another form of numeric assignment. The notation

```
@ var_name[index]  = expression
```

allows you to index into a wordlist variable and replace its contents with numeric data. The variable and corresponding indexed word must already be defined. Let's look at an example. The commands

```
% set d = `date`
% echo $d
Fri Nov 30 21:56:27 PST 1984
% @ d[1] = 5
% @ d[2] = 11
% echo $d
5 11 30 21:56:27 PST 1984
```

replace the strings **Fri** (the fifth day of the week) and **Nov** (the eleventh month) with their numeric equivalents in the wordlist variable **d.** Once we use @ to change the values to numeric data, we can perform arithmetic operations on these values.

Note that it is illegal to use @ with string data. For example, the command

```
% @ d[1] = Friday
@: Syntax error
```

fails because **Friday** is not numeric data.

Arithmetic, Bitwise, and Logical Operators

Let's return now to our task. Here is the first version of the script **timer,** which calculates the hours, minutes, and seconds from the value returned from **uptime.**

```
   % num timer
1  # csh to display hours, minutes, and seconds
2  # Usage: timer
3
4  set tval = `uptime`                # call the uptime program
5  @ time = $tval[3]                  # get the number of seconds
6
7  @ hrs = $time / 3600               # calculate number of hours
8  echo -n "$hrs hours "
9
10 @ time = $time % 3600
11 @ mins = $time / 60                # calculate number of minutes
12 echo -n "$mins minutes "
13
14 @ secs = $time % 60                # calculate number of seconds
15 echo -n "$secs seconds "
16 echo ""                            # print a blank line
```

Line 4 sets shell variable **tval** to the output of the **uptime** program using command substitution. Note that the time in seconds is stored in **$tval[3].** Since this is an integer, line 5 assigns it as numeric data to the shell variable **$time.** The arithmetic operator / performs integer division, and **%** yields the remainder.

Table 7-4 contains a complete list of the arithmetic, bitwise, and logical operators. The arithmetic operators apply only to integer values. The shift operators $>>$ and $<<$ shift the value on the left side left or right by the number of bits specified by the value on the right side of the expression. Vacated bits are filled with zeros. The 1's complement operator $\sim$ inverts the bits (changing 1s to 0s and 0s to 1s) in its expression. The operator **!** merely inverts the logical result of its expression; its value can only be 0 or 1. Similarly, the operators $|$, $\hat{}$, and **&** perform bitwise operations (**or, exclusive or, and**) on their values. For all values, assume the word length of a shell variable to be the word length of the computer (usually 16 or 32 bits). A shell variable can appear on either side of any operator that uses two operands. You may want to work through the examples in Table 7-4 to familiarize yourself with the operators. *Note:* Expressions containing the shift operators $>>$ and $<<$ and the bitwise operators **&,** $|$, and $\hat{}$ require surrounding parentheses. These indicate that the symbols are operators instead of redirection, background execution, pipe, and history modification symbols, respectively.

Although the C shell has numeric operators, it stores all variables as strings. Furthermore, numeric expression evaluation is slow, and only integer arithmetic is possible.

TABLE 7-4 ARITHMETIC, BITWISE, AND LOGICAL OPERATORS

Symbol	Meaning	Example	@ num = 10 echo $r
+	addition	@ r = $num + 4	14
−	subtraction	@ r = $num − 5	5
*	multiplication	@ r = $num * 10	100
/	integer division	@ r = $num / 6	1
%	modulo	@ r = $num % 3	1
>>	right shift	@ r = ($num >> 2)	2
<<	left shift	@ r = ($num << 3)	80
~	1's complement	@ r = ~ $num	− 11
!	logical negation	@ r = ! $num	0
|	bitwise "inclusive or"	@ r = ($num | 7)	15
^	bitwise "exclusive or"	@ r = ($num ^ 7)	13
&	bitwise "and"	@ r = ($num & 6)	2
||	logical "or"	@ r = ($num > 8 || $num < 4)	1
&&	logical "and"	@ r = ($num > 4 && $num < 8)	0

The number on the right is the value of **$r** if **$num** is 10.

Let's try our first version of **timer.** Assume **uptime** returns a value of **3652.**

```
% timer
1 hours 0 minutes 52 seconds
```

The calculation is correct; now we just need a few cosmetic changes. The next version makes the output clearer by dropping unnecessary 0s.

```
     % num timer
1    # csh to display hours, minutes, and seconds
2    # Usage: timer
3
4    set tval = `uptime`                       # call the uptime program
5    @ time = $tval[3]                         # get the number of seconds
6
7    if ($time == 0) then
8        echo timer reset
9        exit
10   endif
11
12   @ hrs = $time / 3600                      # calculate number of hours
13   if ($hrs != 0) then
14       echo -n "$hrs hour"
15       if ($hrs > 1) echo -n "s"
16   endif
17
18   @ time = $time % 3600
19   @ mins = $time / 60                       # calculate number of minutes
20   if ($mins != 0) then
21       echo -n " $mins minute"
22       if ($mins > 1) echo -n "s"
23   endif
24
25   @ secs = $time % 60                       # calculate number of seconds
26   if ($secs != 0) then
27       echo -n " $secs second"
28       if ($secs > 1) echo -n "s"
29   endif
30   echo ""                                   # print a blank line
```

Here we use **if** statements to test for nonzero values and pluralize the units of measure. Let's try it now (for the same value **3652**).

```
% timer
1 hour 52 seconds
```

TABLE 7-5 COMPARISON OPERATORS

Symbol	Meaning	Example	@ num = 5 Evaluation
==	equal to	$num == 5	true
!=	not equal to	$num != 5	false
>	greater than	$num > 3	true
>=	greater than or equal to	$num >= 3	true
<	less than	$num < 3	false
<=	less than or equal to	$num <= 5	true
==	equal to	$str == xyz	true
!=	not equal to	$str != abc	true
=~	matches (BSD only)	$pat =~ [abc]*	true
		(true if $pat starts with **a, b,** or **c**)	
!~	does not match (BSD only)	$pat !~ *c	false
		(true if $pat does not end in **c**)	

The result of evaluating each expression appears at the far right, assuming that **$num is 5**, **$pat** is **abc,** and **$str** is **xyz.**

Comparison Operators

The C shell has three different sets of comparison operators for numbers, strings, and patterns (see Table 7-5). We frequently use comparison operators to check the number or validity of arguments in a shell script.

The operators for numbers are >, >=, <, <=, !=, and a==. You are already familiar with several of these. The following statement, for example, verifies that a script has only one argument:

```
if ($#argv != 1) then            # if number of args is not 1
    echo2 ⟨error message⟩        # display error message
    exit 1                       # exit (status 1)
endif
```

Logical operators can allow you to check for a range of numbers, as in

```
if ($#argv < 3 || $#argv > 5)  then   # number of args must be
    echo2 ⟨error message⟩              # between 3 and 5
    exit 1
endif
```

The operators for strings are == and !=. The following statement (from a **backup** script run daily) nags you on Thursday to do a full system backup on Friday.

```
set d = `date`            # get the current date
if ($d[1] == "Thu") then
```

```
        echo "full system dump on Fri"  |  mail $user
    endif
```

Finally, the pattern matching operators (available only in BSD versions of the C shell) are =~ (match) and !~ (does not match). Patterns may match more than one string. They use the following special characters:

*	Match any string (including null).
[and]	Define a character set.
?	Match a single character.

You must not put these in quotation marks, since the C shell won't recognize their special meanings.

Pattern matching operators are convenient for checking the validity of an argument. For example, suppose a script operates on either a C or assembly language program; that is, the argument must end in either **.c** or **.s.** The following statement checks for this.

```
    if ($argv[1] !~ *.[cs]) then    # if arg doesn't end in .c or .s
        echo2 ⟨error message⟩       # display error message
        exit 1
    endif
```

We can also use pattern matching to check for an option flag beginning with − on the command line.

```
    if ($argv[1] =~ −*) then        # does argument begin with − ?
        ⟨process flags⟩             # process flag arguments
    endif
```

Operator Precedence

The C shell uses precedence rules when evaluating expressions. Suppose you are writing a script to calculate the number of bytes in a file. Each block is 512 bytes, and your file is **$nblks** long plus an offset of 32 bytes. A line in your script is

```
    @ bytes = 32 + $nblks * 512
```

How does the shell evaluate this expression? Does it add 32 to **$nblks** first or multiply **$nblks** times 512? The C shell performs multiplication before addition because * (multiply) has a higher precedence than + (add). Table 7-6 lists the C shell operators in order of precedence with the highest-ranking first.

Note that you may use parentheses to override the evaluation order in an expression.

TABLE 7-6 PRECEDENCE CHART FOR THE C SHELL OPERATORS

Operator	Meaning
( )	change precedence
~	complement
!	negation
* / %	multiply, divide, modulo
+ −	add, subtract
<< >>	left shift, right shift
<= >= < >	relational operators
== != =~ !~	string comparison/pattern matching
&	bitwise "and"
^	bitwise "exclusive or"
|	bitwise "inclusive or"
&&	logical "and"
||	logical "or"

Notes:

1. Precendence decreases down the list. The shell executes operators of the same precedence in the usual left-to-right order.

2. The result of all expressions are strings, representing decimal numbers.

3. You must separate operators from surrounding text with spaces. This does not apply to **&**, **|**, **<**, **>**, or **()**.

For example, the C shell performs the addition before the division in the following statement:

```
@ nblks = ($header + $codesize) / 512
```

7.9 SIZING UP A FILE: FILE INQUIRY OPERATORS

Shell scripts frequently operate on files or directories. For example, our **longlines** script reads files using the **awk** command, and our **numfiles** script reads directories using the **ls** command. We often want to check the status of a file or directory before passing its name to a command. Not only can we thus avoid executing a command that might fail (maybe drastically), but we can also report the error clearly.

We can use the file inquiry operators to do this. Use the following format:

```
if (-opr filename)
```

You can put a space between the left parenthesis and −, but not between − and the inquiry operator (**opr**). The C shell provides many file inquiry operators; Table 7-7 contains a complete list.

Suppose we want to check whether a file exists. (It contains the output of another

TABLE 7-7 FILE INQUIRY OPERATORS

(− **opr** **filename**)
where **opr** is one of the following:

Operator	Meaning
r	read access
w	write access
x	execute access
e	existence
o	ownership
z	zero length
f	plain file (not a directory)
d	directory

command.) If it does, we'll mail it to ourselves; otherwise, we want the script to inform us of the error. The following statement checks for the existence (− **e**) of the file named in the first argument of a shell script.

```
if (-e $argv[1]) then
     mail $user < $argv[1]
else
     echo2 file $argv[1] does not exist
     exit 1
endif
```

We can now make our example shell scripts, **longlines** and **numfiles,** more robust by having them validate their arguments.

The following version of **longlines** checks that the argument is an existing plain file (that is, not a directory or special file) before processing it with **awk.**

```
   % num longlines
1  # report lines over 80 chars
2  # Usage: longlines [file]
3
4  if ($#argv == 0) then          # no arguments so read from
5      awk "length > 80"          # standard input and exit
6      exit 0
7  endif
8
9  if (-f $argv[1]) then          # is argument a plain file?
10     echo $argv[1]\:            # yes; display name and call
11     awk "length > 80" $argv[1] # awk with file name
12  else                          # argument not a plain file
13     echo2 $0\: No file $argv[1] # display error message and
14     exit 1                     # exit with error status
15  endif
```

longlines with no arguments (lines 4 through 7) reads from the standard input. If there is an argument, line 9 checks whether it is a plain file. If so, line 11 passes it to **awk.** If not (the argument may be a directory, a special file, or nonexistent), the script displays the error message "No file" followed by the argument. Note the different form of the **echo2** statement in line 13. We use **$0** for the script name (**longlines**), and we quote the : to avoid the problem with variable modifiers.

To illustrate the use of **longlines,** suppose file **rejectltr** does not exist, and **japanese** is the name of a directory. **longlines** will produce the following messages:

```
% longlines rejectltr
longlines: No file rejectltr
% longlines japanese
longlines: No file japanese
% longlines dict1                                    (no error messages)
dict1:                          .
[All lines longer than 80 characters appear here]
% longlines < dict1                                  (no error messages)
[All lines longer than 80 characters appear here]
```

Occasionally a script may have to test for conditions that are not met. You may, for example, want to verify that a directory does not exist or that a file is unreadable before printing special error messages. In this case, use the logical negation operator (!) along with your file inquiry operator (**opr**):

```
if (! -opr filename)
```

In the script **numfiles,** for example, we want to ensure that **$dir** is a directory. The following version does this.

```
    % num numfiles
1   # csh to count number of files and
2   # directories in current directory or argument 1
3   # Usage: numfiles [directory]
4
5   if ($#argv == 0) then                    # no arguments?
6       set dir = " "                        # use current directory
7   else
8       set dir = $argv[1]                   # use argument 1
9   endif
10
11  if (! -d $dir) then                      # is $dir a directory?
12      echo2 $0\: $dir not a directory.     # no-display error
13      exit 1                               # exit with error status
14  endif
```

```
15
16    echo −n Number of files/directories in $dir\:
17    ls $dir | wc −l                          # process directory $dir
```

Line 11 uses the **−d** file inquiry operator with the logical negation (!) operator. The overall meaning is "if **$dir** is not a directory, report an error." Here is some sample output:

```
% numfiles
Number of files/directories in . : 22
% numfiles ~
Number of files/directories in /u/sara: 43
% numfiles rejectltr
numfiles: rejectltr not a directory.
% numfiles japanese
Number of files/directories in japanese: 12
```

7.10 OVER AND OVER AND OVER AGAIN: foreach

The **foreach** construct allows a script to process a set number of items placed in a list. The format is

```
foreach name ( wordlist )
        command(s)
end
```

Each time through, **foreach** assigns the next item in **wordlist** to the variable **$name. end** marks the end of the **foreach** loop. For example, suppose you want to send invitations to several colleagues. The following statement uses a **foreach** construct with the **mail** command to do this.

```
foreach person ( ann bruce cal marty sam sara)
        echo "Dear $person, \
        You are cordially invited to a Welcome Aboard \
        luncheon for our new employee, Susan Jenkins, \
        to be held Thursday at 12 noon at Jake's in \
        Del Mar. " | mail $person
end
```

This **foreach** loop mails the message enclosed in double quotation marks to each person in the wordlist. We use \ to escape the carriage returns in the **echo** command and pipe **echo** to the **mail** program.

In this example, you entered specific items in the wordlist. You can also use a variable in the **foreach** construct. The **$path** variable, for example, contains a list of directory names. The following sequence produces a formatted long listing of each directory in your **$path** variable.

```
foreach dir ( $path )
        ls −l $dir | pr −h "directory $dir"
end
```

You may also use file expansion characters. For example, to list only the executable files in your current directory, you would apply the **−x** file inquiry operator to all files as follows:

```
foreach file (*)
        if (! −d $file && −x $file) echo $file
end
```

Note that you ignore directory names with the **! −d** operator.

You may use argument (e.g., **$argv[*]**) expansion notation to build a wordlist as well. The following script, called **nfiles,** numbers and formats each file in its argument list.

```
% num nfiles
1    # csh to number and format all files in argument list
2    # Usage: nfiles file(s)
3
4    if ($#argv == 0) then                        # arguments?
5        echo2 "Usage: $0 file(s)"                # no−display error message
6        exit 1                                   # and exit
7    endif
8
9    foreach file ($argv[*])                      # expand argument wordlist
10       if (! −z $file) then                     # file not empty?
11           num $file | pr −h $file              # yes; number and format
12       else
13           echo2 "$file empty."                 # no−inform the user
14       endif
15   end
```

nfiles requires at least one filename. Line 9 uses **$argv[*]** to produce a wordlist of all filenames passed to the script. If a file is not empty, line 11 makes **num** pipe its output to the **pr** command.

Similarly, the following script, called **ndirs,** uses file expansion to number and format each file in the directory named in argument 1 (or the current directory).

```
% num ndirs
1    # csh to number and format all files in directory $argv[1]
2    # (or current directory)
```

```
 3    # Usage: ndirs [dir]

 4

 5    if ($#argv == 0) then                    # no arguments?
 6        set dir = '.'                        # use current directory
 7    else
 8        set dir = $argv[1]                   # use argument 1
 9    endif

10

11    if (! -d $dir) then                      # $dir not a directory?
12        echo2 "$dir not a directory"         # display error message
13        exit 1                               # and exit
14    endif

15

16    cd $dir                                  # change directory to $dir
17    foreach file (*)                         # all files in $dir
18        if (-f $file) num $file | pr -h $file # if a plain file,
19    end                                      # number and format
```

Line 16 changes directories so that the **foreach** statement in line 17 can generate a wordlist from the current directory. Line 18 checks that the filename is a plain file before numbering and formatting it.

Let's look at a script that generates its own wordlist. Script **yearly_report** generates a yearly report by calling program **calc_sum** for each monthly data file. Here we create a wordlist variable, **$names,** to store the names of the months. We then use **$names** in the **foreach** loop. Note that we accumulate all the reports by appending each one to the temporary file, **accntg.temp.** After printing it, we remove it.

```
      % num yearly_report
 1    # csh to generate accounting information
 2    # for each month
 3    # Usage: yearly_report

 4

 5    set names = (Jan Feb Mar Apr May Jun Jul Aug Sep Oct Nov Dec)
 6    foreach month ($names)              # generate report for each month
 7          calc_sum /usr/accntg/$month.data >> /tmp/accntg.temp
 8    end

 9

10    lpr /tmp/accntg.temp                # print temp file accntg.temp
11    rm -f /tmp/accntg.temp              # remove temp file
```

By using argument expansion with the **foreach** loop, we can now modify the **longlines** script to accept more than one filename. This allows us to search several files with a single command. Lines 9 through 17 go through the arguments one by one.

```
% num longlines
1   # report lines over 80 chars long
2   # Usage: longlines [file(s)]
3
4   if ($#argv == 0) then              # no argument?
5       awk "length > 80"              # read from standard input
6       exit 0                         # and exit
7   endif
8
9   foreach file ($argv[*])            # argument expansion
10  if (-f $file) then                 # plain file?
11      echo $file\:                   # display file name
12      awk "length > 80" $file        # call awk
13  else
14      echo2 $0\: No file $file        # not a plain file; error
15      # don't exit–process rest of arguments
16      endif
17  end
```

Line 11 displays the name of each file before the list of lines. As before, we process all file arguments even if there is an error (line 15).

We can also use file expansion with the **foreach** loop to modify the **numfiles** script. It now reports the number of files and directories in the target directory.

```
% num numfiles
1   # counts number of files and
2   # directories in argument 1 or current directory
3   # Usage: numfiles [directory]
4
5   if ($#argv == 0) then              # no arguments?
6       set dir = "."                  # use current directory
7   else
8       set dir = $argv[1]             # use argument 1
9   endif
10
11  if (! -d $dir) then                # not a directory?
12      echo2 $0\: $dir not a directory.   # error message and
13      exit 1                         # exit
14  endif
15
16  echo $dir\:                        # display directory name
17  @ fcount = 0                       # initialize counters
18  @ dcount = 0
19
20  cd $dir                            # change directory to $dir
21  foreach file (*)                   # file expansion
22      if (-f $file) then             # file?
```

```
23              @ fcount++              # increment file counter
24          else if (-d $file) then     # directory?
25              @ dcount++              # increment directory counter
26          endif
27      end
28
29      echo $fcount files $dcount directories    # display results
```

Lines 17 and 18 initialize counter variables **fcount** and **dcount.** Lines 23 and 25 use the increment operator **++** to count the number of files and directories. The file inquiry operators **(−d)** and **(−f)** determine whether an entry is a file or a directory. Here is sample output from the new **numfiles** script:

```
% numfiles ~/bin
/u/sara/bin:
14 files 2 directories
```

7.11 AROUND AND AROUND WE GO: CONDITIONAL LOOPS AND SHIFTING

The C shell also has a **while** statement that you can use for loops with numeric or string variables. Furthermore, the **shift** statement can allow a script to access all the words in a wordlist. We frequently use **shift** in conjunction with a **while** construct.

While Construct

The C shell's **while** loop handles situations where the number of iterations is not known in advance. This loop terminates when the controlling expression becomes false. Its format is

```
while (expression)
        command(s)
end
```

You can use any of the operators in Table 7-5 in **expression.** The C shell keeps executing **command(s)** as long as **expression** is true. Note that it won't execute them at all if **expression** is initially false. As with the **foreach** construct, **end** marks the end of the **while** loop.

Let's go back to our monthly calculations. Assume that **calc_sum** with a **−t** (total) option returns the sum of expenditures for the month. The following script, called **monthly_tot,** calculates a running total of costs up to but not including the current month.

```
% num monthly_tot
1    # csh to total all months up to the current month
2    # Usage: monthly_tot
3
4    set months = (Jan Feb Mar Apr May Jun Jul Aug Sep Oct Nov Dec)
5
6    set d = `date`                          # get current date
7    @ sum = 0                               # initialize sum
8    @ m = 1                                 # and month index
9
10   while ($d[2] != $months[$m])
11       @ sum += `calc_sum -t /usr/accntg/$months[$m].data`
12       @ m++
13   end
14
15   echo "Total costs up to ${d[2]}: $sum"
```

Line 6 stores the current date in a shell variable **$d. $d[2]** is the current month. Line 11 uses the shell variable **$sum** to accumulate the running total. The **+=** operator increments **$sum** by the amount returned by **calc_sum,** enclosed in grave accent marks (command substitution). **$m** indexes into the **$months** wordlist. We use the insulating braces { and } in line 15 to append : (instead of quoting with \).

Shift Statement

The **shift** statement is often helpful in conjunction with **while,** since it allows you to access all argument variables by always referring to the first one. This simplifies argument access notation and provides an alternative to the **foreach** construct.

The format of a **shift** statement is

```
shift
```

or

```
shift varname
```

shift with no arguments operates on **argv.** Otherwise, it operates on variable **varname.** It is an error if **$#varname** (or **$#argv**) is 0.

Let's look at **shift** with no arguments first. It deletes **argv[1],** places **argv[2]** in **argv[1], argv[3]** in **argv[2],** and so on. The script can then loop through all arguments without any change in notation. The shell decrements **$#argv** (the number of arguments) automatically each time you use **shift.**

Here is a script that produces a formatted listing of each directory in the argument list. We check for at least one argument and use the file inquiry operators to make sure each argument is a directory.

```
   % num dirlister
1    # dirlister
2    # usage: dirlister dir(s)
3
4    if ($#argv == 0) then                    # no arguments?
5        echo2 "Usage: $0 dir1 ... dirn"      # error message and
6        exit 1                               # exit
7    endif
8
9    while ($#argv)                           # while there are arguments
10       if (-d $argv[1]) then                # directory?
11           ls -l $argv[1] | pr -h $argv[1]  # list and format
12       else
13           echo2 $0\: No directory $argv[1] # display error
14       endif
15       shift                                # get next argument
16   end
```

Each time through the **while** loop, we refer to the directory name as **$argv[1].** The **shift** statement in line 15 moves the variables and decrements **$#argv.** Thus when there are no arguments left, line 9 causes an exit. The statement

```
while ($#argv)
```

is shorthand notation for

```
while ($#argv != 0)
```

Note that we can either pipe the output to the line printer or save it in a file as follows:

```
% dirlister japanese | lpr
% dirlister ~ ~/bin > dir.out
```

Let's look at the second form of the **shift** statement now. The notation

```
shift varname
```

deletes the first item from the wordlist **varname** and decrements **$#varname.** Let's modify **monthly_tot** to calculate a sum for a range of months using this form of the **shift** statement. We pass a month name (**Jul,** for example), as an argument to the script, which calculates the sum from that month through the end of the year. We use accounting data from the previous year.

```
    % num monthly_tot
1   # csh to total all months from month through end of year
2   # Usage: monthly_tot month
3
4   if ($#argv != 1) then                          # check for 1 argument
5       echo2 "Usage: monthly_tot month"
6       exit 1
7   endif
8
9   set months = (Jan Feb Mar Apr May Jun Jul Aug Sep Oct Nov Dec)
10  @ sum = 0                                       # initialize sum
11
12  while ($argv[1] != $months[1])
13      shift months
14      if ($#months == 0) then                     # illegal input
15          echo2 "$argv[1] not a valid month name"
16          exit 1                                   # error exit
17      endif
18  end
19
20  foreach m ($months)
21      @ sum += `calc_sum -t /usr/accntg_old/$m.data`
22  end
23
24  echo "Total costs from ${argv[1]}: $sum"
```

Line 12 uses a **while** statement to **shift** the wordlist until it finds the specified month. Lines 14 through 17 exit if the input is not a valid month name. This sets up the modified wordlist used in line 20. Note that line 21 accesses the old accounting data through the directory **/usr/accntg_old.** Again, line 24 uses {} to append the colon to **$argv[1].**

We are now ready to write our final version of the **longlines** utility. It will allow us to specify an optional width flag as well as a list of files. We can use **longlines** as follows:

```
% longlines -w 60 taxrec.*
% longlines dict4 appendixA
```

The first example searches all **taxrec** files for lines longer than 60 characters. The second command displays only lines longer than 80 characters (the default) in files **dict4** and **appendixA.**

```
     % num longlines
 1   #
 2   # Report lines longer than specified width
 3   # Usage: longlines [-w width] [file(s)]
 4   # if width is not specified, it defaults to 80
 5
 6   set width = 80                          # default width
 7
 8   if ($#argv > 0) then                    # arguments?
 9       if ("$argv[1]" == '-w') then        # width option
10           shift                           # yes; grab next argument
11           if ($#argv > 0) then            # make sure width is specified
12               set a = $argv[1]
13               if ($a !~ [0-9]* || $a == 0 || $a > 999) then
14                   # valid width?
15                   echo2 $0\: Bad width argument $a
16                   exit 1                  # error exit
17               else
18                   set width = $a          # width is valid; save it
19                   shift                   # grab next argument
20               endif
21           else
22               echo2 $0\: Missing width argument    # no more
23               exit 2                              # arguments
24           endif
25       endif
26   endif
27
28   if ($#argv > 0) then                    # Now process rest of argument list
29       foreach file ($argv[*])             # argument expansion
30           if (-f $file) then              # plain file?
31           echo $file                      # display file name
32           awk "length > $width" $file     # call awk
33           echo ""                         # display blank line
34           else
35           echo2 $0\: No file $file        # not a plain file
36           # don't exit; keep processing list
37           endif
38       end
39   else
40       # no arguments; use standard input
41       awk "length > $width"
42   endif
43   exit 0
```

Note that the **shifts** on lines 10 and 19 allow subsequent parts of the script to disregard the − **w** option. Lines 13 and 14 check that the **width** argument is all digits and is in the range 1 through 999, inclusive.

To avoid confusing our option flag − **w** and the file inquiry operator − **w,** we must quote the flag in line 9. Note that we use double quotation marks around **$argv[1]** (so the shell will expand it). Single or double quotation marks suffice for the constant − **w.** We use double quotation marks instead of single quotation marks on lines 32 and 41 so that the C shell will expand variable **$width.**

7.12 SELECTING ONLY THE BEST: switch

When a variable can take a wide variety of values, we use the **switch** statement to process the different cases. It can replace a long sequence of **if-then-else** statements when there are more than three values. Furthermore, you can use the familiar pattern matching characters *, ?, and [] to construct case patterns. This is particularly important for C shell versions that lack the pattern matching operators !~ and =~. Here is the format of the **switch** construct:

```
switch (string)
       case pattern1:
           command(s)
           breaksw
       case pattern2:
           command(s)
           breaksw

           . . .
       default:
           command(s)
           breaksw
   endsw
```

The C shell performs command, filename, and variable expansion on **string.** It then compares **string** to each pattern until it finds a match. The C shell variable expands **pattern,** but no file expansion occurs with characters *, ?, [, and] since these are **switch**'s pattern matching characters. When the C shell finds a match, it executes all commands up to the next **breaksw** or **endsw** statement. **endsw** marks the end of the entire **switch** construct, and **breaksw** marks the end of a **case** pattern. If it does not find a matching **case** pattern, it executes the commands following the **default** label. If there is no **default** label, execution resumes at the command following the **endsw.** If you omit the **breaksw** statement, the C shell executes all commands under the next **case** pattern as well (until it encounters a **breaksw** or **endsw** statement). This permits more than one **case** pattern to execute the same set of commands.

To illustrate **switch,** we will create a customized script that performs different tasks depending on an option flag. The script, called **report,** uses combinations of several UNIX commands with options. As you will see, the UNIX commands are tedious to type and hard to remember.

Our script generates reports using one of 12 data files, called **/usr/accntg/Jan.data** through **/usr/accntg/Dec.data.** Each file contains entries with four fields: purchase date, tax category, purchase amount, and item description. For example, a portion of file **Jan.data** might look like this:

```
% cat Jan.data
1/1/84          Office/decor          101.50      File:folders
1/5/84          Magazine/books         62.53      UNIX:books
1/10/84         Printing/postage      150.25      stamps
. . .
```

Option −**a** (amount) generates an expenditure report sorted by the amount field (field 3). Option −**c** (category) generates a similar report sorted by the tax category (field 2). Option −**i** (item) sorts by tax category and produces a report containing items and purchase amount only. Finally, option −**s** (sum) totals the purchase amount fields. Here is how we call **report.** The commands

```
% report −a Apr
% report −amt Apr
% report −amount Apr
```

all produce an amount report for April. Similarly, the commands

```
% report −cat Jun
% report −c Jun
```

produce a category report for June. We use the same format with all the options.

```
     % num report
1    # csh to generate report
2    # usage: report −opt month
3
4    if ($#argv != 2) then
5        echo2 "Usage: $0 −option month"
6        echo2 "Options are:  −a expenditure amount"
7        echo2 "              −c expenditure category"
8        echo2 "              −i item report"
9        echo2 "              −s summary report"
10       exit 1
11   endif
12
13   set file = /usr/accntg/$argv[2].data
14   if (! −r $file) then                        # make sure file is readable
```

```
15        echo2 $file unreadable.
16        exit 1
17    endif
18
19    switch ($argv[1])
20       case -a*:                          # sort by amount
21          sort +2 -n -r $file | pr -h \
22             "Expenditure Report by Amount for $argv[2]"
23          breaksw
24       case -c*:                          # sort by category
25          sort +1 -d -f $file | pr -h \
26             "Expenditure Report by Category for $argv[2]"
27          breaksw
28       case -i*:                          # generate item report (2 columns)
29          sort +1 -d -f $file | awk '{print $4, $3}' | pr -h \
30          "Item - Amount Report by Category for $argv[2]"
31          breaksw
32       case -s*:                          # generate summary report
33          awk -f total.awk $file | pr -h "Total for $argv[2]"
34          breaksw
35       default:
36          echo2 Illegal option $argv[1]
37          exit 1
38    endsw
```

Lines 4 through 11 verify the number of arguments and display a help summary if it is
incorrect. Line 14 makes sure that the data file exists and is readable. Lines 19 through
38 contain the **switch** construct, which generates different UNIX commands depending
on **report's** option. Pattern matching in each **case** statement recognizes a word beginning
with a particular option character. For example, we may type − **a**, − **amount**, or − **amt**
for the amount report.

Three options (− **a**, − **c**, and − **i**) use the UNIX **sort** utility. The − **a** option
generates the following **sort** command (line 21),

```
sort +2 −n −r $file
```

This tells **sort** to skip two fields (**+ 2**) and sort numerically (− **n**) in reverse (− **r**) (i.e.,
descending) order. Option − **c** sorts the file by tax category, the second field. The
command (line 25)

```
sort +1 −d −f $file
```

skips one field, sorts by dictionary order (− **d**), and "folds" (− **f**) uppercase and lowercase
letters together. Option − **i** uses this same **sort** command line and then pipes the output
to **awk** (line 29). The **awk** command

```
awk '{print $4, $3}'
```

prints the fourth field followed by the third field. All commands pipe their output to **pr** for formatting. The **−s** option calls **awk** with the following command (line 33):

```
awk −f total.awk $file
```

The **−f** option tells **awk** to read an **awk** script from file **total.awk**. The **awk** script sums all values in field 3 (**$3**) and prints the total at the end. Here is the **awk** script:

```
% cat total.awk
{ sum += $3 }
END { print "Total is " sum }
```

Thus the **switch** construct allows us to write a script that reduces four complex commands to four simple options of one command.

7.13 GETTING OFF THE BEATEN PATH: break, continue, goto

The C shell has three control commands that can alter program flow in a loop. They are **break, continue,** and **goto.** We use **break** and **continue** in **while** or **foreach** loops. **goto** causes execution to resume at a specified label.

break

break causes execution to resume after the **end** statement of the innermost loop. You can use it anywhere inside a **while** or **foreach** loop. One format for **break** inside a **foreach** loop is as follows:

```
foreach n (wordlist)
        if (expression) break
        command(s)
end
echo "Break sends us here"
```

Here we use a simple **if** statement and execute **break** if **expression** is true. Otherwise, the shell executes **command(s)** as long as **expression** is false (and **wordlist** is not exhausted).

When would you need a **break?** Let's return to our initial version of the **monthly_tot** script from Section 7.11.

```
% num monthly_tot
1   # csh to total all months up to the current month
2   # Usage: monthly_tot
3
4   set months =  (Jan Feb Mar Apr May Jun Jul Aug Sep Oct Nov Dec)
5
6   set d = `date`                          # get current date
7   @ sum = 0                               # initialize sum
8   @ m = 1                                 # and month index
9
10  while ($d[2] != $months[$m])
11      @ sum += `calc_sum -t /usr/accntg/$months[$m].data`
12      @ m++
13  end
14
15  echo "Total costs up to ${d[2]}: $sum"
```

How could we include the current month in the total? The following version uses **break** within a **foreach** statement to do this.

```
% num monthly_tot
1   # csh to total all months up to and including current month
2   # Usage: monthly_tot
3
4   set d = `date`                 # get current date
5   @ sum = 0                      # initialize sum
6
7   foreach m (Jan Feb Mar Apr May Jun Jul Aug Sep Oct Nov Dec)
8       @ sum += `calc_sum -t /usr/accntg/$m.data`
9       if ($m == $d[2]) break         # current month so stop
10  end
11
12  echo "Total costs up to ${d[2]}: $sum"
```

Note that line 7 includes the **month** wordlist in the **foreach** statement. Line 8 calls **calc_sum** with the **−t** (total) option. Again, we use {} to insulate the variable name in line 12. Line 9 executes **break** when **$m** is the current month. The shell resumes execution at line 12. This occurs after line 8 adds the total for the current month to **$sum.**

continue

A **continue** statement makes the shell skip the rest of the commands within the innermost loop and resume execution at (just before) the **end** statement. In a **while** loop, the shell tests the control expression and continues the loop if it is still true. In a **foreach** loop, it uses the next item in the wordlist. One format for **continue** within a **while** construct is

```
# format of continue
while (expression1)
        if (expression2) continue
        command(s)
# continue sends us here:
end
```

Here, if **expression2** is true, the shell skips **command(s)** and resumes execution just before the **end** statement. As an example of using **continue,** let's modify the **monthly_ tot** script again. This time we'll call **monthly_tot** with a list of months to exclude from the sum. For example,

% **monthly_tot Apr Sep**

will calculate the sum for all months except April and September. We use last year's data for the calculation.

```
     % num monthly_tot
1    # csh to total all months excluding month_list months
2    # Usage: monthly_tot month_list
3
4    if ($#argv == 0) then                     # arguments?
5         echo2 "Usage: monthly_tot month_list"
6         exit 1
7    endif
8
9    @ sum = 0                                  # initialize $sum
10
11   foreach m (Jan Feb Mar Apr May Jun Jul Aug Sep Oct Nov Dec)
12        set i = 1                             # initialize index to argument li
13        unset match                           # reset flag variable
14          while ($#argv >= $i)
15              if ($argv[$i] == $m) then       # is it a match?
16                  set match                   # set flag variable
17                  break                       # get out of while loop
18              endif
19              @ i++                           # no match so increment index
20          end
21
22        if ($?match) continue                 # skip this month
23        @ sum += `calc_sum -t /usr/accntg_old/$m.data`
```

```
24    end
25
26    echo "Total costs: $sum"
```

Lines 4 through 7 check whether there is a month list. Line 9 initializes the **sum** variable, and line 11 sets up a **foreach** loop for all the months. The wordlist **$argv** contains the months we will exclude. The **while** loop (lines 14 through 20) checks each element of **$argv** against the month **$m** for a match. If they match, line 16 sets variable **match.** We use **match** as a flag; we don't care about its value, only whether it is set (i.e., defined) or unset. The statement

```
    if ($?match) continue
```

says "if **match** is defined, execute the **continue** statement." After setting **match,** line 17 terminates the **while** loop with **break.** (Remember, **break** and **continue** affect only the innermost loop. Therefore, the **break** in line 17 does not affect the outer **foreach** loop. However, the **continue** in line 22 does affect the **foreach** loop because it is the innermost loop.)

When **match** is set, the shell executes the **continue** statement in line 22 and resumes execution at line 11 (the beginning of the **foreach** loop). When **match** is unset, the shell executes line 23 and adds that month's data to the sum.

Using the **while** loop to find months on the excluded list allows us to enter the month list in any order. For example, the commands

```
% monthly_tot Aug Feb May
% monthly_tot May Feb Aug
```

yield the same results.

We now present our final version of the **numfiles** utility. It examines the current directory if no arguments are specified. Note that the loop control expression for the **while** loop on line 13 is always true, so we need **break** as a terminator.

```
      % num numfiles
1     # final version of numfiles
2     # csh to count number of files and
3     # directories in argument list
4     # Allow multiple directories; use current directory if no args
5     # Usage: numfiles [dir(s)]
6
7     if ($#argv == 0) then
8         set dir = "."                      # use current directory
9     else
10        set dir = $argv[1]                  # use argument 1
11    endif
```

```
12
13    while (1)                                 # always true
14
15        if (! -d $dir) then                   # directory?
16            echo2 $0\: No directory $dir.     # No directory; error
17        else
18            echo $dir\:                       # display directory name
19            @ fcount = 0                       # initialize file and
20            @ dcount = 0                       # directory counters
21            foreach file ($dir/*)             # file expansion
22                if (-f $file) then            # file?
23                    @ fcount++                # increment file counter
24                else if (-d $file) then       # directory?
25                    @ dcount++                # increment dir counter
26                endif
27            end                               # end foreach
28            echo $fcount files $dcount directories
29        endif
30        if ($#argv <= 1) then                 # more arguments?
31            break                             # no; exit while loop
32        else
33            shift                             # yes; get next one and
34            set dir = $argv[1]                # assign to $dir
35        endif
36
37    end                                       # end while
```

The script uses a **while** loop that tests for completion at the end instead of at the beginning. We construct this using **1** as the loop control expression. Since 1 is always true, the loop will execute at least once. The test for completion is on line 30. If the current directory is specified, **$#argv** equals 0; otherwise **$#argv** equals 1 when the last directory name has been processed. Until this occurs, lines 33 and 34 shift **$argv** and assign a new value to **$dir** for each directory name in the argument list. The **break** exits from the loop.

This version of **numfiles** allows multiple directory names. Line 21 defines the wordlist as **$dir/*** so that the **foreach** statement can reference files relative to the directory **$dir.** If an argument is not a directory, the script reports the error and continues with the rest of the argument list. Here is some sample output from **numfiles:**

```
% numfiles ~ ~/cshell rejectltr ~/cshell/ch6
/u/sara:
43 files 6 directories
/u/sara/cshell:
39 files 2 directories
numfiles: No directory rejectltr
/u/sara/cshell/ch6:
27 files 0 directories
%
```

goto

A **goto** statement has the form

```
goto word
```

The shell file and variable expands **word,** producing a string of the form **label.** The shell resumes execution after the line specified by

```
label:
```

goto is single word. You can use it anywhere in a script; it is not limited to loops.

The following statements detect a filename argument that begins with a digit and transfer execution to an error label **err.** We use **goto** as an alternative to **break** or flag variables when exiting from a loop. Furthermore, **goto** may exit from more than one loop (not just the innermost).

```
while (expression1)
    while (expression2)
        if ($argv[1] ~= [0-9]*) goto err
        command(s)
    end
end
exit 0                          # normal exit
err:
    echo2 filename starts with digit
    exit 1                      # error exit
```

Use **goto** statements sparingly in C shell scripts. A maze of them makes scripts difficult to understand or modify. However, you may want to use **goto** to exit from a deeply nested control structure. This avoids having to include flags within the expressions (for example, **expression2**) or **break** statements. We use **goto** statements most often in error detection.

7.14 TALK TO YOUR SCRIPT: READING DATA FROM THE TERMINAL

You can interact with a C shell script while it is running. Berkeley versions of the C shell supply the special notation $<. The C shell substitutes a line from standard input for $<. Other UNIX versions (such as XENIX) provide a program called **gets** for the same purpose. If your version has neither, compile our C program **gets.c** (see Appendix D for its source).

Reading a Line with $< (BSD)

One way to read a line of input using **$<** is to put it on the right-hand side of the **set** command. Precede the **set** statement with **echo −n** and some text if you want a prompt. The following example displays a prompt, reads a line of user input, and sets the input string **$name.**

```
echo −n "Please enter a filename: "
set name = $<
```

The C shell treats a multiword input line as a single word. That is, **$name** will always contain a single string (**$#name** will be 1). Note that if you just press the RETURN key, **$#name** is still 1.

You may wish to index the words as a wordlist. One way to do this is to assign the input variable using parentheses. The following example reads a line of input and assigns **$line** to the wordlist variable, **$names.**

```
echo −n "Please enter source filenames: "
set line = $<
set names = ($line)
```

If you typed the filenames **scan.c** and **grafix.s,** you could now reference them separately as **$names[1]** and **$names[2].**

Another way to index the words is to expand **$line** in a **foreach** construct, as in

```
echo −n "Please enter source filenames: "
set line = $<
foreach file ($line)
     # process $file
end
```

Reading a Line with gets

One way to use **gets** is to put it in command substitution marks and assign it to a variable. For example, the following statements assign the input line to variable **$line:**

```
echo −n "Please enter source filenames: "
set line = `gets`
```

In this approach, **$line** is automatically a wordlist variable if you type more than one word. If you put double quotation marks around `` `gets` ``, however, the C shell makes **$line** a single-word variable.

The following script displays a menu and lets the user select a program to run. The input is one or two letters followed by the RETURN key. We use pattern matching in the **case** expressions to allow either uppercase or lowercase letters. Note that you must type a carriage return to end the **$<** (or **gets**) command.

```
        % num menus
 1      # csh script to show a menu program
 2
 3      set d = /usr/bus_utils              # business package directory
 4      set menu = $d/menu                  # menu file
 5
 6      while (1)                           # always true
 7          cat $menu                       # display menu
 8          echo -n "      Enter your response —— > " #prompt
 9          set a = $<                      # read input
10          switch ($a)
11              case [aA]:
12                  $d/acctg                # accounting package
13                  breaksw
14              case [gG][lL]:
15                  $d/genledg              # general ledger package
16                  breaksw
17              case [pP]:
18                  $d/payroll              # payroll package
19                  breaksw
20              case [fF]:
21                  $d/filer                # filer package
22                  breaksw
23              case [wW][pP]:
24                  $d/wordpro              # word processer
25                  breaksw
26              case [qQ]:
27                                          # leave menu program
28                  exit 0
29                  breaksw
30              default:
31                  echo2 $0\: No program for $a
32                  breaksw
33          endsw
34      end
```

The file in variable **$menu** contains the menu's text. The directory in variable **$d** contains all of our programs that we use in lines 4, 12, 15, 18, 21, and 24. This script provides a simple interface for selecting from a number of packages. When the package finishes, the script displays the menu again. The user types **q** or **Q** followed by a carriage return to exit from the **menu** script.

7.15 A COMMANDING SCRIPT: MAKING A SCRIPT INTO A COMMAND

Once you have created a new command or tool by writing a shell script, you should save it in a public command directory. Many UNIX systems use the directory **/usr/local** for locally written tools. Alternatively, place it in your own command directory (e.g., ~·/**bin** or ·~/**tools**) to add it to your private arsenal. If **$path** contains

```
% echo $path
~/bin /usr/ucb /bin /usr/bin /usr/local  .
```

then the command

```
% cp longlines ~/bin
```

will copy **longlines** to directory **bin** under your home (~) directory. The C shell keeps an internal table for finding commands. It builds this table when you login. When you add a command to a **$path** directory, the existing table does not include it. To force the shell to rebuild (**rehash**) its table, execute the command

```
% rehash
```

The C shell will then be able to find commands entered in the current session. Alternatively, you can logout and log back in.

7.16 HINTS AND CAUTIONS

C shell syntax can be confusing. Watch the following:

■ When using **if-then-else** constructs, be sure **then** is on the same line as **if, else** is on a line by itself, and the terminating **endif** is on a line by itself. Don't forget to balance each **if** with an **endif.**

■ Terminate each **while** and **foreach** construct with an **end** statement on a line by itself. Take extra precautions when you nest **while** or **foreach** loops to include the correct number of **end** statements. Indenting nested loops will help you keep track of them.

■ A **break** statement only exits from the innermost **while** or **foreach** statement. The following statements illustrate the execution path.

```
while (expression1)          # outer while loop
    while (expression2)      # inner while loop
```

```
            statement(s)
            break
            statement(s)
        end                           # end of inner while
    echo break sends control here...
    end                               # end of outer while
```

■ If you forget a **breaksw** statement in a **switch** construct, execution continues (falls through) to the next **breaksw** or **endsw** statement.

■ Numeric expressions have many syntax restrictions. For example, in the statement

% **@ num = ($check >> 8)**

you must include a space after @ and around the =. You must use parentheses around the expression because it contains a shift operator. Also, remember to use @ when you want to store a number. For example, consider the following statements:

% **echo $check**
5
% **set num = ($check >> 8)**
% **echo $num**
5 >> 8

Although the **set** command is correct syntactically, it stores the string **5 >> 8** in variable **$num,** not the value of that expression.

■ Watch for violations of an index's range. For example,

```
    echo $argv[5]
```

is an error if the number of arguments is four or less. Similarly, there must be at least one argument before you can use the **shift** statement.

■ Do not put patterns in quotation marks when using the pattern matching operators = ~ and !~. For example, in

```
    if ($argv[1] =~ "*.c") then
```

the C shell will not recognize the pattern matching character ***.** The following line is correct:

```
    if ($argv[1] =~ *.c) then
```

■ Since the pattern matching operators (= ~ and !~) are only available under BSD versions of the C shell, you must use a **switch** construct for pattern matching under other versions. Suppose you want to verify that a script's argument is the name of a C source file (it ends in **.c**) or assembly source file (it ends in **.s**). The following statements use the pattern matching operator = ~:

```
if ($argv[1]  -~ *.[cs]) then  # if argument ends in .c or .s
        # process $argv[1]
else
        echo2 error message      # error in filename
        exit 1
endif
```

Use the following statements if your version does not have the pattern matching operators:

```
switch ($argv[1])             # check argument
    case *.[cs]:              # does it end in .c or .s
        # process $argv[1]
        breaksw
    default:
        echo2 error message    # error in filename
        exit 1
endsw
```

■ You must use quotation marks around expressions that the shell might confuse with file inquiry operators. In the statement

```
if ("$argv[1]" == "-w") then
```

we need quotation marks around **$argv[1]** as well as the string **−w.** Otherwise, the C shell expects a following filename to match the −w file inquiry operator. In fact, you should always quote a string in such a construct since the user might type −w (or another file inquiry operator) rather than, say, a filename.

■ Don't use undefined variables. If you want to check whether a variable is defined, put the test on the preceding line. For example, in the statement

```
if ($?line) set com = ($com $line)
```

if **line** is not defined (i.e., if **$?line** is false), the shell will flag **$line** as an error. Instead, the assignment statement must appear on another line, as follows:

```
if ($?line) then
        set com = ($com $line)
endif
```

Similarly, the following statement yields a subscript out of range error when **$#argv**
is 0:

```
if ($#argv != 0 && $argv[1] == "stop") then
```

Even though the shell evaluates **$#argv != 0** first, it still parses **$argv[1]** when **$#argv**
is 0. In this case, we must create a nested if statement:

```
if ($#argv != 0) then
        if ($argv[1] == "stop") then
                    . . .
        endif
endif
```

■ Finally, the first symbol of a C shell script must be **#.** Otherwise a different
shell (with different syntax) will attempt to execute your script.

7.17 KEY POINT SUMMARY

We can create our own tools by writing C shell programs or scripts. Scripts may contain
C shell commands, UNIX programs, and calls to other scripts.

The C shell is a rich programming language with many constructs patterned after
the C language. A C shell script may contain any of the following features:

■ Comment lines (lines that the C shell ignores)

■ Text output for reporting information or diagnostic messages

■ Program arguments

■ An exit status reported to the shell

■ Program flow control using **if-then-else, while, foreach,** or **switch** constructs

■ Expressions and operators including C shell variables, numeric expressions,
arithmetic, logical, bitwise, and file inquiry operators

■ Interaction via the standard input

■ Any C shell basic command form, including redirection, pipes, sequential execution, background execution, and command groups

To create scripts, enter the text with an editor (or redirect input directly from the
keyboard using **cat** if your typing is perfect). To make the file executable, use the UNIX
chmod command. To execute the script, just type the file's name. Scripts can result in
useful new commands if you place them in a public tools directory (e.g., **/usr/local**) or
in your own tools directory (e.g., **~/bin**).

8

Advanced Programming Techniques

As with any kind of programming, there are many tips and tricks that can help you write better C shell scripts. This chapter describes some of these as well as methods for designing and debugging scripts and making them run faster.

We also explain how to program the C shell directly from the keyboard. This lets you create loops at your terminal, prompt for input, and run UNIX commands. An important technique is a generalized way to create unique names for temporary files. This keeps you from inadvertently overwriting existing files. It also prevents multiple users from accessing the same temporary file simultaneously.

To handle unexpected conditions, you may want a script to recognize interrupts. Recall that normally a script stops and returns to the C shell when you press the DEL or RUBOUT key. However, this could leave behind results or extra temporary files. We therefore need ways either to exclude interrupts or to perform cleanup operations.

By now you have seen the value of input redirection. One drawback is that it generally requires a special file for each script. One way to avoid this is by supplying the input from the shell script file itself.

Occasionally, you may want to turn off file expansion during script execution. This makes quoting easier. Some tasks may also need to create recursive scripts. We discuss both of these topics.

Like all other programs, new (and even old) shell scripts often contain errors. The C shell has options you can use for debugging when executing shell scripts. Several of these display intermediate output to help pinpoint errors quickly. Debugging options can even help you learn how scripts operate.

Finally, we discuss how to make shell scripts more efficient. A particularly useful tool is the **time** command, which reports timing statistics for its arguments.

8.1 A TIME FOR AD-LIBBING: LOOPING AT THE TERMINAL

You can use **while** or **foreach** loops at the terminal without a shell script. This lets you do tasks without creating executable scripts. For example, suppose you want to remove all subdirectories from your current directory. You type

```
% foreach f (*)
?
```

The **foreach** loop has the file expansion character * inside the wordlist. The C shell responds with **?,** telling you it expects further input. Until you type **end,** the shell includes each statement you enter in the loop. In this example, it executes the loop body for each file in the current directory.

Next we type

```
? if (-d $f) rm -r $f
? end
```

The shell processes the files in the current directory, one at a time. Using the file inquiry operator (**-d**), the shell removes each directory (along with its contents) using the **rm -r** (recursive remove) command.

Suppose we have a set of outdated files in our current directory. We want to delete files with a December 14 date. The brute force approach is to type

```
% ls -l > list
```

examine **list,** and issue **rm** commands for the appropriate files. Let's try an interactive approach:

```
% foreach f (*)
? if (-d $f) continue
? set fn = `ls -l $f | grep "Dec 14"`
? if ($#fn) rm -i $f
? end
```

Here we use a **foreach** statement to access all the files. The second statement ignores directories. The third uses command substitution to look for the December 14 date in a long listing of the current file; if **$#fn** is nonzero (if the file has a December 14 date), we issue an **rm** command. Note that we use the **-i** option (interactive), which prompts us before actually removing the file. After we type the **end** statement, the interactive session begins:

```
? end
a.words.bk: y
b.words.bk: y
```

```
build.1: y
build.2: y
intr.2: y
intr.4: y
pnames: n
test: n
update: y
```

Here we removed all December 14 files except **pnames** and **test.**

Suppose we now want to search a file for several patterns. We want to display the line containing the pattern as well as the line number. The command we want executed is

```
% grep -n $pat ttape.c
```

where **ttape.c** is the input file and **$pat** is a shell variable containing the pattern. The **grep** option **-n** displays line numbers along with the lines of text. We want this command executed in a loop with the search patterns specified interactively. First, we create an infinite loop with

```
% while (1)
?
```

Again, the shell displays **?,** indicating it is waiting for input. Next we enter our search pattern and use it with the **grep** command:

```
? echo -n "Input search pattern: "
? set pat = `gets`
? if ($#pat == 0) break
? grep -n $pat ttape.c
? end
```

echo -n prompts for the search pattern, and `gets` reads it from the standard input. Next we use an **if** statement to see if the C shell read anything. A return by itself will set **$ #pat** to 0, and the **break** statement will terminate the **while** loop. Otherwise, the next line uses the typed input **$pat** in a **grep** command. Using **gets** together with **if** and **break** allows us to specify as many patterns as we like.

Because we are entering the loop bodies interactively, we cannot edit anything except the current line. Therefore, these loops should be kept short and simple.

8.2 STAKING OUT YOUR OWN TERRITORY: USING /tmp

Scripts often create files to hold the output of UNIX commands. Output redirection makes the C shell create a file with a specified name. This is fine if you intend to keep the new file. But what if it is of only temporary interest?

Creating Temporary Files

Suppose we are using a utility program to transfer ASCII files to and from another UNIX system. This utility puts an extra line feed in front of each line before transmitting it. This results in the new file having a blank line before each data line.

To illustrate, suppose we send a telephone list to the remote machine. The received file appears as follows:

```
% cat ~/phone.numbers
                                              (blank line)
Andrews Bill 201 5347689
                                              (blank line)
Hill Art 805 4445620
                                              (blank line)
Johnson Bill 415 5283941
                                              (blank line)
Johnson Mary 303 8583911
                                              (blank line)
 .  .  .
```

To correct this, we use **awk** to delete every other line. We store the condensed text in a temporary file, then rename it to the original:

```
% awk "NR%2 == 0" ~/phone.numbers > tmp
% mv tmp ~/phone.numbers
```

NR is a special **awk** variable that contains the current line or record number. The expression "**NR%2 == 0**" (**NR** modulo **2** equals **0**) is true if the line number is even. **%** determines the remainder from integer division. **awk** thus copies every other line to the standard output. Afterward, we rename **tmp** to the original phone list.

All is well as long as there isn't already a file **tmp** in the current directory. If there is, the C shell will either overwrite it or (if you have set **noclobber**) force you to repeat the commands using a different name. Either case creates problems. Using this approach, you must also be able to create files in the current directory. This may not be the case if you happen to be in a directory that you don't own.

One way to give the temporary file a unique name is by using the process ID, called **$$.** We can type

```
% awk "NR%2 == 0" ~/phone.numbers > tmp$$
% mv tmp$$ ~/phone.numbers
```

Note that we append the process ID to the filename. If, for example, the current process ID of your C shell is 1452, these commands become

```
% awk "NR%2 == 0" ~/phone.numbers > tmp1452
% mv tmp1452 ~/phone.numbers
```

Although this technique works well for redirecting commands to your own directory, problems arise when you try to create temporary files in arbitrary directories (where you may lack write permission). What you need is a public "place" in the UNIX file system for temporary files. As an example, let's create a public tool, **rmxlf** (remove extra line feeds), to process files sent from the remote machine. This script requires a temporary file.

The /tmp Directory

By convention, **/tmp** is a public temporary storage directory. If you examine the permission bits with

```
% ls -ld /tmp
drwxrwxrwx 5 root system 200 Dec 20 14:39 /tmp
```

you will find that all users can read and write in it. The size of this storage area depends on how many users your machine supports. The system editors (**vi**, **ex**, and **ed**) all use **/tmp** to store copies of files being edited. Some systems regularly delete all **/tmp** files to keep it free from debris. So **/tmp** is an ideal place to store temporary files for scripts.

Note, however, that the temporary filename must be unique to avoid problems when two people use the utility at the same time. A conventional method for naming files in **/tmp** from shell scripts is as follows: Concatenate the script's name with the current process ID. This identifies the command that created the file and makes the filename unique. Remember, process identification numbers are unique within the entire UNIX system. **$0** contains the command (file) name, and **$$** is the process ID.

Since **$0** may contain an absolute pathname, we use **:t** (for tail) qualifier to extract just the filename. Unfortunately, the C shell does not process **:t** with **$0,** so we must create a new variable. The following statements within a shell script called **rmxlf** found in, for example, **/u/sara/bin** first assign the command name to a shell variable **com.** We then use **$com:t** to obtain the filename. We finally concatenate the process ID (**$$**):

```
set com = $0
set tf = /tmp/$com:t.$$
```

For a process ID of 16024, the statements

```
echo $com
echo $tf
```

produce the strings

```
/u/sara/bin/rmxlf              (for $com)
/tmp/rmxlf.16024               (for $tf)
```

This assures a valid pathname for **tf.**

Let's use this technique in the script **rmxlf:**

```
     % num rmxlf
1    # csh script to remove extraneous blank lines from file.
2    # Awk deletes every other line.
3    # We create a temporary file each time we squeeze a new file.
4    # We replace the original file with the temp file.
5    #
6    # Usage: rmxlf file(s)
7    #
8
9    if ($#argv == 0) then               # no arguments?
10       echo2 'Usage: rmxlf file(s)'
11       exit 1
12   endif
13
14   set com = $0                        # command name
15   set tf = /tmp/$com:t.$$             # temp filename
16
17   foreach file ($argv[*])             # argument expansion
18       awk "NR%2 == 0" $file > $tf     # delete every other line
19       mv $tf $file                    # replace original file
20   end
```

Line 9 assures that the script has at least one file argument. Line 14 stores the command name in **com.** Line 15 stores the temporary filename in **tf.** Line 17 uses a **foreach** statement to loop through all arguments. Note that each iteration of the loop creates the same temporary file (line 18) and renames it (line 19). Now you can execute **rmxlf** from anywhere in the file system since the temporary file is placed in **/tmp,** not in the current directory.

If we run **rmxlf** on the telephone list, we see the following:

```
% rmxlf ~/phone.numbers
% cat ~/phone.numbers
Andrews Bill 201 5347689
Hill Art 805 4445620
Johnson Bill 415 5283941
Johnson Mary 303 8583911
 .  .  .
```

8.3 PREPARING FOR THE UNEXPECTED: INTERRUPT HANDLING

You can interrupt most (foreground) UNIX commands with a single keystroke. The DELETE key terminates a command and returns control to the C shell.

We typically use interrupts to stop a "runaway" job or to terminate a command early. You will use interrupts more often if your version of the C shell has no job control and therefore does not let you stop a job temporarily with **control-Z.**

Interrupting Scripts

UNIX commands can be interrupted. What about scripts? By default, the interrupt key immediately terminates a script and returns control to the C shell. This is usually all right. You may, however, want to transfer control to a different place in your script when an interrupt occurs. Here you can execute statements before returning control to the C shell. We refer to such statements as an *interrupt handler*.

What statements should you place in an interrupt handler? Typically, you would display messages or, more often, remove temporary files created by the script. This allows you to "clean up" before returning to the C shell. You can also use **exit** with a nonzero status to indicate abnormal termination.

Let's illustrate this with an example. Suppose we have a database of Japanese-English dictionary files. Each one has two fields: a Japanese word followed by the corresponding English word. A colon separates the fields to allow internal spaces. Each file contains Japanese words starting with the same letter; thus file **a.words** contains words starting with **a**, **b.words** with **b**, and so forth. Our task is to reverse the fields in each file, placing the English word first.

The script **build** places the English words first in each dictionary file. We use **awk** to swap the fields. The files **a.words, b.words,** and so on, are all in directory ~/**dictionary.** Here is the text for **build:**

```
     % num build
 1   #
 2   # build new dictionaries by reversing fields
 3   # Usage: build
 4
 5   set tf = /tmp/$$                       # use to build tmp filenames
 6   cd ~/dictionary                        # goto dictionary directory
 7
 8   echo "Building dictionary"
 9   foreach file (?.words)                 # file expansion
10       echo $file\:                       # reverse fields using awk
11       awk -F: '{print $2 ":" $1 }' $file > $tf$file
12   end
13
14   echo "Renaming original files"
```

```
15    foreach file (?.words)              # move all tmp files to
16        mv $tf$file $file                # current directory
17    end
```

Line 5 sets up variable **tf** for use in the temporary filenames in line 11. Line 9 initiates a loop for each dictionary file. Line 10 displays the filename, and line 11 calls **awk** to build the new file. The notation **tffile** generates a unique filename in the **/tmp** directory for each dictionary file. In this case **$0** is unnecessary since we concatenate the dictionary name instead. For example, the statements

```
awk -F: '{print $2 ":" $1 }' a.words > /tmp/123a.words
awk -F: '{print $2 ":" $1 }' b.words > /tmp/123b.words
```

show the **awk** commands for the first two dictionary files (assuming the process ID is 123). After we build the temporary files, lines 15 through 17 move them to the current directory, overwriting the originals.

What happens if we interrupt this script? It terminates, and control returns to the C shell. This may leave many files in the **/tmp** directory or, worse still, may leave part of the dictionaries unconverted. We need a way to detect interrupts so that we can stop the script in a controlled manner.

The C shell provides the **onintr** (on interrupt) command to process interrupts within shell scripts. The command

```
onintr label
```

transfers control to **label** when an interrupt occurs. This command usually appears at the beginning of a script. It is in effect only while the script is executing. Elsewhere in your script, include the following:

```
label:
    command(s)
```

label: should be on a line by itself. Any number of commands may follow it. Typically, an **exit** statement with nonzero status is the last command. You can then check whether your script was interrupted by examining **$status** in the calling shell.

Let's modify the **build** script to remove all temporary files if it is interrupted.

```
    % num build
1   #
2   # build new dictionaries by reversing fields
3   # Usage: build
4
5   onintr catch                        # prepare to catch interrupts
6
7   set tf = /tmp/$$                     # use to build tmp filenames
```

```
 8    cd ~/dictionary                      # goto dictionary directory
 9
10    echo "Building dictionary"
11    foreach file (?.words)               # file expansion
12        echo $file\:                     # reverse fields using awk
13        awk -F: '{print $2 ":" $1 }' $file > $tf$file
14    end
15
16    echo "Renaming original files"
17    foreach file (?.words)               # move all tmp files to
18        mv $tf$file $file                # current directory
19    end
20    exit 0                               # normal exit
21
22    catch:                               # interrupt handler
23        set nonomatch                    # prevent file expansion errors
24        rm -f $tf?.words                 # remove temporary files
25        exit 1                           # error exit
```

Line 5 tells the C shell to transfer control to label **catch** when the script is interrupted. Line 23 sets the predefined C shell variable, **nonomatch.** What does this do? Let's assume we interrupt the script before the shell creates the temporary files. Line 24 removes the files using **rm -f** (forced remove). If there are no files to remove, however, the file expansion in **$tf?.words** fails, and the shell reports the error:

```
No match.
```

The statement

```
set nonomatch
```

tells the C shell to ignore filename expansion errors. **nonomatch** is in effect only during execution of lines 24 and 25.

Line 20 provides the normal exit path. Note that control would fall through to the interrupt handling statements if we omitted this statement.

As long as the script receives the interrupt before the **foreach** loop in line 17, all is well. But if a move operation is interrupted, the result could be an incompletely copied file in our permanent directory and the removal of the good copy from **/tmp.** We must handle this situation differently. Lines 17 through 19 are *critical* code that cannot be interrupted.

The C shell lets you disable interrupts using the notation

```
onintr -
```

placed on a separate line. If this is the first statement, the entire script will be impervious to interrupts. You can also use **onintr -** to shield part of a script.

Let's modify **build** to shield the critical code.

```
      % num build
   1  #
   2  # build new dictionaries by reversing fields
   3  # Usage: build
   4
   5  onintr catch                     # prepare to catch interrupts
   6
   7  set tf = /tmp/$$                  # use to build tmp filenames
   8  cd ~/dictionary                  # goto dictionary directory
   9
  10  echo "Building dictionary"
  11  foreach file (?.words)           # file expansion
  12      echo $file\:                 # reverse fields using awk
  13      awk -F: '{print $2 ":" $1 }' $file > $tf$file
  14  end
  15
  16  onintr -                         # disable interrupts
  17
  18  echo "Renaming original files"
  19  foreach file (?.words)           # move all tmp files to
  20      mv $tf$file $file            # current directory
  21  end
  22  exit 0                           # normal exit
  23
  24  catch:                           # interrupt handler
  25      onintr -                     # ignore further interrupts
  26      set nonomatch                # prevent file expansion errors
  27      rm -f $tf?.words             # remove temporary files
  28      exit 1                       # error exit
```

Before the critical move operations begin (lines 19 through 21), line 16 forces the C shell to ignore interrupts. Now you can safely terminate this script at any time before line 16. The second **onintr -** command (line 25) prevents the shell from processing multiple interrupts needlessly.

The last form of **onintr** is the statement

```
onintr
```

on a line by itself. This form restores the default action (terminate and return to the prompt). You can use it to cancel other modes of interrupt handling.

A further modification of **build** makes it ask the user whether to display the new dictionary. We'll use **pr** to format the new files and **more** to page the data on our terminal. We reenable interrupts so that you can interrupt this last operation. Here's the text:

```
      % num build
  1   #
  2   # build new dictionaries by reversing fields
  3   # Usage: build
  4
  5   onintr catch                        # prepare to catch interrupts
  6
  7   set tf = /tmp/$$                     # use to build tmp filenames
  8   cd ~/dictionary                      # goto dictionary directory
  9
 10   echo "Building dictionary"
 11   foreach file (?.words)              # file expansion
 12       echo $file\:                    # reverse fields using awk
 13       awk -F: '{print $2 ":" $1 }' $file > $tf$file
 14   end
 15
 16   onintr -                            # ignore interrupts
 17
 18   echo "Renaming original files"
 19   foreach file (?.words)              # move all tmp files to
 20       mv $tf$file $file               # current directory
 21   end
 22
 23   onintr                              # restore interrupts
 24
 25   echo -n "Display new dictionary? "  # prompt for display
 26   set answer = `gets`                 # read answer
 27   if ($answer == 'y') then            # yes--then
 28       pr ?.words | more               # page the display
 29   endif
 30   exit 0                              # normal exit
 31
 32   catch:                              # interrupt handler
 33       onintr -                        # ignore further interrupts
 34       set nonomatch                   # prevent file expansion errors
 35       rm -f $tf?.words                # remove temporary files
 36       exit 1                          # error exit
```

Line 23 reenables interrupts using **onintr** by itself. We no longer need the interrupt handler (**catch**), since the temporary files have been moved. Line 25 prompts for the display option, and line 26 reads the response. If we type **y,** line 28 formats the converted files and pages them on the terminal. At any time we may press the interrupt key to return to the C shell.

Interrupting Shared Scripts

Interrupting shared scripts (ones that many users may access) creates special problems. Such scripts often have mechanisms for preventing users from interfering with one another. The scripts must deactivate these mechanisms properly if they are interrupted (or prevent interrupts altogether). Otherwise, the result can be a universal lockout. A lockout mechanism (we call it a *lock file*) enforces single-user access. Before a program accesses shared data (such as a database file), it creates a lock file to keep other users out.

Suppose we write a script, **archiver,** that copies a database file to floppy disk. Our script must first check whether a lock file is present to ensure that no other program is using the database. To do this we use the UNIX program **ln** (link) to create a link to an existing file called the "base" file. If the link operation fails, the lock file already exists (someone else is currently running **archiver** or another program that modifies the database). If the link succeeds, we've successfully created the lock, preventing other programs from running. These programs must wait until we are through copying and remove the lock file. We use **ln** because it can create a file and test for its existence in one operation.

The database, lock, and base files are all in **/usr/data.** We must be careful to manage the lock file correctly. If we exit the script without removing the lock file, everyone will be locked out of the database. It's like locking all the car doors and leaving the keys inside. Here is the text for **archiver:**

```
% num archiver
1    # archive /usr/data/database to floppy
2    # Usage: archiver
3
4    set lock = /usr/data/lock          # lock file
5    set base = /usr/data/base          # base file
6    onintr -                           # prevent interrupts
7
8    ln $base $lock >& /dev/null        # attempt to link lock file
9    if ($status) then                  # nonzero status means busy
10       echo2 Database busy ...        # deny access
11       exit 2                         # error exit
12   endif
13
14   # if link succeeds we've created lock
15   onintr cleanup                     # enable interrupts
16   cp /usr/data/database /dev/fd0     # archive to floppy
17   onintr -                           # prevent interrupts
18   rm -f $lock                        # remove lock
19   exit 0                             # normal exit
20
21   cleanup:                           # interrupt handler
22       onintr -                       # disallow further interrupts
23       rm -f $lock                    # remove lock
24       exit 1                         # error exit
```

Lines 4 and 5 set the lock and base shell variables to pathnames in the **/usr/data** directory (the base file already exists). Line 6 prevents interrupts until we establish the lock. Line 8 attempts to link the lock file to the base file, redirecting standard and diagnostic output to **/dev/null** (to discard error messages). If the link succeeds, **$status** is 0 and the **if** statement in line 9 is false. If it is true, (**$status** is nonzero), the link failed, so we display a busy message and exit.

Line 15 enables interrupts, so we can stop the script during the copy operation if necessary. Line 16 copies the database from **/usr/data.** When the copy operation is complete, line 17 prevents interrupts, line 18 removes the lock, and line 19 exits with normal status. An interrupt (during the copy) causes control to transfer to line 21. Here we disable further interrupts and remove the lock file. Now we may terminate the script. We make the status 0 for normal completion and 1 for an interrupt.

8.4 USING CANNED RESPONSES: HERE DOCUMENTS

The C shell provides alternative ways of supplying standard input to commands. Suppose you want to mail a memo to a colleague. You've already learned several ways to do this. If the memo is short, you simply type the following:

```
% mail bill
type your memo here..
ˆD
```

The **mail** command accepts keyboard input until you press a **control-D.** This approach has its limitations, however. Once you press RETURN, you cannot correct any typing errors. Moreover, you cannot use shell variables in your text. Suppose you just installed a program for Bill. You have set the following shell variables:

```
% set d = /usr/include/src
% set f = $d/remote.c
```

You then notify Bill with a memo.

```
% mail bill
I just installed that C program you wanted.
You'll find it in the $d directory.
It's called $f:t.
ˆD
%
```

Poor Bill. When he reads his mail, he sees just what you typed! (And he still doesn't know what the file's name is or where it resides.)

You could simply create a file for the memo. You would then drop it in Bill's "mailbox" using input redirection:

```
% mail bill < memo
```

The problem here is that you end up with an unnecessary file you may forget to remove. Furthermore, accessing shell variables and using command substitution strings is clumsy with this approach. Is there an alternative?

The C shell allows in-line input redirection using the symbols <<. We call such input a *here document*. The C shell calls the program and passes text from your script directly to it as standard input. The format for a here document is as follows:

```
command [argument(s)] << word
    command input


        .  .  .

word
```

The << symbol specifies in-line input redirection. The marker **word** indicates the beginning and end of the input. It can be a single character or a word. You should choose something that does not appear in the text. The ending **word** should be on a line all by itself (no spaces before or after it). If we quote **word,** the shell does not perform command substitution or file or variable expansion on the input. Otherwise, it does, and you must quote special characters (such as **$** and *****) with \.

Using a here document, let's mail our message to Bill again.

```
% mail bill << +
I just installed that C program you wanted.
You'll find it in the $d directory.
It's called $f:t.
+
```

Here we use **+** as the marker word; the second **+** terminates the **mail** command. The message Bill receives is

```
I just installed that C program you wanted.
You'll find it in the /usr/include/src directory.
It's called remote.c.
```

Surely this is more helpful than the unexpanded version. Here documents work with any UNIX command that reads from the standard input.

Suppose you are writing a script that sends mail to a list of users. It contains the statement

```
mail $user < message
```

This means you must create and maintain the message file. Here documents, on the other hand, let you put the message text directly into the script, as in

```
mail $user << !
Today's group meeting is canceled.
!
```

The **!** character serves as the label. Since the **mail** command uses the text as input, you do not need a message.

Here's another example. Suppose the script **fstat** reports the current status of your file system. First, it reports current disk usage in blocks, starting from your home directory. Next it uses the **find** command to report the full pathnames of all core files. These core files are typically large, resulting from a system dump when UNIX detects errors. Last, **fstat** reports the pathnames of all zero-length files.

fstat may take a while to execute, so we put it in the background and display the output. Here's the command sequence:

```
% (fstat > fsav; beep)&
2256
 .  .  .  .  .  .  .
% cat fsav
==============================
Current disk storage (blocks  home_dir):
400     /u/sara
==============================
Core File pathnames:
/u/sara/projw/core
/u/sara/csh/scripts/core
==============================
Zero-Length File Pathnames:
/u/sara/book/appendix/APP.G
/u/sara/m/xx
/u/sara/remote/lockf
```

Here is the **fstat** script:

```
% num fstat
1   # csh script to report current file status
2   # Usage: fstat
3
4   cat << EOF
5   ================================
6   Current disk storage (blocks  home_dir):
7   `du -s ~ `
8   ================================
9   Core File pathnames:
10  `find ~ -name core -print`
11  ================================
12  Zero-Length File Pathnames:
13  `find ~ -size 0 -print`
14  EOF
```

The entire script is just a here document. Line 4 uses the **cat** command to read lines of text as standard input from the script. We use **EOF** for the starting and ending labels at lines 4 and 14, respectively. We use command substitution strings (lines 7, 10, and 13) to produce the formatted output.

Let's enhance **fstat** to report file status for other users. The following script, called **usfst** (user file status), mails current file status information to users on a mailing list. It uses a here document with the **mail** command.

```
% num usfst
1   # csh script to report current file status to users
2   # Usage: usfst
3
4   set mlist = (paul gail sara marty bruce)
5
6   foreach person ($mlist)                    # loop on mail list
7   mail $person << EOF
8
9   NOTE:   Current file status summary. Please
10          delete any unwanted core or zero-length
11          files.
12  = = = = = = = = = = = = = = = = = = =
13  Current disk storage (blocks  home_dir):
14  `du -s ~$person`
15  = = = = = = = = = = = = = = = = = = =
16  Core File pathnames:
```

```
17      `find ~$person -name core -print`
18      = = = = = = = = = = = = = = = = = = = = = = = =
19      Zero-Length File Pathnames:
20      `find ~$person -size 0 -print`
21      EOF
22      end
```

Line 4 creates the mailing list of user names. Line 6 sets up the loop to mail each user the summary information in the here document (lines 8 through 21). We specify each user's home directory with ~ in lines 14, 17, and 20.

We can also use a here document to call the editor from a script file. Suppose we have a large application package written in C. We decide to change the global constant **MAXPROP** to a global integer **maxprop.** Since C distinguishes between uppercase and lowercase names, we must change each occurrence of **MAXPROP** to **maxprop** in all our (many!) source files. (By convention, C programmers usually reserve uppercase identifiers for constants.) A script is a sensible alternative to editing each source file and issuing global substitution commands.

We decide to write a general utility **gsub** (global substitute) that substitutes argument 2 for all instances of argument 1 in the named files. We call the **ex** editor to perform the actual substitution and place the editor commands in a here document.

Now to change our source files, we need only give the single command

```
% gsub MAXPROP maxprop *.c
```

The C shell expands *.c to match all files ending in **.c**—our C source files. **MAXPROP** is the target pattern and **maxprop** the replacement.

Here is the **gsub** script:

```
% num gsub
1    # substitute pattern2 for pattern1 in file(s)
2    # usage: gsub old_pat new_pat file(s)
3
4    if ($#argv < 3) then          # must have a least 3 arguments
5        echo2 "Usage: $0 old_pattern new_pattern file(s)"
6        exit 1
7    endif
8
9    set old = "$argv[1]"          # quotes necessary to retain blanks
10   set new = "$argv[2]"          # and special characters
```

```
11
12    shift                          # remove old_pat
13    shift                          # remove new_pat
14
15    foreach f ($argv[*])           # loop over all files
16        ex - $f << EOF
17            1,\$s/$old/$new/g
18            w
19            q
20    EOF
21    end
```

gsub expects at least three arguments: **old_pattern**, **new_pattern**, and at least one file. The patterns may contain special characters (blanks, *, ?, [ ], etc.), so we quote them in lines 9 and 10. (However, since we use / as the pattern delimiter, the patterns may not contain /.) To make the **foreach** simpler, we save the first two arguments in **$old** and **$new,** respectively. Two **shifts** then make all of the remaining arguments target files.

Line 16 calls the **ex** editor. The **-** option suppresses interactive output. Variable **$f** contains the input filename. **EOF** is the end of input label.

Lines 17 through 19 contain the input to **ex.** Note that we cannot put comments in a here document because they would become input to the program. Since we did not put **EOF** in quotation marks in line 16, the shell will expand **$old** and **$new.** For the same reason, we must quote the initial $ in line 17 with \ so the C shell won't try to expand **$s.** The editing commands have the following meanings:

1,$	for lines 1 through the last
s/$old/$new/g	Substitute each **$old** with **$new.**
w	Write out the file.
q	Quit the editor.

The ending label **EOF** must appear left-justified on a line by itself.

gsub is not limited to single-word patterns. You can use it as follows:

```
% gsub "System III" "System V" *.doc
% gsub "PORT*" "port*" *.c
```

The first example changes all occurrences of **"System III"** to **"System V"** in our **.doc** files. We want the C shell to expand **.doc,** so we do not quote it. We must, however, quote substitution patterns to retain the internal spaces.

The second example involves patterns containing the special character **∗**. Unless we quote them, the C shell attempts file expansion. Lines 9 and 10 preserve the quoting so the subshell executing the script will not attempt file expansion either. We pass them unaltered to **ex** via the here document.

Not only has **gsub** helped with a tedious task, but we have also gained a new tool!

8.5 CALLING YOURSELF TO TASK: RECURSIVE SCRIPTS

Shell scripts can call UNIX commands and other shell scripts. In both cases the parent shell creates a subshell to execute the command. Shell scripts can also call themselves. That is, the C shell can create a subshell to run another copy of the calling script. We call this *recursion*.

When is recursion desirable? Whenever a task operates on items that must be processed in the same way and the number of times this must be done is unknown in advance. A typical example is a script that operates on all files in a directory, including subdirectories. Each time it encounters a directory, it calls itself again. In this way, we "recurse" through a file system. Let's illustrate this with an example.

Suppose we have a subdirectory file system in our home directory. We may have generated it from tape, floppy disk, or another directory. The file system, called **projw,** contains subdirectories as well as files. The command

```
% ls -ld projw
drwxr-xr-x 6 paul other  208 Dec 27 15:01 projw
```

shows that the **projw** directory belongs to group **other.** Our task is to write a shell script to change the **projw** directory and all its subfiles to a new group name.

We'll call the script **projchg.** To change to a new group, say **system,** we'll issue the command

```
% projchg system projw
```

The approach is straightforward. The first call to **projchg** uses the **projw** directory. We'll change directories and use the **chgrp** command to change all the files in directory **projw** to the new group. Next we'll examine all the files. When we encounter a subdirectory, we'll call **projchg** recursively, this time with the subdirectory name. What happens? The shell simply goes through the entire process again. The script terminates when all files and directories in the starting directory file system (**projw**) have a new group name.

Here's the **projchg** script:

```
% num projchg
1    # Recursive csh to change groups (project IDs)
2    # for a directory subtree
3    # Usage: projchg group dir
4
5    if ($#argv < 2) then                      # correct arguments?
6        echo2 "Usage: projchg group dir"
7        exit 1
8    endif
9
10   if (! -d $argv[2]) then                   # is it a directory?
11       echo2 "$argv[2] not a directory"
12       exit 1
13   endif
14
15   grep "$argv[1].*$user" /etc/group > /dev/null  # check group
16   if ($status) then                         # is it valid?
17       echo2 "$argv[1] not a valid group"
18       exit 1
19   endif
20
21   cd $argv[2]                               # change directories
22   chgrp $argv[1] *                          # chgrp for all files
23   foreach f (*)                             # loop over all files
24   if (-d $f) then                           # is it a directory?
25       projchg $argv[1] $f                   # yes--call projchg again
26   endif
27   end
```

Lines 5 through 13 check that there are enough arguments and that the second argument is a valid directory name. Line 15 verifies that argument 1 is a valid group name for **$user,** our login name. The **/etc/group** file contains this information; the statement

```
grep "$argv[1].*$user" /etc/group
```

uses **grep** to search for the target group name (**$argv[1]**) followed by any number of characters (**.***) and our username (**$user**). (We discard the output to **/dev/null**.) **grep** will only match a line containing both in that order. If the requested group name does not exist, **$status** will be 1 (nonzero), and the script exits at line 18. Otherwise, all input parameters are valid, and the real work begins.

Line 21 changes the directory to **$argv[2],** the target directory. Line 22 changes all the files and subdirectories to the new group name. Line 23 uses file expansion within a **foreach** loop. If a file is a directory (line 24), line 25 makes the recursive call to **projchg** with **$f** (the subdirectory name) and **$argv[1]** (the group name). The entire process repeats using the subdirectory name.

How does the script return? When there are no more subdirectories or files in the current directory to process, the **foreach** loop terminates (line 27). The shell then returns control to the previous **projchg** (for the next directory up), and execution continues. This is a different directory (hence a different set of files). When it finishes changing all subdirectories and files in the top directory (**projw**), the script terminates.

You can verify the changes with the command

```
% ls -lR projw
```

which lists recursively all files and directories starting at **projw.**

Two notes concerning **projchg:** (1) **projchg** does not change the group name of the directory passed to the script, only the files and subdirectories underneath it. (2) Since **projchg** changes directories and then calls itself, you must install it in one of your **$path** directories. Otherwise, the shell won't find the **projchg** command. (The alternative is to use an absolute pathname, such as ~/**bin/projchg** in line 25.)

8.6 EASY QUOTING: noglob

Sometimes you want special characters and filenames left alone rather than expanded. For example,

```
% echo do you have my new UNIX book?  |  mail marty
```

fails because of the special character **?**. Commands like these must be quoted to prevent filename expansion. Recall that the C shell does filename expansion before executing any commands (in this case, **echo**). You must quote each filename expansion character using single or double quotation marks or a backslash.

There is another way to control filename expansion. Whereas quoting affects only the current command, the built-in shell variable **noglob** affects filename expansion for all subsequent commands. (*Globbing* is another name for file expansion; hence **noglob** is an abbreviation for "no globbing.") The command

```
% set noglob
```

turns off file expansion. The shell will then not expand the characters *, ?, [ ], { }, and ~ (for home directory). When **noglob** is set, all commands use these characters literally. The command

```
% unset noglob
```

restores the C shell's filename expansion mechanism. (*Note:* **noglob** does not affect pattern matching arguments.)

If you use **noglob** in a script, it is not necessary to unset it as the last statement, since **noglob** is only in effect while your script is running. You can still use quoting and other special characters.

As an example of the use of **noglob,** consider a script **pnames** that displays the full pathname of all files with a given name in your home directory and in all subdirectories. This can be done with the UNIX **find** command, but we would rather type

```
% pnames diff
```

instead of

```
% find $home -name diff -print
```

Here's the first version of **pnames:**

```
    % num pnames
1   # csh to display full pathnames for input filenames
2   # Usage: pnames file
3
4   set noglob                           # turn off file expansion
5   if ($#argv == 0) then                # no arguments?
6       echo2 Usage: $0 file
7       exit 1
8   endif
9
10  find $home -name $argv[1] -print     # display pathnames
```

Note that line 4 sets **noglob** to disable filename expansion. This allows the C shell to pass **$argv[1]** unexpanded to the **find** command (line 10). Here's some sample output from **pnames:**

```
% pnames diff
/u/sara/projw/diff
/u/sara/csh/diff

% pnames "*diff*"
/u/sara/projw/diff
/u/sara/projw/diff.c
/u/sara/csh/diff
/u/sara/scripts/sdiff
/u/sara/scripts/sdiff.s
```

Without **noglob,** we must quote **$argv[1]** in line 10. Otherwise, the shell filename expands **$argv[1]** before **find** sees the argument.

Let's enhance **pnames** to search not only our own directory system but also each directory in our **$path** variable (~**/bin**, **/bin**, **/usr/bin**, **/usr/local**, and **.**). This is useful to avoid duplicating command names. We use **find** again, changing only the starting point:

```
    % num pnames
1   # csh to display full pathnames for input filenames
2   # Usage: pnames file
3
4   set noglob                              # disable file expansion
5   if ($#argv == 0) then                   # no arguments?
6       echo2 Usage: $0 file
7       exit 1
8   endif
9
10  echo Searching for $argv[1] in $home\:
11  find $home -name $argv[1] -print
12  foreach dir ($path)
13      echo Searching for $argv[1] in $dir\:
14      find $dir -name $argv[1] -print
15  end
```

We add **echo** statements (lines 10 and 13) to report which directory **find** is currently searching. The **foreach** loop (lines 12 through 15) uses the **$path** wordlist to extract directories. Because line 4 sets **noglob,** we need not quote **$argv[1]** in lines 10, 11, 13, and 14.

Here's what the output looks like:

```
% pnames "*diff*"
Searching for *diff* in /u/sara:
/u/sara/projw/diff
/u/sara/projw/diff.c
/u/sara/csh/diff
/u/sara/scripts/sdiff
/u/sara/scripts/sdiff.s
Searching for *diff* in /u/sara/bin:
Searching for *diff* in /bin:
/bin/diff
/bin/diff3
/bin/sdiff
Searching for *diff* in /usr/bin:
/usr/bin/bdiff
/usr/bin/sccsdiff
/usr/bin/diffmk
Searching for *diff* in /usr/local:
Searching for *diff* in .:
```

Of course, you could just put double quotation marks around each **$argv[1]** in the script. Obviously, **set noglob** is faster and less error-prone.

Note that **set noglob** turns off filename expansion only. We still may need quotation marks to preserve blanks or escape other special characters (e.g., parentheses, redirection symbols, history command symbols).

8.7 CORRECTING THE ERRORS OF YOUR WAYS: DEBUGGING C SHELL SCRIPTS

When you run a shell script, you type its name and arguments on the command line. The C shell executes the command

```
% script [script arguments]
```

by calling the program **/bin/csh** (the C shell). Your script and its arguments are themselves arguments to **/bin/csh.** You may also call **csh** explicitly. The command

```
% csh script [script arguments]
```

is equivalent to typing your script's name and arguments.

The explicit call to **csh** is useful because of its debugging options. This section describes them.

Debugging with -n (Syntax Checking)

Let's write a script called **lscripts** that reports which of its arguments are shell scripts. This may sound a bit circuitous, but it can be useful to distinguish scripts from programs. For example, we can use

```
% lscripts *
```

to list scripts in our current directory. If

```
dict1 gets lscripts monthly_tot num numfiles
```

are the files in our current directory, we want the output to be

```
dict1: no
gets: no
lscripts: yes
monthly_tot: yes
num: yes
numfiles: yes
```

Let's look at the text for **lscripts** (containing errors):

```
     % num lscripts
1    # list script files
2    # usage: lscripts file(s)
3
4    if ($#argv == 0 then
5        echo2 "Usage: lscripts file(s)"
6        exit 1
7    endif
8
9    foreach f ($argv[*])                         # argument expansion
10       if (-e f) then                           # does file exist?
11           set sc = `file $f | grep "commands text "`
12           if ($#sc == 0) then
13           echo $f: yes                         # if script, display
14           else                                   its name
15               echo $f: no                      # otherwise, no
16           endif
17       else
18           echo2 "file $f does not exist."      # error message
19       endif
20   end
```

Lines 4 through 7 check that at least one argument exists. Lines 9 through 20 are a **foreach** loop using argument expansion. Line 10 makes sure the current file exists, and line 18 displays an error message if it doesn't. Line 11 does the real work. It uses **file** and **grep** to determine if the current file is a shell script. If so, the output of **file** is "commands text". Lines 13 and 15 display the filename and either "yes" or "no".

The C shell has a debugging option that is useful for checking syntax. You should use this option for new scripts. While it won't find all errors, it does catch many common problems such as mismatching parentheses, brackets, and **end** and **endif** statements. The format is

```
% csh -n script
```

The **-n** option makes **csh** read the script, looking for syntax errors. It does not execute anything, so you don't need to supply arguments. Since it only parses the commands, the C shell will not flag errors detectable only during execution. For example, it won't flag a missing **then** in an **if-then-else,** report an incorrect file inquiry operator, or perform any range checking.

The C shell stops at the first error it finds when you use **-n.** Thus you may have to repeat the process several times. Let's try it on **lscripts:**

```
% csh -n lscripts
Too many ('s.
```

The shell reports an error, but the message is far from informative. We know that a parenthesis is missing, but where? We could add **echo** statements to **lscripts,** but this is tedious. Let's see if the C shell can help.

Debugging with -v (Verbose)

The **-v** option tells the C shell to display each line in the script before performing file, variable, or command substitution. You can combine **-v** with **-n** to locate a syntax error. The shell still only parses each statement; for example,

```
% csh -vn lscripts
1
2
3
4   if ( $#argv == 0 then
5   Too many ('s.
```

We number the lines for reference. Note that the **-vn** option displays blank lines for both comments and blank lines (the first three lines of our script). Line 4 reveals the error (missing right parenthesis). Let's fix it and try again.

```
% csh -vn lscripts
1
2
3
4   if ( $#argv == 0 ) then
5   echo2 "Usage: lscripts file(s)"
6   exit 1
7   endif
8
9   foreach f ( $argv[*] )
10  if ( -e f ) then
11  set sc = `file $f | grep "commands text "`
12  if ( $#sc == 0 ) then
13  echo $f: yes
14  Variable syntax.
```

We have another syntax error in line 13, an unescaped semicolon. Since this error also occurs in line 15, we'll fix both instances and try again.

```
% csh -vn lscripts
1
2
3
4   if ( $#argv == 0 ) then
```

```
 5    echo2 "Usage: lscripts file(s)"
 6    exit 1
 7    endif
 8
 9    foreach f ( $argv[*] )
10    if ( -e f ) then
11    set sc = `file $f | grep "commands text"`
12    if ( $#sc == 0 ) then
13    echo $f\: yes
14    else
15    echo $f\: no
16    endif
17    else
18    echo2 "file $f does not exist."
19    endif
20    end
```

The **-vn** option reports no errors; our script is syntactically correct. Let's be brave and run it now.

```
% lscripts *
file dict1 does not exist.
file gets does not exist.
file lscripts does not exist.
file monthly_tot does not exist.
file num does not exist.
file numfiles does not exist.
```

The **-v** option is useful for another reason. Used without **-n,** it tells what statements the shell is executing. Let's execute **lscripts** again using **-v** alone. To shorten the output, we restrict the arguments to just **num** and **numfiles.**

```
    % csh -v lscripts num*
 1
 2
 3
 4    if ( $#argv == 0 ) then
 5
 6    foreach f ( $argv[*] )
 7    if ( -e f ) then
 8
 9    echo2 "file $f does not exist."
10    file num does not exist.
11    endif
12    end
13    if ( -e f ) then
14
```

```
15   echo2 "file $f does not exist."
16   file numfiles does not exist.
17   endif
18   end
```

This display shows which lines the C shell executes. Note that the output of **echo2** appears at lines 10 and 16. The reason **lscripts** thinks the files don't exist is straightforward. The **if** statement in lines 7 and 13 is always false because we typed **f** instead of **$f.**

Back to the editor for another attempt. Let's execute it directly.

```
% lscripts *
dict1: no
gets: no
lscripts: no
monthly_tot: no
num: no
numfiles: no
```

We're getting close, but we still have an error. **lscripts** can't even recognize itself! We'll run the **-v** option again for **num** and **numfiles.**

```
% csh -v lscripts num*
1
2
3
4    if ( $#argv == 0 ) then
5
6    foreach f ( $argv[*] )
7    if ( -e $f ) then
8    set sc = `file $f | grep "commands text"`
9    if ( $#sc == 0 ) then
10
11   echo $f\: no
12   num: no
13   endif
14   else
15   end
16   if ( -e $f ) then
17   set sc = `file $f | grep "commands text"`
18   if ( $#sc == 0 ) then
19
20   echo $f\: no
21   numfiles: no
22   endif
23   else
24   end
```

This display shows that the script is now executing the correct statements. The **file** and **grep** commands are processing the filenames (lines 8 and 17). Lines 9 and 18 are the new suspects. To proceed, we need to know **sc**'s values at execution time.

Debugging with -x (Echo)

The **-x** option tells the C shell to display each line in the script after file, variable, and command substitution but before execution. This is a handy way of displaying the run-time values of script variables. It's most useful when combined with the **-v** option. Let's try it.

```
% csh -vx lscripts num*
1
2
3
4    if ( $#argv == 0 ) then
5    if ( 2 == 0 ) then
6
7    foreach f ( $argv[*] )
8    foreach f ( num numfiles )
9    if ( -e $f ) then
10   if ( -e num ) then
11   set sc = `file $f | grep "commands text"`
12   set sc = `file $f | grep "commands text"`
13   grep commands text
14   file num
15   if ( $#sc == 0 ) then
16   if ( 3 == 0 ) then
17
18   echo $f\: no
19   echo num: no
20   num: no
21   endif
22   endif
23   else
24   else
25   end
26   end
27   if ( -e $f ) then
28    if ( -e numfiles ) then
29   set sc = `file $f | grep "commands text"`
30   set sc = `file $f | grep " commands text"`
31   grep commands text
32   file numfiles
33    if ( $#sc == 0 ) then
34   if ( 3 == 0 ) then
35
36   echo $f\: no
```

```
37    echo numfiles: no
38    numfiles: no
39    endif
40    endif
41    else
42    else
43    end
44    end
```

Use this option sparingly—it can produce a large amount of output. It shows the result of variable substitution for each statement. Lines 16 and 34 reveal our error. The **if** statement is false because the wordlist is nonzero for a shell script. We must reverse the logic; instead of checking whether **$#sc** is 0, we must check whether it's nonzero. The statement

```
    if ($#sc) then
```

is true when **$#sc** is nonzero. Here's the corrected script (finally!):

```
      % num lscripts
 1    # list script files
 2    # usage: lscripts file(s)
 3
 4    if ($#argv == 0) then
 5        echo2 "Usage: lscripts file(s)"
 6        exit 1
 7    endif
 8
 9    foreach f ($argv[*])                        # argument expansion
10        if (-e $f) then                         # does file exist?
11            set sc = `file $f | grep "commands text"`
12            if ($#sc) then
13                echo $f\: yes                   # if script, say yes
14            else
15                echo $f\: no                    # otherwise, no
16            endif
17        else
18            echo2 "file $f does not exist."     # error message
19        endif
20    end
```

8.8 AS TIME GOES BY: TIMING YOUR SCRIPTS

Once you are familiar with C shell programming, you will want to learn ways to make scripts run faster. This requires an understanding of UNIX commands as well as how the shell works. This section discusses shell script efficiency and how to determine the execution time of scripts.

The first step in making shell scripts run faster is recognizing the difference between UNIX commands and C shell built-in commands. An **ls** command, for example, makes the shell create a subshell to execute the program **/bin/ls**. A **cd** command, however, makes the C shell change directories without creating a subshell. We invoke these commands in the same way, but the C shell executes them differently.

You should use built-in commands whenever possible to save the time required to create a subshell. Refer to Appendix C for a complete list.

Using file expansion may also provide you with a shortcut in execution time. Suppose you want to generate a list of files whose names begin with **pn.** The statement

```
set flist = `ls pn*`
```

uses **ls** with command substitution to generate the list and store it in variable **flist.** The statement

```
set flist = pn*
```

does the same thing. Which is faster? The second form is, because the C shell does not have to generate a subshell to perform file expansion.

It is often difficult to tell if you have improved a script. For example, let's consider a script that uses pathname and directory searching. The script **shcom1** lists the names of all shell scripts from the UNIX directories **/bin**, **/usr/bin**, and /**etc.** It uses the **file** and **grep** commands.

```
   % num shcom1
1    # csh to list standard UNIX shell scripts
2    # Usage: shcom1
3
4    file /bin/* | grep "commands text"
5    file /usr/bin/* | grep "commands text"
6    file /etc/* | grep "commands text"
```

We use file expansion for each full pathname as an argument to the **file** command. Compare this to another implementation, **shcom2.**

```
   % num shcom2
1    # csh to list standard UNIX shell scripts
2    # Usage: shcom2
3
4    foreach d (/bin /usr/bin /etc)        # loop over directories
5        cd $d                             # change directories to
6        file * | grep "commands text"     # find the shell scripts
7    end
```

shcom2 uses a different strategy. Line 4 sets up a **foreach** loop (a built-in command) to process the UNIX command directories. Line 5 changes directories, and line 6 executes

file for all files in the current directory. Script **shcom2** displays' the script filename only, whereas **shcom1** displays the full pathname.

The time Command

Which script is faster? Rather than rely on our intuition (or toss a coin), let's use a tool to measure execution speed.

The C shell **time** command reports the execution statistics of a command. You can use it for any executable command, including your shell scripts. The format is

```
time command
```

Just put the word **time** in front of your script's name and arguments. **time** prints the following statistics:

> Time spent in the system
> Time spent executing the command
> Elapsed (real) time to execute the command
> Percentage of CPU to real time used

time reports its data in seconds on the diagnostic output. This lets you redirect standard output and still see execution times on the screen. Let's try it for **shcom1.** We redirect its output to **/dev/null**, since we are only interested in execution speed.

```
% time shcom1 > /dev/null
6.1u 15.9s 0:32 68%
```

Times vary with system load and the number of users. On a single-user system, these statistics show that the **shcom1** script took 32 seconds (real time) to execute. User time (**u**) was 6.1 seconds, and system time (**s**) was 15.9 seconds. **shcom1** used the CPU for 68 percent of the elapsed time.

Now let's time **shcom2.**

```
% time shcom2 > /dev/null
4.9u 12.4s 0:26 66%
```

Surprised? **shcom2** is faster (4.9 seconds of user time compared to 6.1 seconds for **shcom1** and 12.4 seconds of system time compared to 15.9 seconds). This is because **shcom1** uses full pathnames. The **file** command must therefore process a full pathname for each argument. This takes longer.

A word about timing scripts: Always consider user and system times combined, not elapsed times. Running a script when there are many users on the system will increase its elapsed time (real time) but have little effect on user and system times. This is because these times reflect the amount of time UNIX needs to execute your script, regardless of the number of users on the system. The elapsed time, on the other hand, reflects system load.

Optimizing Shell Scripts: An Example

In Section 8.5 we wrote a recursive shell script **projchg** to change the group names of all files and subdirectories below a target directory. Let's see if we can make this script run faster.

      projchg is recursive; it processes all subdirectories at each directory level. We let the C shell handle the recursion by making **projchg** call itself. Is there an alternative? Since the UNIX **find** command has recursion built in, we can use it instead.

      Let's alter our design strategy. First, we use the **find** command to locate the directory names. Next we loop over these directory names. For each one we'll change the group name and all its files. Here's the revised script **projchg2**.

```
    % num projchg2
 1  # csh to change groups (project IDs) for a directory subtree
 2  # Usage: projchg2 group dir
 3
 4  if ($#argv < 2) then                       # correct no. of arguments?
 5      echo2 "Usage: projchg group dir"
 6      exit 1
 7  endif
 8
 9  if (! -d $argv[2]) then                     # is it a directory?
10      echo2 "$argv[2] not a directory"
11      exit 1
12  endif
13  # check for valid group:
14  grep "$argv[1].*$user" /etc/group > /dev/null
15  if ($status) then                          # is it valid?
16      echo2 "$argv[1] not a valid group"
17      exit 1
18  endif
19
20  foreach d (`find $argv[2] -type d -print` )  # find subdirs
21      chgrp $argv[1] $d/*                    # change group for all files
22  end
```

Lines 1 through 18 are the same as in **projchg.** Line 20 uses **find** to generate all directory names from the starting directory (**$argv[2]**). Line 21 changes the group name for all files in directory **$d.**

      We can illustrate the **find** command with an example. Suppose you called **projchg2** as follows:

```
    % projchg2 system ~/telcom
```

The **find** command uses the **-type d** option to produce the directory names underneath the **telcom** directory. For example, you might see

```
/u/sara/telcom
/u/sara/telcom/src
/u/sara/telcom/src/asm
/u/sara/telcom/doc
/u/sara/telcom/doc/nroff
```

Instead of displaying these directory names, however, **find** supplies them to the **foreach** statement.

Which is faster? Let's time each one for a large directory subsystem (10 subdirectories, 200 files).

```
% time projchg system telcom
43.6u 28.6s 1:55 62%

% time projchg2 system telcom
6.5u 19.3s 0:50 51%
```

As you can see, **projchg2** is significantly faster. The knowledge of how the **find** command works allowed us to improve our shell script.

8.9 MAKING THE BEST OF IT: C SHELL SCRIPT GUIDELINES

One of the pleasures of UNIX is its vast arsenal of commands, utilities, and connecting tools (pipes, input/output redirection, etc.). Chances are you can solve your problem by simply putting the pieces together in the right way. When you have a job to do, what's the best design strategy? When should you write a C shell script as opposed to, say, a C program?

In this section we offer guidelines and a few ground rules that will help you decide. There is no substitute for experience, of course, but a few hints certainly can't hurt. We'll begin by looking at areas where the C shell is adept as a problem solver but point out its deficiencies as well. Should you elect to write a script, what is a good design framework? Finally, we'll look at ways to make shell scripts execute faster.

Don't Reinvent the Wheel

You should write a C shell script rather than a C program if your task can be solved with UNIX commands. Becoming familiar with UNIX commands that process files is a step in the right direction. A task that processes lines of text is especially suited to a script because many UNIX commands process lines of text (e.g., **grep**, **sort**, **uniq**, **awk**). For example, our **longlines** script (from Chapter 7) is really just the UNIX **awk** command.

We added structure for processing more than one file and an option for specifying a width.

A task that deals mostly with numeric or character data is not suitable for a script. A script that converts hexadecimal numbers to decimal, for example, requires character-by-character processing. We can write such a tool in the C shell, but it will execute slowly. The C programming language is more suitable.

But we can certainly justify writing a script in the C shell initially and rewriting it in C if speed is a concern. Since the C shell offers high-level control structures, it is easy to use. We pay for this ease of use with a high overhead. We benefit because we can design and program a tool in much less time.

Why Write a Script?

First of all, a shell script is easy to create and maintain. All you need is your favorite editor. You don't need a compiler, linker, or loader, and you don't have to worry about maintaining object files. When you make a change, you simply rerun the script. This saves time and gets you going quickly. Moreover, shell scripts are generally short in length, yet they have 'programming constructs similar to high-level languages. You store shell scripts in source form, which requires minimal storage. You can use them as system commands, just like UNIX commands.

A Framework for Your Scripts

Once you decide to write your script, there are some basic guidelines that you should follow. A good C shell script should take advantage of the shell user interface. It should allow you to use redirection and pipes, if appropriate. This means that your scripts should read from the standard input if no arguments are specified and write to the standard output. This lets the user specify through redirection or piping the destination of the output. The script should write all diagnostic messages to the diagnostic output using a utility such as **echo2** (see Appendix D).

The first thing your script should do is check for the correct number and form of its arguments. It should check for the existence of files and/or directories when appropriate. If it detects an error, use the following usage format:

```
echo2 "Usage: $com:t arguments"
```

where **$com:t** is the (tail-only) name of the script and **arguments** is a script-specific description of the expected argument list. Put brackets [ ] around optional arguments. For example, the usage statement for the **gsub** script is

```
echo2 "Usage: $com:t old_pattern new_pattern file(s)"
```

and **longlines** is

```
echo2 "Usage: $com:t [-w width] [file(s)]"
```

If the script is used improperly elsewhere, error messages should be as informative as possible and should include the name of the script that detected the error. For example, **longlines** might use the following message statement when it encounters a bad width argument:

```
echo2 $com:t\: Bad width argument $a
```

This message specifies the script name (**$com:t**) and the offending width argument (**$a**).

These forms have two advantages: (1) You can rename the script later without modifying the error messages, and (2) including the name in the error message identifies which command detected the error. For example,

```
% sort taxrec[1-5] | longlines 8X | pr -n
longlines: Bad width argument 8X
```

shows you that the error is not from the **sort** or **pr** command.

Use **exit** statements in your scripts with the same status conventions followed by standard UNIX commands. If your script terminates normally, use **exit 0.** When you exit under error conditions, use nonzero status (**exit 1**). This allows your scripts to be used with the conditional command operators (**&&** and ‖).

A script should prevent such execution time errors as "Subscript out of range" or "Badly formed command." You do this by thinking of boundary conditions and situations where subscripts or commands yield run-time errors. For example, the statement

```
if ($#argv && $argv[1] == "-i") then
. . .
```

results in the execution time error "Subscript out of range" if there are no arguments. Even though we check for arguments with **$#argv,** the C shell parses the entire line and finds the reference for **$argv[1].** To avoid this error, you must embed the **if** statements as follows:

```
if ($#argv) then
    if ($argv[1] == "-i") then
```

This ensures that there are indeed arguments in **argv** before you reference the first element (**$argv[1]**).

A script that needs to store temporary files should use the /**tmp** file system. The script should be responsible for removing these files. Any tools that we write, either for ourselves or for others, should be as general as possible. Yet the tools should perform only one task. For example, our **gsub** utility globally substitutes one text pattern for another in one or more files. Perhaps the inspiration for this script came from the need to change all occurrences of the word **UNIX** TO **XENIX** in many files. Although it's tempting simply to write a script that does this very specific task, we decide that the need for such a utility might come up again. So we make the script more general by making the substitution patterns arguments.

Moving Toward Efficiency

Efficient shell programming can mean different things. There are efficient ways to code scripts, run them, even use them. Generally speaking, minimizing your use of the following features will make your shell scripts run faster:

> Process creation
> Pathname searches
> Arithmetic processing
> Character processing

In addition, C shell scripts start up faster when you suppress execution of the ~/**.cshrc** file. When combining commands in a pipeline, you can decrease execution time depending on how you arrange the commands. Let's examine each of these techniques in detail.

Process Creation. The C shell creates a new process to execute each external command. Using built-in C shell commands or file expansion (if appropriate) always executes faster than executing an external UNIX program.

For example, the statement

```
foreach f (`ls` )
```

executes slower than the functionally equivalent

```
foreach f (*)
```

because the shell creates a subshell to execute **ls.** With *, the shell performs only file expansion (it does not create a subshell).

Pathname Searches. Long pathname searches can add overhead to your script. Consider the following statement:

```
ls -l /u/sara/japanese/{dict1,dict2,dict3}
```

Although we use the terse form to save on typing, the C shell still executes

```
ls -l /u/sara/japanese/dict1 /u/sara/japanese/dict2 \
      /u/sara/japanese/dict3
```

To find each file, the shell must look in directory /**u,** then subdirectory **sara,** and finally subdirectory **japanese.** We increase our pathname search overhead.

Contrast this with the following (functionally equivalent) statement:

```
cd /u/sara/japanese
ls -l dict1  dict2  dict3
```

We change directory to /**u/sara/japanese** and then do a long listing of three files in that directory: **dict1, dict2,** and **dict3.** Once the C shell changes directories, finding the pathnames for **dict1, dict2,** and **dict3** requires looking in a single place (the current directory). This approach decreases the search time for pathnames. Furthermore, since **cd** is a built-in command, we have not added much overhead.

As another example, it is more efficient to use a construct such as

```
cd $dir
foreach file (*)
   〈process $file〉
end
```

than

```
foreach file ($dir/*)
   〈process $file〉
end
```

For the same reason, this reduces pathname search overhead and uses file expansion in the current directory to create the filenames.

Arithmetic Processing. A program that performs mainly arithmetic operations should not be written in the C shell. For example, suppose we need a program that converts hexadecimal integers to decimal. We call **htoi** (hexadecimal to integer) as follows:

```
% htoi 12ab
4779
```

The decimal equivalent of **12ab** (hex) is **4779.** This utility needs to examine each character in the argument and perform addition and multiplication operations to convert to base 10. Writing this program in C instead of the C shell results in a utility that executes much faster.

Character Processing. Accessing individual characters in shell variables is also slow. Although there is no built-in command to do this, we can use the UNIX program **expr.** Suppose we have a C shell script, **config,** used to configure a software system. We specify an argument to build different systems. Here we give argument **ts7.** The script extracts the number following **ts.** Using **expr,** we can assign all characters following **ts** to shell variable **n,** as follows:

```
set n = `expr $argv[1] : 'ts\(.*\)'`
```

Since **expr** is not a built-in command, this statement executes slowly.

Combining Commands in a Pipeline

The following command sorts file **tax**, searches for lines that contain the word **"business expense"**, and prints the result:

```
% sort tax  |  grep "business expense"  |  lpr
```

However, it is more efficient to **grep** first and **sort** second. The end result is the same, but running **grep** first leaves less work for **sort** to do. (Why sort lines in a file that will be excluded anyway?) Therefore, a more efficient form of this command is

```
% grep "business expense" tax  |  sort  |  lpr
```

Putting commands that diminish the output first in a pipeline is a technique that you should use interactively as well as in your scripts.

Fast Shell Startup

Each time the C shell prepares to execute a script, it searches for the file ~/**.cshrc** and executes it. This allows us to use our aliases and any locally defined variables during the subsequent execution of the shell script. However, in many cases we do not need these aliases or local variables (especially scripts used by many people). Startup time can be significantly reduced by eliminating this step.

To prevent the C shell from executing your ~/**.cshrc** file, use the following format:

```
% csh -f script [script arguments]
```

For example, the statement

```
% csh -f longlines table.4
```

runs the **longlines** script on the file **table.4** without reading your ~/**.cshrc** file. Remember, you must not use any aliases in your scripts or this method won't work.

This is inconvenient to type each time. Furthermore, it places the burden on the user of knowing when the shell must execute ~/**.cshrc** for each script. Using an alias helps:

```
% alias longlines 'csh -f ~/tools/longlines'
```

We precede the call to **longlines** with **csh -f.** Note that we use the full pathname for the **longlines** file (to prevent an alias loop error). We do not need to specify any arguments (in this case) since the shell will append them automatically. We can create such aliases for the scripts we use most often.

Berkeley versions (2.9, 4BSD) of the C shell provide an alternative method. Include the statement

```
#! /bin/csh -f
```

as the first line in your C shell script. There must not be a space after the initial **#,** but the space following **!** is optional. You must specify the full pathname for the shell (**/bin/csh**).

You now execute your script as usual. When the C shell creates a subshell to run your script, it automatically leaves out searching and execution of the ~/.**cshrc** file.

For example, the following version of **longlines** implements this directive:

```
% cat longlines
#! /bin/csh -f
# script to demonstrate -f option
if ($#argv == 0) then
   awk "length > 80"
else
   foreach f ($argv[*])
        awk "length > 80" $f
   end
endif
```

A final thought on efficient C shell programming: Sometimes the most important factor is creating a script that gets the job done with little effort. Therefore, it may not always be a worthwhile goal to modify a working script to make it more efficient.

8.10 HINTS AND CAUTIONS

■ Be careful with naming conventions when you create more than one temporary file in your shell scripts. For example, in the statements

```
set com = $0
. . . . . .
sort +1 -d -f $file > /tmp/$com:t.$$
. . . . . .
awk -f total.awk $file > /tmp/$com:t.$$
. . . . . .
```

we use the same temporary file for the **sort** and **awk** commands. This can be an error if **sort**'s temporary file is not moved or copied before the **awk** command executes. The script should be organized as follows:

```
set com = $0
set tf1 = /tmp/$com:t1.$$
set tf2 = /tmp/$com:t2.$$
. . . . . . .
sort +1 -d -f $file > $tf1
. . . . . .
awk -f total.awk $file > $tf2
. . . . . .
```

Here we declare two temporary files using a numbering notation for shell variables **tf1** and **tf2.** This not only guarantees unique filenames but also saves on typing and mistakes (we type **$tf1** and **$tf2** instead of their longer counterparts).

■ Recall that background tasks ignore interrupts from your keyboard. If your shell script submits a background job, the interrupt key terminates your script but not the job. Study the following script:

```
onintr catch                        # prepare to catch interrupts
set com = $0
set tf = /tmp/$com:t.$$              # temp filename
. . . . . .
sort +1 -d -f $file > $tf           # sort in foreground
. . . . . .
nroff -ms app.* > appendix&         # format in background
. . . . . .
exit 0

catch:
    rm -f $tf                       # remove temp file
    exit 1                          # error exit
```

The **sort** command runs in the foreground and stores its output in a temporary file. The **nroff** command runs in the background. If you strike the interrupt key after the **nroff** command, the script deletes the temporary file (denoted by **$tf**), but the **nroff** command continues to run. Can you have your script terminate the background job as well?

Most versions of the C shell (not BSD) have a built-in shell variable (called **child**) that holds the process ID of the last background process. You can use it with a **kill** command to stop the job. Here's the revised script:

```
onintr catch                        # process interrupts
set com = $0
set tf = /tmp/$com:t.$$              # temp filename
. . . . . .
sort +1 -d -f $file > $tf           # sort in foreground
. . . . . .
```

```
nroff -ms app.* > appendix&          # format in background
set job1 = $child                    # save PID
. . . . . .
exit 0

catch:
    rm -f $tf                        # remove temporary file
    if ($?job1) then                 # job1 defined?
        kill -9 $job1                # terminate background job
    endif
    exit 1                           # error exit
```

Now the interrupt handler removes **sort**'s temporary file and terminates the background job (**nroff**) if it exists. We saved the background job's process ID in variable **job1** for use in the interrupt handler. We can easily extend this approach to handle multiple background jobs.

■ While **onintr** - always ignores interrupts in shell scripts, the **onintr label** format does not work correctly with some commands. If you press the interrupt key in this situation, the offending command terminates, and the system returns control to the next statement in your shell script. Examine the following script:

```
    % num formatter
1   #
2   onintr catch                     # prepare to catch interrupts
3   nroff *.doc > book               # format document files
4   exit 0                           # normal exit
5   catch:                           # process interrupt
6       rm -f book                   # remove partial format
7       exit 1                       # error exit
```

If you press the interrupt key during the **nroff** command, **nroff** terminates, and the shell resumes execution at line 4 (and thus it doesn't catch the interrupt). One solution is to examine the **status** variable after returning from the **nroff** command. If its value is nonzero, you received an interrupt (or some other abnormal event occurred). In this case transfer control to **catch** and process the interrupt as usual. Here is the (admittedly ad hoc) solution:

```
    % num formatter
1   #
2   onintr catch                     # prepare to catch interrupts
3   nroff *.doc > book               # format document files
4   if ($status) goto catch          # check status
5   exit 0                           # normal exit
6   catch:                           # process interrupt
```

```
7       rm -f book                      # remove partial format
8       exit 1                          # error exit
```

It is a good idea to experiment with the commands you use in a script file that uses interrupt handling. The **sort** and **cc** commands also behave this way.

■ Always setting **noglob** in shell scripts can be a mixed blessing. Its merit depends on how you modify your script. We've seen how we can add statements that use file expansion characters without quoting them when we set **noglob.** Suppose we add these statements to the same script:

```
cd $argv[1]
foreach f (*)
.  .  .  .  .  .
end
```

We intend to change directories and create a wordlist from the files in the current directory (**$argv[1]**). Since **noglob** is set, however, the C shell does not expand *. What should we do? One solution is to use the **ls** command to generate the list of files. The statements

```
cd $argv[1]
foreach f (`ls`)
.  .  .  .  .  .
end
```

do the job, but this approach creates a subshell to run **ls.** A better solution (and one that is faster) toggles the **noglob** variable just for the time that we need it. The statements

```
cd $argv[1]
unset noglob        # enable file expansion
foreach f (*)
.  .  .  .  .  .
end
set noglob          # disable file expansion
```

create the list of files and still maintain **noglob** for the rest of the script.

■ **noglob** also affects commands that read input (such as `gets` and $<). Suppose a script with **noglob** unset prompts for pattern names. These pattern names can include regular expressions (which use the characters * and [ ]—these have different meanings from their file expansion counterparts!). The following shell script statements can produce an error:

```
echo -n "Enter a pattern: "
set pat = $<
echo Substituting $pat in file $argv[1]
```

(Use `gets` if your C shell lacks **$<**.) As long as the pattern you type does not contain special characters, all is well. The sequence

```
Enter a pattern: maxlen
Substituting maxlen in file addprop.c
```

works as advertised. But the sequence

```
Enter a pattern: maxlen*
```

fails. (Quoting the input has no effect on file expansion; the read command includes any quotation marks as part of the input.) Since **noglob** is unset, the C shell attempts file expansion before executing the **echo** command. You may see errors such as

```
echo: No match.
```

or

```
Substituting in file addprop.c
```

If you set **noglob** in this script, no file expansion occurs for read input commands. You may set it for the entire script or bracket the code that needs it, as we did before:

```
set noglob         # disable file expansion
echo -n "Enter a pattern: "
set pat = $<
echo Substituting $pat in file $argv[1]
unset noglob       # enable file expansion
```

The alternative is to quote the read command and all instances of **$pat** in the script.

■ **noglob** is useful with quoted wordlists. Suppose a script prompts for a list of patterns that may contain special characters. Here's an example:

```
Enter a pattern list: dict[1-4] *.doc
```

Assume that this script does not have **noglob** set. You must include the following statements to read your pattern list correctly (using **$<**):

```
echo -n "Enter a pattern list: "
set pat = $<
foreach pattern ($pat:x)
  grep "$pattern" $argv[1]
end
```

To prevent file expansion, we create a quoted wordlist using the **:x** modifier with **$pat** and quote **$pattern** in the **foreach** loop. (Recall from Section 4.4 that the **:x** modifier quotes a variable and expands it into separate words.) If you use `gets` in this same example, you will need to quote it as well as the **$pat** and **$pattern** variables.

We can remove all this quoting using **noglob.** We can write the same script (with **noglob** set) as follows:

```
set noglob        # disable file expansion
echo -n "Please enter a pattern list: "
set pat = $<
foreach pattern ($pat)
    grep $pattern $argv[1]
end
unset noglob      # enable file expansion
```

■ If your shell scripts use aliases from your ~/.**cshrc** file, you may need additional debugging tools. The C shell includes the **-V** and **-X** options for this purpose. These options are equivalent to **-v** and **-x,** respectively, except the C shell displays lines in your ~/.**cshrc** file as well as the script file. Use the following formats:

```
% csh -V script [script arguments]
% csh -X script [script arguments]
```

■ If your shell scripts do not use aliases from your ~/.**cshrc** file, you can combine the **-f** option (fast startup) with the other debugging options. The alias

```
% alias dbug 'csh -fvx'
```

allows you to **dbug** your scripts quickly by typing, for example,

```
% dbug lscripts num*
```

■ In scripts that do not use aliases, make recursive calls using **csh** with the **-f** option. These will execute faster. Furthermore, call the script using an absolute pathname so that the C shell does not have to search the directories in **$path.** For example, in **projchg** (see Section 8.5), the statement

```
/bin/csh -f ~/bin/projchg $argv[1] $f
```

calls **projchg** recursively without reading your ~/.**cshrc** file and without searching **$path.**

■ Be careful when you change directories within a script. There may be situations in which this is not acceptable. For example, suppose we call **numfiles** (from Section 7.13) as follows:

```
% numfiles ../bill tools realestate
```

Recall that **numfiles** gives a file and directory count for each directory argument. Suppose **numfiles** uses these statements to process the files in each directory:

```
foreach dir ($argv[*])        # loop on each directory name
    cd $dir                   # change directory
    foreach file (*)          # file expansion
        (process $file)
    end
end
```

There's no problem as long as the directory names have full pathnames. But the script fails for relative pathnames. (Remember, once you execute a **cd** command, all subsequent relative pathnames are invalid.)

The alternative form, though less efficient, solves this problem. Look at the difference:

```
foreach dir ($argv[*])           # loop on each directory name
    foreach file ($dir/*)        # file expansion
        (process $file)
    end
end
```

In this case we simply use the directory as specified on the command line. This allows a directory to be a relative pathname.

Can we be more efficient and still solve our problem? For a better solution, we prefix the current working directory on all relative pathnames before issuing a change directory command (and thus force each directory to conform to its absolute pathname form). Or we could return to the original working directory each time to ensure that all subsequent relative pathnames are valid.

The following script fragment processes a list of directories by changing to the directory and then returning to the original before processing the next directory.

```
set save = $cwd         # save current working directory
foreach dir ($argv[*])  # loop on each directory name
    cd $dir             # change directory
    foreach file (*)    # file expansion
        <process $file>
    end
    cd $save            # return to original directory
end
```

Use the statement

```
set save = `pwd`                        # save current working directory
```

if your C shell does not have the predefined **$cwd** shell variable.

■ When doing interactive shell programming, don't expect the history mechanism to help you. It stores only the first line. Also, shell variables in interactive scripts remain set afterward. For example

```
% foreach f (*)
? set oldf = `ls -l $f | grep "Apr 11"`
? if ($#oldf) cp $f bkup
? end
```

copies only April 11 files to a backup directory. The shell variable **oldf** is still in your current shell. To release it, use

```
% unset oldf
```

8.11 KEY POINT SUMMARY

Shell scripts are a viable alternative to programming languages. They can use UNIX commands for text processing and file input/output tasks. In addition, they can:

use the UNIX public directory, **/tmp,** for temporary files
enable and disable file expansion
send stored text to a program as standard input

C shell scripts should conform as much as possible to standard UNIX command format and the shell interface. Interrupt handlers (see Table 8-1) allow you to execute commands before your script terminates. Shell scripts can be recursive.

TABLE 8-1 SUMMARY OF INTERRUPT CONTROL COMMANDS

onintr	Terminate script and return control to invoking shell (default action).
onintr -	Ignore interrupts. In effect until script terminates or until changed by another **onintr** command.
onintr label	Transfer control to **label** when an interrupt is received.

The **onintr** commands do not affect detached (background) commands.

TABLE 8-2 USEFUL **csh** OPTIONS

-f	Does not search for or execute commands in ~/. **cshrc**
-n	Parses commands but does not execute them
-v	Echoes command input after history substitution (verbose option)
-x	Echoes commands after variable substitution but before execution (echo option)
-V	Sets verbose option before reading ~/. **cshrc**
-X	Sets echo option before reading ~/. **cshrc**

The C shell provides options for debugging scripts (see Table 8-2). Use these options to pinpoint syntax as well as execution-time errors. Use the UNIX **time** command to measure your script's execution time.

Make scripts more efficient by reducing shell startup time and minimizing arithmetic and character processing. Use built-in commands whenever possible and avoid full pathname searches.

9

Customizing the C Shell

Many people work on a variety of UNIX systems. One system could run on a micro-computer, another on a mainframe. Users want to work on each system in the same way. They also want to take advantage of (or compensate for) each system's features and create a comfortable working environment. The user interface is a key ingredient in meeting these goals.

The C shell lets you customize the UNIX interface by defining system parameters and terminal settings. You can create your own custom environment when you login. This includes terminal settings, aliases, and special shell scripts. It requires a familiarity with the C shell's special files (**.cshrc, .login, .logout**) and with the interaction between the C shell and UNIX.

This chapter presents sample login sessions. We then examine the special files' building blocks—the C shell's predefined variables, UNIX environment variables, and the shell's built-in commands. You will see how these work and how they interact. You will then be able to use the C shell's customizing options to meet your own needs.

9.1 YOUR WISH IS MY COMMAND: A SAMPLE CUSTOMIZATION SESSION

A short working session on the terminal will illustrate how to personalize the C shell environment. Suppose we want to login, compile a program, send mail, and logout. We'll login under the name **sara.** The system responds with

```
Hello, sara !
Welcome to UNIX
Today is Fri Jan 4 08:15 PST 1985
Last logout: Thu Jan 3 20:05 PST 1985
There are 4 users logged on.
1%
```

Besides the friendly greetings (a bit much for some people's tastes), the C shell displays the date and time and the date and time of our last logout. This record could help identify unauthorized use of our account. The shell then tells us how many users are currently logged on. This shows if the system is busy or if we have it to ourselves.

The final line displays the prompt. We made it include the event number we need for history commands.

Let's issue a few commands.

```
1% dir
japanese source tools unix_course
2% cd source; ls *.c
echo2.c gets.c
```

The **dir** command is an alias, not a standard UNIX utility. Note that it is available automatically. Command 2 changes directory to **source** and lists all files ending in ∗**.c**.

Next we'll compile **gets.c**.

```
3% cc -o gets gets.c >& errs
errs: File exists.
4% ^errs^! errs
cc -o gets gets.c > & ! errs
```

Command 3 reports that we are about to overwrite an existing file (the **noclobber** option is set). We don't care, so we change the command to override **noclobber**. Command 4 uses the history correction character ˆ to replace **errs** with **! errs** in the previous command. Now the C compiler redirects compilation errors to **errs**.

When the compilation finishes, we type

```
5% cat !$
cat errs
6% mv gets /usr/local
```

We display the **errs** file by using the history command **!$** to designate the last argument of the previous command. The **errs** file is empty; hence the compilation was successful. We move the object file **gets** to the **/usr/local** directory.

Next we send mail.

```
7% mail bruce
I installed a new version of gets in /usr/local.
Try it and let me know of any problems.
^D
^D
Use "logout" to logout.
8% who | grep bruce
9% bye
Logging out at: Fri Jan 4 08:30 PST 1985
```

Since the message is short, we type it directly from the keyboard and terminate it with **control-D.** Our fat fingers (or a bouncy keyboard) have struck again. We mistakenly press **control-D** twice. The C shell responds that we must use the **logout** command (luckily, the **ignoreeof** option is set). Otherwise, the first **control-D** terminates the **mail** command and the second **control-D** terminates our login shell! We're not ready to logout yet. We use the **who** and **grep** commands to see if Bruce is currently logged in. No output indicates that Bruce has gone home. When we're ready to leave, we type **bye** (an alias for the **logout** command). The C shell then displays a logout message with the date and time.

As you can see, the C shell is both an aid and an error catcher. This is no accident; in fact, we set up our C shell to include the following features automatically:

```
A prompt with the event number
Aliases dir and bye
noclobber set
ignoreeof set
Special messages at login and logout
```

We will now describe how to customize the C shell to produce these automatic settings and display special messages. We'll show you how to run commands, display messages, and set special C shell and environment variables. We use three special files to do this; let's examine **.cshrc** first.

The .cshrc File

After you login, UNIX calls the C shell to execute your commands. However, before displaying the prompt, the C shell must do some work. It first searches for a file **.cshrc** in your home directory. If it is there, the C shell executes the commands stored in it. Here is the **.cshrc** file we used in the foregoing session:

```
     % num ~/.cshrc
  1  # .cshrc file - Version 1
  2
  3  # Set up shell variables
  4  set history = 10                        # set up history list
```

```
 5    set prompt = '\!% '                      # put event number in prompt
 6    set ignoreeof                            # logout protection
 7    set noclobber                            # redirection protection
 8
 9    # Setup aliases
10    alias al alias                           # short for alias
11    al bye logout                            # signoff
12    al dir \
13    'set d = `ls -1F \!* | grep /` ; if ($#d) echo "$d:gh"; unset d'
14    al h history                             # short for history
15    al ldir 'ls -l \!* | grep "^d" '         # long list directories
16    al nusers \
17    '(set a = `who|wc -l` ;echo "There are $a users logged on. ")'
```

First we define some shell variables. Line 4 makes the history list size 10. Line 5 puts the event number in the prompt. Lines 6 and 7 set **ignoreeof** and **noclobber** for extra protection. Next we define our aliases. Line 10 defines a short form of alias itself (this is like abbreviating the word *abbreviation*). Lines 11 and 12 define the aliases **bye** and **dir,** respectively, and lines 14 and 15 define aliases for **history** and a long listing of directory names. Although we did not use them in our sample session, they are available. Line 17 defines the alias **nusers** to report the number of users currently logged in.

This file is important. It defines shell variables and aliases so that they are available automatically when we login. It also has another function. Since the C shell executes **.cshrc** every time it executes a script, this makes aliases and default settings available to scripts. We may, for example, use **dir** or **ldir** in a script. Thus the C shell may execute our **.cshrc** file many times during a session.

The .login File

Next the C shell executes file **.login** in your home directory if it is available. **.login** is executed only once each session. Here is the **.login** file we used:

```
      % num ~/.login
 1    # .login - Version 1
 2
 3    # Greetings and Salutations
 4    echo Hello, sara !
 5    echo Welcome to UNIX
 6    echo -n "Today is "; date
 7    echo -n "Last logout: "; cat ~/.lastlog
 8
 9    nusers
```

Lines 4 through 7 display the login messages using the UNIX commands **echo, date,** and **cat.** You can also execute scripts or even aliases defined in the **.cshrc** file. Line 7 displays the contents of the file ~/**.lastlog.** It contains the date and time of our last session. We'll see shortly how **.lastlog** obtains this information. Line 9 executes the alias **nusers** to display the number of users logged in. We can use aliases in our **.login** file because **.cshrc** has already been executed.

The .logout File

When you're ready to end your session, you execute **logout** (alias **bye** in our case). The C shell executes **.logout** in your home directory if available. Here is the **.logout** file used in the sample session:

```
% num ~/.logout
1   # .logout - Version 1
2
3   echo -n "Logging out at: "
4   date | tee ~/.lastlog
```

Lines 3 and 4 display a message. Because we pipe **date**'s output to the **tee** utility, the date appears on the terminal and in the file ~/**.lastlog.** This is how we record our last logout time for **.login** to display.

We can add to these special files. By using other C shell variables, UNIX environment variables, and built-in commands, we can increase our control over the C shell's behavior. Let's examine these options one at a time.

9.2 CUSTOMIZATION WITH PREDEFINED VARIABLES

One way to customize the C shell is with special shell variables. We can set them in many ways. We can, for example, tell the C shell how often to check for incoming mail, whether to report execution statistics for commands that take more than a certain amount of time, and what to use as a prompt. We can change the order and location of directories the shell searches for commands. We can even change the characters used to edit commands from the history list.

To do all this we use the **set** command. The notation

```
set variable = string
```

initializes **variable** to **string.** We will draw variables from a special list called the C shell's *predefined variables*.

Some of these have default settings (that is, they are initially the same for every user), while others get their values from UNIX user information files (such as **/etc/passwd**). Appendix B contains a complete list of predefined variables. In this section we discuss the ones you are most likely to use in a C shell setup file.

path

path contains a list of directory names. The C shell uses it to search for commands. On most systems the default setting is

```
( .  /bin /usr/bin )
```

where **.** (dot) is your current directory. When you type

```
% who
```

for example, the C shell searches the directories in the **path** variable. It finds **who** in the **/bin** directory and executes program **/bin/who.** The **/bin** and **/usr/bin** directories contain most UNIX commands.

You will probably want to add directories. Many installations use directory **/usr/ local** for locally written or modified commands. You may also have a private tools directory. In your **.cshrc** file, the command

```
set path = (  ~/bin /bin /usr/bin /usr/local   . )
```

includes these directories in your search path. Since **path** is a wordlist variable, we must use parentheses with **set.** On a Berkeley (BSD) system, add the **/usr/ucb** directory to include its utilities.

Note that we put our current directory (.) last. The C shell searches **path** from left to right, so you should order its entries carefully. Placing ~/**bin** first allows us to execute private versions of UNIX commands. Placing /**bin** and /**usr/bin** near the front decreases the C shell's search time for UNIX commands.

The C shell doesn't bother with **path** if you enter a command's full pathname. Thus the shell will always find the command

```
% /bin/who
```

no matter what **path**'s value is. (*Note:* The more directories **path** includes, the longer the C shell must spend searching for commands, especially mistyped ones.)

cdpath

The wordlist **cdpath** is, like **path,** a list of directory names. However, the shell uses **cdpath** only with **cd, pushd,** and **popd.** When you change directories using one of these three commands, the C shell searches **cdpath**'s list for the specified name. To illustrate this, suppose directory **japanese** is a subdirectory of **lang** in your home directory. You haven't set **cdpath.** If you type

```
% cd japanese
japanese: No such file or directory
```

from your home directory, the C shell looks for **japanese** in the current directory. Since it's not there, the shell reports an error. Now if you define **cdpath** as

```
set cdpath = (~/lang)
```

the C shell will also search the ~/**lang** directory if necessary.

UNIX's hierarchical file system lets you divide major work areas into separate directories. Users who partition their work this way will find **cdpath** very useful. By including all directories in it, a user can conveniently change to a subdirectory in a major work area by specifying only the directory name. Like **path, cdpath** must be a wordlist containing absolute pathnames.

home

The **home** variable contains the absolute pathname of your home directory. The C shell initializes it from the value passed by the login program. The C shell uses it when you type **cd** with no arguments and when you use ~ in a command.

shell

By default, the C shell initializes **shell** to **/bin/csh** (its own name). The shell executes this file when you run a script or issue a command that creates a subshell. Normally you will not change **shell.**

mail

mail is another wordlist variable. It can be a single word (containing the name of your mail file) or a wordlist (containing multiple mail filenames). For example, the following statement in your **.cshrc** file defines **/usr/spool/mail/sara** as your mailbox:

```
set mail = (/usr/spool/mail/sara)
```

The C shell checks this file regularly to inform you when you have mail. The default interval is system-dependent but is typically 10 minutes. If you receive mail while you are logged on, the C shell displays

```
You have new mail.
```

You'll receive this message only after a command has completed. The shell does not barge in to **vi** to tell you to read your mailbox.

Furthermore, you can make the C shell check your mailbox more often. Putting a number (in units of seconds) as the first word in the mail variable changes the default time interval. For example, the following statement changes the interval to 60 seconds for Sara's mail file:

```
set mail = (60 /usr/spool/mail/sara)
```

The smaller the number, the sooner you will be notified when new mail arrives, but the more drain you will place on your system.

You may also specify multiple mail files. For example, the statement

```
set mail = (60 /usr/spool/mail/sara /usr/spool/uucp/mail/sara)
```

checks a mailbox on the network as well as your system mailbox. In this case, the C shell displays

```
New mail in /usr/spool/uucp/mail/sara
```

when you receive mail over the network.

Suppose you stay logged in for days at a time (a possibility for privileged users who have a dedicated UNIX line to their offices). You may find it useful to include the message-of-the-day file, **/etc/motd,** in your mail variable. That way you're informed of changes in the system message file. It is also useful to include **/usr/msgs.**

history

The **history** variable is the number of commands you want the C shell to save in the history list. The default value is **unset,** which makes the C shell remember only the last command. The statement

```
set history = 10
```

saves the last 10 commands in the history list.

histchars

Set variable **histchars** to the two characters you want to use to issue history commands. If **histchars** is unset, these characters are !^ . This means you use ! to issue most history commands and ^ for the special history correction command. You can define **histchars** in the **.cshrc** file as follows:

```
set histchars = "#:"
```

Now you would use # to issue history commands and **:** to make the history correction. For example,

```
% #3
```

repeats command 3, and

```
% #cat
```

repeats the most recent command beginning with **cat.**

savehist

Use this variable to preserve your history list between login sessions. The default value is **unset.** Set **savehist** to the number of commands you want the C shell to save for the next login session. For example, the statement

```
set savehist = 5
```

saves the last five commands you typed before logging out. The C shell saves them in a file called **.history** in your home directory.

When you login, the C shell will place these commands in the active history list without executing them. If you use this mechanism, you might want to put the command **history** in your **.login** file. The shell will then display the active history list at the beginning of each session.

Not all versions of the C shell have **savehist.**

prompt

By default, **prompt** is '**% '** (note the space). You can, as we have seen, include the history character **!** to display the event number. The statement

```
set prompt = '\!% '
```

sets the prompt to the event number followed by **%.** Other common choices include a different character, as in

```
set prompt = '> '
```

or a display of the current directory, as in the alias

```
alias cd 'cd \!*; set prompt = "<$cwd> "'
```

ignoreeof

As noted earlier, the variable **ignoreeof** protects you from logging yourself out accidentally by typing **control-D.** By default, **ignoreeof** is **unset.** When set, you must use **logout** to logout of the system. If unset, you may also use **control-D.**

noclobber

The **noclobber** variable keeps you from overwriting existing files with output redirection. It also prevents file creation during output append operations (using >>). You must use ! with > or >> to override this protection temporarily. Since the default value is **unset,** use the statement

```
set noclobber
```

to put this protection in effect.

time

If **time** is set (the default is **unset**), any command that takes more than the specified number of seconds in CPU time displays resource utilization statistics. For example,

```
set time = 3
```

displays timing statistics when any command takes more than three seconds of CPU time. (CPU time is user time plus system time.) Suppose we give the command

```
% spell proposal.85 > spellfile
1.8u 1.5s 0:27 11%
```

The second line indicates that **spell** took 1.8 seconds of user time, 1.5 seconds of system time, and 27 seconds of real time, with a ratio of 11 percent user plus system time to real time. The shell displays the resource statistic since this command took longer than three seconds of CPU time (it took 3.3 seconds). On UNIX systems that charge for CPU time, this can help you to monitor the execution times of commands. A word of caution: UNIX's time measurements are not very reliable or reproducible.

Special Files Revisited

Let's add some of the features we've learned to our **.cshrc** and **.login** files. Here's the next version of **.cshrc:**

```
% num ~/.cshrc
1   # .cshrc file - Version 2
2
3   # Set up shell variables
4   set path = ( ~/bin /bin /usr/bin /usr/local .)
```

```
 5    set cdpath = (~/proj1 ~/proj2)
 6    set mail = (30 /usr/spool/mail/sara)
 7    set history = 10                # set up history list
 8    set savehist = 5                # save for next login
 9    set prompt = '\!% '             # put event number in prompt
10    set time = 3                    # enable command timing (3 secs)
11    set ignoreeof                   # logout protection
12    set noclobber                   # redirection protection
13
14    # Setup aliases
15    alias al alias                  # short for alias
16    al bye logout                   # signoff
17    al dir \
18    'set d = `ls -1F \!* | grep /`; if ($#d) echo "$d:gh"; unset d'
19    al gt 'set d1 = `/bin/pwd`;cd \!^'    # go to a new directory
20    al gb 'set d2 = `/bin/pwd`;cd $d1;set d1=$d2;/bin/pwd'
21    al h history                    # short for history
22    al ldir 'ls -l \!* | grep "^d" '   # long list directories
23    al nusers \
24    '(set a = `who|wc -l` ;echo "There are $a users logged on.")'
```

Line 4 makes the search path include **/usr/local** and our own tools directory (~/**bin**).
Line 5 lets us change to subdirectories in ~/**proj1** and ~/**proj2** from anywhere in the
file system. Line 6 names our mailbox file and tells the C shell to check for mail at 30-
second intervals (we're very anxious!). Line 8 tells the C shell to save our last five
commands when we logout, and line 10 provides timing statistics for commands requiring
more than three seconds of CPU time.

Note that we did not change the **home** or **shell** variables. We also added **gt** and
gb (from Section 6.2) to our alias list.

Here's the next version of **.login:**

```
      % num ~/.login
 1    # .login - Version 2
 2
 3    # Greetings and Salutations
 4    echo Hello, sara !
 5    echo Welcome to UNIX
 6    echo -n "Today is "; date
 7    echo -n "Last logout: "; cat ~/.lastlog
 8
 9    stty intr ^C                    # interrupt now cntrl-C
10    nusers
```

The only change is that we added the **stty** command in line 9. This changes our interrupt
key to **control-C.**

Displaying Your Shell Variables: Using set

The **set** command with no arguments displays the shell variables and their current values. Here is the list for our current setup files.

```
% set
argv        ()
cdpath      (/u/sara/proj1 /u/sara/proj2)
history     10
home        /u/sara
ignoreeof
mail        (30 /usr/spool/mail/sara)
noclobber
path        ( /u/sara/bin /bin /usr/bin /usr/local .)
prompt      !%
savehist    5
shell       /bin/csh
status      0
time        3
```

The **argv** and **status** variables are not used to customize the C shell.

9.3 CUSTOMIZATION WITH ENVIRONMENT VARIABLES

Special information, like your login directory, the location of your mailbox, and your terminal type, are all part of your user environment. A set of special variables, called *environment variables,* maintains this data. UNIX can pass (*export*) these to programs executed from the shell. Unlike C shell variables that are accessible only within the shell, environment variables are available to both your current shell and subsequent programs (such as scripts, editors, and mail programs).

When you execute a program (such as the editor or **mail**), UNIX gives it the values of all environment variables. The **vi** editor, for example, uses **TERM** to determine what type of terminal you're using. While you're in **vi,** you may want to "escape" temporarily by creating a new shell. **vi** obtains the correct program name from **SHELL.**

Although environment variables are not built into the C shell, you can define them (or change their values) from it. The notation

```
setenv VARNAME string
```

defines **VARNAME** to be an environment variable and initializes it to **string.** By convention, the variable name is in uppercase. The C shell maintains certain environment variables, and you may also create your own. Let's examine the predefined ones first.

TERM

The **vi** editor and the **more** command use your terminal's cursor-positioning commands. The **TERM** variable makes these terminal-independent. **TERM** is set to a code that defines your terminal type. The login program sets it from information in the file /**etc**/ **ttytype** (see Appendix F for its format). This file maps terminal types to ports on your UNIX system. When ports are hard-wired to certain terminals, the login program can preset **TERM** for you.

However, some ports may be dial-up or network lines. In this case you must tell the C shell what type of terminal you are using. The command

```
setenv TERM vt100
```

for example, sets **TERM** to **vt100.**

Some UNIX systems provide the **tset** (terminal setup) command. This lets you use different ports and terminals to access the same UNIX system.

For example, if we always sign on to a UNIX system using an ADM3A on line **tty01,** we can simply let the login program initialize **TERM** from /**etc/ttytype.** However, suppose we use either a VT100 with dial-up access or the console port (a HeathKit-19). Now we need to call **tset** as follows:

```
tset - -m 'dialup:vt100'
```

This says to map (**-m**) a dial-up port to **vt100;** otherwise, use the default mapping in /**etc/ttytype.** The **-** option says to send the terminal name to the standard output. This allows us to use **tset** with command substitution and assign the terminal type to **TERM,** as in

```
setenv TERM `tset - -m 'dialup:vt100'`
```

Now **TERM** is set correctly in both cases.

HOME

The **HOME** variable contains the absolute pathname of your home directory. The login program initializes this from the home directory field in the UNIX password file (/**etc**/ **passwd**). Your working directory is initially **$HOME** when you login.

The predefined C shell variable **home** takes its value from the **HOME** environment variable.

PATH

The environment variable **PATH** contains the same information as the C shell **path** variable, but in a different format. By default, the login program sets **PATH** to

```
:/bin:/usr/bin
```

The C shell maintains both **path** and **PATH** variables. When you change **path,** the C shell updates **PATH** automatically. This permits the information stored in **path** (and **PATH**) to be exported to other programs.

PATH's notation is different from **path**'s to maintain compatibility with other shells. Note that **PATH** is not a wordlist; it is a string of directories (full pathnames separated by colons). An empty field (the colon at the far left) denotes your current directory.

Suppose we change **path** to include the following directories:

```
set path = (~/bin /bin /usr/bin /usr/local   .)
```

The C shell updates **PATH** accordingly. The command

```
% echo $PATH
/u/sara/bin:/bin:/usr/bin:/usr/local:
```

reflects the change.

LOGNAME or USER

Both of these environment variables hold the user's login name. Some versions of the C shell use **LOGNAME,** others use **USER.** The login program initializes **USER** (or **LOGNAME**) from the UNIX password file (**/etc/passwd**). It comes in handy to personalize commands and shell scripts.

SHELL

The environment variable **SHELL** contains the absolute pathname of your shell. By default, this variable is undefined, and other programs will assume your default shell is **/bin/sh,** the Bourne shell. Therefore, you should initialize **SHELL** to the C shell variable **shell** (which is **/bin/csh,** the C shell, by default). Some UNIX programs (such as **vi, ex,** and **mail**) allow the user to "escape" temporarily by executing a subshell. These utilities use the environment variable **SHELL** (if it's defined) to call the correct program.

MAIL

The **MAIL** variable contains the pathname of your mail file. This is the value used by the **mail** command; the C shell uses the **mail** variable to see if you have any new mail. For example, the command

```
setenv MAIL /usr/spool/mail/sara
```

specifies Sara's mailbox for her **mail** command. The conventional value for **$MAIL** is **/usr/spool/mail/$USER.**

EXINIT

This is an important environment variable if you use the **ex** or **vi** editors. Both check **EXINIT** and initialize from options specified in it. There are over 40 options you can set automatically using the notation

```
setenv EXINIT 'options'
```

We enclose **options** in single quotation marks to make it a single word and to quote special characters.

Suppose you want to set the editor options **autoindent, shiftwidth = 4,** and **showmatch.** This makes **vi** automatically indent each typed line, indent nested control structures, and match parentheses and braces. To do this, define **EXINIT** as

```
setenv EXINIT 'set ai sw=4 sm'
```

When you then execute **vi** (or **ex**), it presets these options.

TERMCAP

Once your **TERM** variable is set to your terminal code, **vi** and other utilities (such as **more**) will work properly. This is because these programs access a database to read the cursor-positioning codes for your terminal. The environment variable **TERMCAP** holds the name of this database. Its default value is **/etc/termcap.**

If you need to install a terminal which has no **TERM** code in the **/etc/termcap** database, you must write your own. Since other users need **/etc/termcap,** you shouldn't debug new code in it. The **TERMCAP** variable lets you work in your own local database. For example,

```
setenv TERMCAP ~/new.termcap
```

makes **vi** read the cursor codes from file **new.termcap** in your home directory. You can change this file and test it until your terminal works correctly. You can then add the new entry to the **/etc/termcap** database.

Special Files Revisited

Since UNIX automatically exports environment variables to programs, you need not put them in your **.cshrc** file. Initialize them in your **.login** file instead. Logging in will then preset them to the values you want. Here's a version of **.login** that includes predefined environment variables, plus one we define ourselves, **TTYLINE.**

```
        % num ~/.login
  1     # .login - Version 3
  2
  3     # Greetings and Salutations
  4     echo Hello, $USER !
  5     echo Welcome to UNIX
  6     echo -n "Today is "; date
  7     echo -n "Last logout: "; cat ~/.lastlog
  8
  9     # Environment Variables
 10     setenv SHELL /bin/csh                   # C shell
 11     setenv MAIL /usr/spool/mail/$USER    # mailbox
 12     setenv EXINIT 'set ai sm wm=10 sw=4 aw'
 13     setenv TTYLINE `tty`                    # save port number
 14
 15     setenv TERM `tset - -m 'dialup:tvi920'`
 16
 17     stty intr ^C                            # interrupt now cntrl-C
 18     nusers
```

Lines 4 through 7 contain the greeting, as before. Note the change in line 4; we refer to the user as **$USER** (a nice, personalized touch—the UNIX equivalent of "occupant"). Line 10 defines our **SHELL** as **/bin/csh** (C shell), and line 11 initializes **MAIL** using **$USER.** Line 12 defines the following default options for **vi: autoindent (ai), show matching** parentheses and braces (**sm**), **wrap margin** for 10 characters (**wm = 10**), **shiftwidth** for four spaces (**sw = 4**), and **auto-writes** from buffer to disk (**aw**).

Line 13 defines our own environment variable, **TTYLINE.** It gets its value from the **tty** command using command substitution. For example, if we logged in on the system console,

```
    setenv TTYLINE `tty`
```

sets **TTYLINE** to **/dev/console.** We declare this variable for use in driver programs that check the terminal device line. In these programs, we reference it as **$TTYLINE.**

Line 15 sets our environment variable **TERM.** Ordinarily, we login on a dedicated port with a VT100 terminal. In this case the **tset** program will use the default mapping in **/etc/ttytype.** However, we also have a modem connected to **/dev/tty01** on our UNIX system. When we login on the dial-up line, **tset** will use the code **tvi920,** which we then assign to **TERM.**

If your UNIX system does not include the **tset** program, you can set **TERM** from the value returned by the command **tty.** For example, since the login program sets **TERM** from the default mappings in **/etc/ttytype,** you only have to worry about non-hard-wired ports. In this example, you would check whether the value returned by **tty** was **/dev/ tty01** and set **TERM** to **tvi920.** The following statement does this:

```
    if ($TTYLINE == /dev/tty01) setenv TERM tvi920
```

Note that we do not set **PATH** or **HOME.** Since we set **path** in **.cshrc,** it's unnecessary to set **PATH.** Its value is set to **path. HOME** is preset to our home directory by default, and we have no reason to change it.

Displaying Your Environment Variables: Using env

Use the **env** command (**printenv** in some versions) to display the values of your environment variables. Here's the list for our current setup files.

```
% env
HOME=/u/sara
PATH=/u/sara/bin:/bin:/usr/bin:/usr/local:
TERM=vt100
TZ=PST8PDT
USER=sara
SHELL=/bin/csh
MAIL=/usr/spool/mail/sara
EXINIT=set ai sm wm=10 sw=4 aw
TTYLINE=/dev/console
```

9.4 CUSTOMIZATION WITH BUILT-IN COMMANDS

We've seen how to customize the C shell using predefined shell variables and environment variables. You may use the C shell's built-in commands as well. You've seen the value of some of these already, such as **alias** and **set.** We include both in our **.cshrc** file.

Another built-in command, **setenv,** defines or modifies environment variables. We include this in our **.login** file. Let's look at a few other built-in commands that might help customize our C shell environment. We'll examine their functions, purposes, and uses.

umask

Suppose we login and create a directory called **astro** (a project code name). We create several files in this new directory, one of which we'll call **tblk.c.** Let's look at the permission bits for directory **astro** and file **tblk.c:**

```
% ls -ld astro
drwxr-xr-x  2 sara    system    32 Jan 12 20:02 astro
% ls -l tblk.c
-rw-r--r--  1 sara    system   464 Jan 12 20:02 tblk.c
```

All users can access the **astro** directory, but only **sara** (the owner) can create or remove files. Likewise, all users can read **tblk.c,** but only **sara** can modify it. You may wonder who set these permission bits, and, more important, how do we determine their initial settings?

Our **astro** project is sensitive to security issues (we don't want our competitors to know how badly things are going). We therefore want to define permission bits in our C shell environment as follows: We want directories to be accessible only to the owner (**sara**) and group (**system**). We also want only the owner and group to be able to read the files. Furthermore, only the owner should be able to modify (write to) files. How can we do this?

The **umask** (user mask) command allows you to specify permission settings for new files or directories. **umask** uses the same access codes as **chmod;** the format is

```
umask [nnn]
```

nnn is an octal code obtained by summing access codes for each access group. Read access is 4, write access is 2, execute or search access is 1. Therefore, a permission code of 6 allows read and write access (**rw-**). A permission code of 5 allows read and search access (**r-x**). We specify a file's mode with three numbers: the user's access code, the group's access code, and everyone else's.

By default, files use mode 666 (**rw-rw-rw**). which gives everyone read and write access. Directories take the mode 777 (**rwxrwxrwx**). This gives all users read, write, and search permission.

To change these settings, use **umask** to *disable* the unwanted access. UNIX uses the complement of the umask **and**ed with the file and directory modes. Therefore, if your **umask** is 000, its complement is 777. Thus files remain mode 666 and directories 777. Table 9-1 contains the permission settings for each **umask** value for files and directories. Suppose you want to keep others from writing in your files and directories. You need to turn off the write bit (2). The command

```
umask 002
```

does the job. The three digits apply to the owner, group, and others, respectively. The owner and group accesses are unchanged (0), but write permission (2) is removed for

TABLE 9-1 umask VALUES AND PERMISSION SETTINGS

umask	File Permission	Directory Permission
0	**rw-**	**rwx**
1	**rw-**	**rw-**
2	**r--**	**r-x**
3	**r--**	**r--**
4	**-w-**	**-wx**
5	**-w-**	**-w-**
6	**---**	**--x**
7	**---**	**---**

the others. You may omit leading zeros. Since **umask** applies both to directories and files, the mode for newly created files is now 664 (**rw-rw-r--**), and the mode for directories is 775 (**rwxrwxr-x**).

Let's change **umask** for the **astro** project group. Recall that we want directories to be accessible (readable) only by the owner and system group and files to be readable by owner and group as well. We must specify a **umask** value of 0 (leave alone) for owner, 2 (remove write access) for group, and 6 (remove read and write access) for others. In our **.cshrc** file we put the statement

```
umask 26
```

Now new directories and files will have the correct settings. Suppose we create a directory called **mercury** and a file **memo.** The commands

```
% ls -ld mercury
drwxr-x--x  2 sara    system    32 Jan 12 20:02 mercury
% ls -l memo
-rw-r-----  1 sara    system   464 Jan 12 20:02 memo
```

show the proper permission bits for directory **mercury** and file **memo.**

umask with no arguments reports the current setting. For example, the command

```
% umask
26
```

shows us that our setting is as advertised.

We can be even more restrictive. We may, for example, turn off all access permission for others and allow read and search access only to users in our group. The **umask** argument for this setting is

```
umask 027
```

which creates directories with mode 750 and files with mode 640.

Even better, you may forbid access by anyone. The **umask** argument is

```
umask 777
```

Now this produces a truly secure system. Even you can't read or write in it. While it may be a bit difficult to use, it surely eliminates worries about leaks or snooping.

Remember, all **umask** arguments apply to the default of 777 for directories and 666 for files.

exit

We have already used the **exit** command extensively in our scripts. We can also use **exit** to help maintain our environment. It terminates shells just as it terminates scripts. Let's look at an example.

Suppose we want to change some predefined shell variables temporarily or even create new ones. We need to debug new commands in a directory in our search path. We also want to set a time limit on our commands. These tasks require changing both the **path** and **time** shell variables.

If we change them in our current shell, we'll have to restore them when we're done. As a last resort, we could logout. A simpler solution is to create a new C shell by executing the **csh** command. Our original shell doesn't go away, it just goes to "sleep" until we finish our chores. The advantage is that we can modify the new shell's variables and simply **exit** (return to our login shell) when we're through. The login shell's variables remain unchanged.

Suppose our current (login) shell has **path** set as follows and **time** unset:

```
16% echo $path
/u/sara/bin /bin /usr/bin /usr/local  .
```

Let's create a new shell:

```
17% csh
1%
```

The new shell executes ~/.**cshrc** before displaying the prompt. We are now at event number 1 because the history list starts over. (This number won't be 1 if you have a ~/.**history** file.) **$path** and **$time** have the same values as in the login shell. Suppose we set them as follows:

```
1% set path = (~/test $path)
2% set time = 3
3% echo $path
/u/sara/test /u/sara/bin /bin /usr/bin /usr/local  .
4% echo $time
3
```

We now do our test work. When we're finished, we use the **exit** command to return to our original shell, as follows:

```
59% exit
60% 18%
```

Note that the prompt has returned to the next event number for the login shell. We can verify that **path** and **time** are unchanged by issuing the commands

```
18% echo $path
/u/sara/bin /bin /usr/bin /usr/local  .
19% echo $time
time: Undefined variable.
```

source

The **source** command is a valuable tool for working in your current shell environment. Its format is

```
source name
```

where **name** is a C shell script. When you execute this command, your C shell reads and executes the commands in **name.** The difference from normal execution is that no subshell is created. You can therefore use **source** to modify your current environment.

The most common application is updating special files (**.cshrc** and **.login.**) If you add a new alias to **.cshrc,** for example, the command

```
% source ~/.cshrc
```

executes all commands in **.cshrc** in your current environment. This adds the new alias to your repertoire. You can test new versions of **.login** in the same way.

You can also use **source** within aliases in order to call scripts in the current shell. For example, in our implementation of **pushd** and **popd** detailed in Section 11.10, the aliases use **source** to call the scripts.

exec

You can also use the **exec** command to modify your current environment. This format is

```
exec command
```

Using **exec** makes UNIX replace your current shell with a process that runs **command.** Your current shell doesn't wait for **command** to finish to display its prompt; it just disappears. When **command** finishes, UNIX logs you out. So don't run **exec** from your login shell! Watch what happens when you use **exec** with the **date** command:

```
% exec date
Sun Jan 13 11:39:46 PST 1985
login:
```

Not very friendly, is it? Since you replaced your login shell with the **date** command (the program **/bin/date**), UNIX logged you out.

The real value of **exec** is in your **.login** file. Instead of logging in to a C shell, you can substitute your own program. If you include an **exec** statement as the last statement of your **.login** file, you'll replace the C shell. For example,

```
% cat .login
 .  .  .  .
exec ~/.menu
```

runs a menu program from your home directory. This can be a C program or a script. When you **exit** from **menu,** you will logout. Section 11.7 provides an example using this technique.

limit

Some UNIX systems charge for resources. If your C shell has the **limit** command, you can specify resource limits for your processes. The most common resource to limit is **cputime.** This prevents "runaway" processes from using all your account funds and perhaps saddling you with a bill that exceeds the national debt.

The forms of the limit command are

```
limit [resource] [maxvalue]
unlimit [resource]
```

resource is a predefined resource name recognized by the C shell, and **maxvalue** is its maximum allowed value. The **limit** command with no arguments displays limited resources and their limit values. **unlimit** removes limits, either on a particular resource (if specified) or completely (no arguments). We discuss the **cputime** resource only. Refer to your C shell manual for information on other resources.

To limit a process to 600 seconds of CPU time, for example, use the command

```
limit cputime 600
```

You may abbreviate **cputime** as **cpu.** With this limit in effect, the C shell terminates any process it creates that exceeds the limit. For example, it would terminate an **nroff** command that ran too long as follows:

```
% nroff -ms *.doc | lpr
Execution time exceeded.
```

Most processes won't exceed the limit. However, an editing session or lengthy formatting task could easily overrun it. To bypass the limit, remove it with the **unlimit** command, as in

```
% unlimit cpu; vi doc/intro
```

This removes any CPU limitations until you issue another **limit** command. Another solution is to create an alias for each command that might overrun your allocation. The alias can remove the limitation, call the command, and restore the limit. For example, you could use the following alias for **vi:**

```
alias vi 'unlimit cpu; /bin/vi \!*; limit cpu 600'
```

The call of **vi** uses the absolute path to avoid an alias loop.

We can define a similar alias for **nroff,** but we must allow for a pipe construction.

The following alias (you can put this in **.cshrc** as well) uses parentheses to place the command in a subshell, making it unnecessary to restore the CPU limit:

```
alias nroff '(unlimit cpu; /usr/bin/nroff \!*)'
```

Let's look at how this alias works. When we issue the command

```
% nroff -ms *.doc | lpr
```

The C shell expands it to

```
( unlimit cpu; /usr/bin/nroff -ms *.doc ) | lpr
```

You may want to make your default CPU limit an environment variable. If so, set the initial limit and define an environment variable (call it **CPU**) in your **.login** file. For example, the commands

```
setenv CPU 600
limit cpu $CPU
```

set the **CPU** environment variable, then use **limit** to set the maximum CPU limit. The limit is defined when you login.

Now our aliases can change the limit and restore it by referring to the value **$CPU**. For example, we can modify the alias for **vi** as follows:

```
alias vi 'unlimit cpu; /bin/vi \!*; limit cpu $CPU'
```

9.5 MAKING IT PERSONAL: CREATING YOUR OWN SPECIAL FILES

We are now ready to discuss the mechanics of creating or modifying your own special files. We will also show you how to create alternative **.cshrc** files.

A new UNIX user must determine what initialization tasks the system performs automatically. First, make sure your standard interface is the C shell. Your prompt will probably contain a **%.** To verify this, look at your entry in the password file using the command

```
% grep "^$USER" /etc/passwd
sara:9vlKMPVf8MBYc:202:50:ext 405:/u/sara:/bin/csh
```

You may need **$LOGNAME** instead of **$USER.** Is the last field **/bin/csh**? If yes, you are running the C shell. If not, you need to execute the program **chsh** (change default shell). If this command is unavailable, have your system administrator change the last field in **/etc/passwd.**

Now determine if a **.cshrc, .login,** or **.logout** file already exists in your home directory. The command (issued from the home directory)

```
% ls -la
```

will show these filenames if they exist. If you plan to modify them, make copies first in case your changes don't work. For example,

```
% cp .cshrc csh.save
% cp .login login.save
% cp .logout logout.save
```

will archive all three special files. Once you have a stable revision, you can remove the backup copies.

Using source to Change the Special Files

After you change the special files, you must test them. Suppose you modify ~/**.cshrc.** The command

```
% source ~/.cshrc
```

makes the C shell execute ~/**.cshrc** directly (it does not create a new C shell). This means that any new variables or aliases you create will exist in your current (login) shell.
If you modify ~/**.login,** you can test it similarly. The command

```
% source ~/.login
```

executes the statements in your ~/**.login** file directly. If you use newly defined aliases in ~/**.login,** be sure to **source** ~/**.cshrc** first and then ~/**.login.** Otherwise, **.login** will not know about these newly defined aliases.
Testing a new **.logout** file is just as simple. The command

```
% source ~/.logout
```

executes the statements in your ~/**.logout** file.

When One .cshrc File Isn't Enough: A New Environment

We can use the **csh** command to create a new environment with an alternative **.cshrc** file. We control which special file the shell executes by simply renaming the desired one **.cshrc.** Before exiting from the new shell, we restore the original filenames. We do all this work in a script when we want to change environments.
Suppose you are working on several projects and need separate environments for each of them. You want to login under one configuration, then change to a new environment when necessary. Here's how to provide this capability.

Let's define a special environment for project **projm.** We create a special file with the predefined variables, environment variables, and commands needed for **projm** and copy it to our home directory. We call this file ~/.**cshrcprojm.** We then include the following script (**projm**) in our private **bin** directory:

```
     % num projm
 1   # .csh to create new working environment
 2   # for project m
 3   # Note: this file, called projm, must
 4   #  have a corresponding special file, called
 5   #          ~/.cshrcprojm
 6   # Usage: projm
 7
 8   set w = `who | grep $USER`
 9   if ($#w > 5) then
10       echo2 "Already logged on...can't change environments"
11       exit 1
12   endif
13
14   mv ~/.cshrc ~/.cshrcsav           # save current environment
15   mv ~/.cshrcprojm ~/.cshrc         # rename project m environment
16   csh                               # create a new C shell
17   mv ~/.cshrc ~/.cshrcprojm         # restore project m file
18   mv ~/.cshrcsav ~/.cshrc           # restore original .cshrc
```

Lines 3 through 6 establish the ground rules for running this script. Note that script **projm** expects a special file (**.cshrcprojm**) in our home directory.

This script prevents us from logging in to UNIX more than once and running **projm.** Line 8 stores the output of **who** and **grep** in variable **w.** Lines 9 through 12 determine if we're logged in more than once by examining the number of words in **w** and exiting if we are.

Line 14 saves our original **.cshrc** file. Line 15 renames the project special file **.cshrc.** When line 16 executes the **csh** command, the shell reads the newly named file. We stay in this new shell until we type **exit.** At this point, the **csh** "program" terminates, and the shell passes control to line 17. Here we save the **project m .cshrc** file and restore the original.

Using this method, we need not worry about restoring the original environment. All we must do is rename the special files. The environment changes occurred in the new shell created by the **csh** command.

Special Files Revisited: A Last Time

Here are the final versions of our special files. You can use them as templates for your own set. We'll start with the ~/.**logout** file.

.logout. Our **.logout** file has new features. It now checks the date and, if it's Friday, runs a background script that gathers statistics about disk usage and files. Let's look at **.logout,** then examine the background script.

```
   % num .logout
1  # .logout - Version 2
2  nohup                              # run after logout
3  set d = `date`
4  if ($d[1] == "Fri") then           # is it Friday?
5      ~/.fstat&                      # run file status
6  endif
7
8  echo -n "Logging out at: "
9  date | tee ~/.lastlog
10 banner UNIX
```

nohup (line 2) allows background jobs to continue to run after logout. Line 3 runs **date** and assigns its output to variable **d.** If it's Friday, we execute script ~/**.fstat** in the background (line 5). Lines 8 and 9 display and save our logout time as before, and we sign off using the **banner** command. This displays a familiar logo on our terminal screen.
Here's the ~/**.fstat** script.

```
   % num ~/.fstat
1  # csh script to report current file status
2  · # This script is run from our ~/.logout file
3
4
5  mail $USER << EOF
6
7  NOTE: Current file status summary. Please
8        delete any unwanted core or zero-length
9        files.
10 ==================================
11 Current disk storage (blocks home_dir):
12 `du -s ~`
13 ==================================
14 Core File pathnames:
15 `find ~ -name core -print`
16 ==================================
17 Zero-Length File Pathnames:
18 `find ~ -size 0 -print`
19 EOF
```

This script is like the **usfst** script in Chapter 8. It's just a here document using the **mail** command.
   .login. Since our **.logout** file now sends us mail, we modify our **.login** file to read

it. We check to see if the date is Monday; if so, we read the mail. There's sure to be some, namely the disk usage statistics from last Friday. What an exciting way to start a new week! Here's the script:

```
       % num .login
   1   # .login - Version 4
   2
   3   # Greetings and Salutations
   4   echo Hello, $USER !
   5   echo Welcome to UNIX
   6   echo -n "Today is "; date
   7   echo -n "Last logout: "; cat ~/.lastlog
   8
   9   # Environment Variables
  10   setenv SHELL /bin/csh                    # C shell
  11   setenv MAIL /usr/spool/mail/$USER        # mailbox
  12   setenv EXINIT 'set ai sm wm=10 sw=4 aw'
  13   setenv TTYLINE `tty`                     # save port number
  14
  15   setenv TERM `tset - -m 'dialup:tvi920'`
  16
  17   stty intr ^C                             # interrupt now cntrl-c
  18   nusers
  19   set d = `date`
  20   if ($d[1] == "Mon") then                 # time to check mail
  21      if (-e $mail[2]) mail                 # mail?-read it!
  22   endif
```

Lines 20 through 22 do the job. If the date is Monday and there is mail, **.login** calls the **mail** command. Note that we assume that the **mail** variable contains a time option. If you use a single filename, change line 21 to

```
if (-e $mail) mail     # mail? read it!
```

   .cshrc. This version of **.cshrc** introduces only a few minor changes. We've added aliases to give it a more personal flavor.

```
       % num .cshrc
   1   # .cshrc file - Version 3
   2
   3   umask 027                    # no writes to group; nothing to others
   4
   5   # Setup shell variables
   6   set path = ( ~/bin /bin /usr/bin /usr/local .)
   7   set cdpath = (~/proj1 ~/proj2)
```

```
 8    set mail = (30 /usr/spool/mail/sara)
 9    set history = 10                 # set up history list
10    set savehist = 5                 # save for next login
11    set prompt = '\!% '              # put event number in prompt
12    set time = 3                     # enable command timing (3 secs)
13    set ignoreeof                    # logout protection
14    set noclobber                    # redirection protection
15
16    # Setup aliases
17    alias al alias          # short for alias
18    al bye logout           # signoff
19    al dir\
20    'set d = `ls -1F \!* | grep /`; if ($#d) echo "$d:gh"; unset d'
21    al gt 'set d1 = `/bin/pwd`;cd \!^'   # go to a new directory
22    al gb 'set d2 = `/bin/pwd`;cd $d1;set d1=$d2;/bin/pwd'
23    al h history            # short for history
24    al ldir 'ls -l \!* | grep "^d" '       # long list directories
25    al nusers \
26    '(set a = `who|wc -l`;echo "There are $a users logged on.")'
27
28    al cx 'chmod +x'         # make it executable
29    al dbug 'csh -fvx'       # for debugging shell scripts
30    al proof 'nroff -ms \!* | more' # page nroff document
```

This version uses **umask** to change the default permission settings for new files and directories. Line 3 makes the default permissions 750 for directories and 640 for files. Lines 28 through 30 define three new aliases: **cx** to create executable files, **dbug** to debug C shell scripts easily, and **proof** to format and proofread a document by paging it on the screen.

9.6 PUTTING IT ALL TOGETHER

Some versions of the C shell include a built-in shell variable called **cwd** (current working directory). We could use **pwd** to obtain this information, but it is slower because it is not built in. You can even use **cwd** to create a faster **pwd** command with the following alias:

```
alias pwd 'echo $cwd'
```

Since **echo** is built in, this command runs in the current shell.

If your C shell lacks **cwd,** you can create it. The result is not quite as nice as having **cwd** maintained inside the C shell, but it is still useful.

The first thing you must do is store your current working directory in the **cwd** variable. The following alias definition does this:

```
alias cd 'cd \!*;set cwd = `/bin/pwd`'
```

When you change directories, you follow **cd** with the **pwd** command. Using command substitution, you store the directory name in **cwd.** In the alias argument, you use the notation \!* to implement **cd** by itself (change to your home directory) and the full pathname **/bin/pwd** to eliminate a pathname search. This gives both generality and execution speed.

Some issues are still unresolved. What is **cwd**'s value when we login? Can we use it in a shell script? With what we have done so far, the answer is no. We must revise our shell environment to handle these situations.

Let us consider our **.cshrc** file. Recall that the C shell reads it first when we login and every time we run a shell script (unless we use **csh -f**). If we initialize **cwd** here, it will have a value at login and when we run a subshell. Here's our first solution:

```
% cat .cshrc
. . . .
set cwd = `/bin/pwd`    # run the UNIX command
. . . .
alias cd 'cd \!*;set cwd = `/bin/pwd`'
```

In addition to setting **cwd** when we change directories, we include it on a separate line in the **.cshrc** file. This initializes it when we login or run a shell script. Shell scripts can then access it.

Although this does the job, its overhead is high. You'll notice the longer startup time for scripts. This is because the C shell must execute **pwd** every time it reads the **.cshrc** file. In general, it's not a good idea to execute UNIX (non-built-in) commands in this file. Let's see if we can modify the **.cshrc** file to give the same results faster.

We want to include **cwd** in our environment. That way we can fetch it without running a command. We'll create an environment variable **CWD** to hold our current directory and store its value in our shell variable. Here's the next approach:

```
% cat .cshrc
. . . .
set cwd = $CWD              # get from environment
. . . .
alias cd 'cd \!*;set cwd = `/bin/pwd`;setenv CWD $cwd'
```

Instead of executing **pwd,** we get the current working directory from **CWD.** This is much faster. We also change our alias definition for **cd.** To make sure our environment variable **CWD** is always current, we use **setenv** to give it the value of **cwd.** When we change directories, we have the current directory name stored in both the environment variable **CWD** and our shell variable **cwd.**

We have only one other task. What is **CWD**'s default value, and where is it initialized? When we login, we should set **CWD** to our home directory. The setup command

```
setenv CWD ~
```

defines **CWD** and initializes it properly. But this doesn't solve the problem of where to initialize it. We can't, for instance, put it in our **.login** file, because the C shell reads **.cshrc** first. We need another way to set **CWD**.

Most UNIX systems with the C shell have a systemwide startup file that the shell reads before executing the **.cshrc** file. The system administrator uses this file to install systemwide defaults (e.g., a **umask** setting or an environment variable). The name of this file varies. Check your local documentation or browse through the **/etc** directory for a likely file. A common name is **/etc/cshrc** (see Appendix F).

Including the **setenv** command here means that environment variable **CWD** will be defined before the shell executes **.cshrc** and that the **cd** and **pwd** aliases will work correctly. And we will have met our original goal: to install a workable alternative when the predefined **cwd** variable does not exist.

9.7 HINTS AND CAUTIONS

■ When you change your **path** variable, be sure to maintain it as a wordlist. The command

```
set path = " ~/bin /bin /usr/bin /usr/local . "
```

sets the **path** variable to the desired pathnames, but you can no longer execute commands. For example,

```
$ who
who: Command not found.
```

shows that the C shell is now unable to locate the **who** command. The correct format is

```
set path = ( ~/bin /bin /usr/bin /usr/local .)
```

■ Suppose you want to add the **/etc** directory to your **path** shell variable. Its current value is

```
path          ( ~/bin /bin /usr/bin /usr/local .)
```

The notation

```
set path = (/etc $path)
```

helps avoid typing mistakes and does the job. The **path** variable is now

```
path          (/etc ~/bin /bin /usr/bin /usr/local . )
```

- You may want to read your mail automatically when you log in. The statements

```
if (-e $mail) then
    echo Opening your mail
    mail
endif
```

in your **.login** file call the **mail** program if you have mail.

Be careful with this construct if your **mail** variable is set for a time interval other than the default. Suppose **mail** is set as follows:

```
set mail = (60 /usr/spool/mail/sara)
```

The **if** statement will fail since **mail** is a wordlist and we have not referenced the file name correctly. In this case use the following statements:

```
if (-e $mail[2]) then
    echo Opening your mail
    mail
endif
```

- You cannot use the **:** modifiers with environment variables. Suppose we set an environment variable **TTYLINE** to our terminal device and then search the **/etc/ttytype** file to find the entry for our port. We assign the output of the **tty** command to **TTYLINE.** This produces the full pathname of our device, as follows:

```
% setenv TTYLINE `tty`
% echo $TTYLINE
/dev/tty32i
```

We may then try the following statements in our **.login** file:

```
setenv TTYLINE `tty`
set dialup = `grep "dialup $TTYLINE:t" /etc/ttytype`
if ($#dialup) setenv TERM vt100
```

The first statement defines **TTYLINE.** The second searches **/etc/ttytype** for our port to see if it's labeled "dialup". If so (that is, if variable **dialup** has at least one entry), we set our **TERM** variable to **vt100,** the terminal type we use on dial-up lines.

Unfortunately, this code does not work because **$TTYLINE:t** expands to the full
device name with **:t** appended to it. Instead, we must use a shell variable, as follows:

```
setenv TTYLINE `tty`
set ttyline = $TTYLINE
set dialup = `grep "dialup $ttyline:t" /etc/ttytype`
if ($#dialup) setenv TERM vt100
```

■ To change directories automatically at login time, simply include a **cd** command
in your **.login** file. For example,

```
% cat .login
 .  .  .  .
cd projm
```

starts out in the ~/**projm** directory when you login.

■ Your **TERM** code may be anywhere in the /etc/**termcap** database. Since **vi** and
ex search /etc/**termcap** sequentially, it will take them a long time to find your code if it
is at the very end. One way to solve this problem is to move your code. However, other
users may not appreciate the effects on their response times, so you may want to use the
environment variable **TERMCAP** instead. First, locate your **TERM** code:

```
% grep -n $TERM /etc/termcap
```

This will provide the starting line number in the database for your terminal code. Next
find the number of lines in the database:

```
% wc -l /etc/termcap
```

This will tell you how far "down" your **TERM** code is. Now simply create your own
local **termcap** file. Copy the /etc/**termcap** file to your home directory and edit it. Remove
all entries except your own (you may want several). Finally, change the **TERMCAP**
variable:

```
% setenv TERMCAP ~/termcap
```

Now **vi** only has to search the small local **termcap** file instead of the public one. Then
put the setup command in your **.login** file.

■ Be careful when executing scripts with the **source** command. Any shell variables that you define will remain in your current shell. The following script sets a variable **d** to a pathname:

```
% cat setup
# csh script
set d = ~/dictionary
. . . . .
```

Suppose you create a shell variable in your login shell with the same name and a different pathname. When you run the **setup** script, you'll change your local copy of **d:**

```
% set d = /usr/local/src
% source setup
% cp $d/* bkup
```

Since we use the **source** command to run **setup, d** changes, and **cp** therefore uses the wrong directory. Eliminating the **source** command solves the problem:

```
% set d = /usr/local/src
% setup
% cp $d/* bkup
```

The **setup** script now runs in a new shell, and its **d** variable does not affect the one in your login shell.

■ You may want to remove aliases or variable definitions from your ~/**.cshrc** file. When you test your new file with the command

```
% source ~/.cshrc
```

the old aliases and variables will still be in your shell environment. Unless you logout and login, you must delete them explicitly with the **unalias** command. For example,

```
% unalias ldir
```

removes alias **ldir,** and

```
% unset cproj
```

removes variable **cproj** (current project). Now when you **source** your new ~/**.cshrc** file, these items won't be included in your environment.

■ If you include **nohup** as the first command in your **.logout** file, any scripts that you execute will continue to run after you logout. With this arrangement you don't have to include **nohup** in the scripts themselves.

9.8 KEY POINT SUMMARY

Use the following guidelines to set up your **.cshrc, .login,** and **.logout** files:

- Use the **.cshrc** file to define C shell characteristics. These include primarily aliases and C shell variables (e.g., **history, noclobber, ignoreeof**). Placing these commands in **.cshrc** makes them always available to your script files and new shells.
- Place environment variable definitions in **.login.** UNIX makes these variables available to other programs, including a C shell that executes a script.
- Place commands that you want executed once at login in **.login.** Otherwise, the shell will execute these commands each time you execute a script file.
- Place commands that set up terminal characteristics in **.login.** The **stty** command tells UNIX (as opposed to the C shell) about your terminal settings. You need to do this only once. Use **tset** for port configurations.
- Avoid using commands in your **.cshrc** file that are not built in. Using other commands increases the startup time for shell scripts.

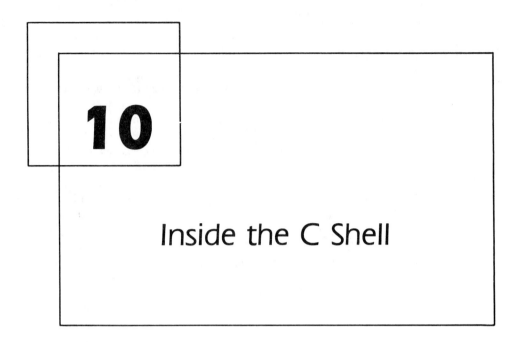

Inside the C Shell

This chapter delves inside the C shell and examines how it implements its features. Our goal is to give you the knowledge necessary to understand, debug, and use complex commands—and to satisfy any idle curiosity you may have. We will answer the following questions:

- How does the C shell implement redirection, pipes, and background execution?
- When are shell scripts, aliases, and shell variables available?
- How does the C shell treat built-in commands (such as **cd**), external programs (such as **who**), and aliases (such as **dir**)?

The answers to these questions are both interesting by themselves (well, to some people at least) and crucial to understanding the C shell's behavior. Eventually, some command you enter will produce a strange result or error message. Then you must try to determine why it failed. This chapter presents the tools you'll need for your sleuthing work.

Let's look at a few examples of problem commands. None gives an obvious error message.

1. Suppose we want to record in a file **dstat** the date, disk usage, and filenames for directory ~/**projw/code**. To avoid typing the directory name repeatedly, we save it in a shell variable. We type

```
% (date;set d = ~/projw/code;du -s $d; ls -l $d) > dstat
```

The command works as expected. But when we type

```
% ls -ld $d
d: Undefined variable.
```

the C shell complains that **d** is undefined. How can this be when the previous command defined it?

2. Suppose we define an alias **nu** to report the number of users currently logged in. We type

```
% alias nu 'echo `who | wc -l` users logged in'
```

Using command substitution, we pipe the output of **who** to **wc** and put the result in an **echo** command. A typical result is

```
% nu
5 users logged in
```

We now create a C shell script **ustat** that uses **nu**. Here are several lines from **ustat**:

```
% cat ustat
. . .
echo -n "Today is "; date
nu
. . .
```

Executing **ustat**, however, produces the following error:

```
% ustat
Today is Wed Feb 20 10:37:18 PST 1985
nu: Command not found.
```

What happened to **nu**?

3. Suppose we compile a C program **gets.c** in our **utils** directory. We redirect compilation errors to the file **compile_log**:

```
% (cd utils; cc -o gets gets.c) >>& compile_log
```

Now let's list the files in **utils**:

```
% ls utils
gets.c gets
```

Where did **compile_log** go?

We will answer these puzzling questions at the end of this chapter.

10.1 THE C SHELL'S JOB: PARSING ORDER

Chapters 3 through 6 described many C shell features: issuing commands, input/output redirection, and history, alias, command, variable, and filename substitution. Each has special symbols. For example, **$** means variable substitution, **!** and **^** history command substitutions, **>** and **<** redirection, **`** command substitution, **|** a pipe, and **&** a background job. Furthermore, single quotation marks, double quotation marks, and the backslash all indicate quoting.

Not surprisingly, the order in which the C shell deals with special characters affects its results. We call this the *parsing order*. This section describes how the C shell reads command lines and in what order it handles things.

Step 1: History Substitution

The C shell starts with history command substitution. That is, it interprets the special characters **!** and **^**.

Suppose we issue the following commands:

```
1% ls /usr/include
2% set ifiles = `!!`
set ifiles = `ls /usr/include`
```

After displaying the files from directory **/usr/include**, we decide to assign them to a variable **ifiles**. To do this we use the history redo command (**!!**) within command substitution marks. Since the C shell performs history substitution first, it expands **!!** before doing command substitution. In fact, it displays the command after substituting for **!!**.

Step 2: Finding Words

The C shell next divides the command line into words. What is a word? It is any character string delimited by a blank or a tab. Furthermore, the shell treats the special characters **&**, **|**, **;**, **>**, **<**, **(**, **)**, **&&**, **||**, **>>**, and **<<** as words (unless they are quoted).

Suppose we type the command

```
3% (date;du -s ~)>>logfile&
```

The C shell divides it into words like this:

```
( date ; du -s ~ ) >> logfile &
0   1   2  3  4 5 6 7    8      9
```

Quotation marks allow words to contain spaces, as in

```
4% grep "Bill Johnson" info.*
```

The C shell considers this as three words:

```
grep  "Bill Johnson" info.*
 0        1           2
```

Note that the file expansion character * is unexpanded at this point.

Step 3: Updating the History List

After the shell breaks the command into words, it places it on the history list. This allows you to reference each word separately. Recall from Chapter 6 that history commands typically operate on words from the history list.

Typing the history command after issuing the first four commands yields the following list:

```
5% history
   1  ls /usr/include
   2  set ifiles = `ls /usr/include`
   3  ( date ; du -s ~ ) >> logfile &
   4  grep "Bill Johnson" info.*
   5  history
```

Note that the C shell inserts spaces to separate words.

Step 4: Parsing the Sequence of Words

Following history substitution, breaking the command into words, and updating the history list, the C shell parses the command in the following order:

1. Quoting with ' and "
2. Alias substitution
3. I/O redirection, background execution, and pipes (recognized but not processed)
4. Variable substitution
5. Command substitution
6. Filename expansion

Quoting occurs first and filename expansion last. This order is often the cause of surprising results. Let's look at a few examples.

■ Although the C shell parses double and single quotation marks at the same time, they provide different levels of quoting. We can use either method to quote filename expansion, redirection, background execution, and pipe characters. Only single quotation marks, however, quote variable expansion and command substitution characters. Therefore, we must use single quotation marks in the following alias definition:

```
% alias cd 'cd \!*; set cwd = `/bin/pwd`; setenv CWD $cwd'
```

In addition, note that we must quote the history command **!*** with **** to prevent expansion even within single quotation marks. This is because history substitution occurs before the C shell processes quoting.

■ After the C shell processes history characters, quoting, and aliases, it next checks for redirection, pipes, and background requests. The command

```
% who > temp
```

for example, uses simple output redirection. The C shell places **who**'s output in a file called **temp**. The command

```
% date; who > temp
```

behaves differently. Here the output of the **date** command appears on the terminal. The C shell places the output of **who** in **temp** as before. Thus redirection affects only a single command or a command group.

In contrast, consider

```
% date; who &
[1] 129
```

Background execution applies to the entire command line, not just to the last command.

Note that the C shell recognizes the special characters for redirection, pipes, and background jobs but defers processing them, as we will see later in this chapter. During parsing, the C shell just removes these special characters from the argument list (they are not part of the command's arguments) and notes their presence.

■ The C shell next expands shell variables. This occurs late in the parsing order. Suppose we want to append the file **dict1** to the file ~/**vault**/**words**. Because we intend to append other material to this file, we save its name in a shell variable along with the redirection symbol to reduce typing. We quote the string to preserve spaces.

```
% set out = '>> ~/vault/words'
```

Now, instead of typing

```
% cat dict1 >> ~/vault/words
```

we type

```
% cat dict1 $out
[contents of dict1 appear here ... ]
cat: cannot open >>
```

What went wrong? We wanted the C shell to expand **$out** to specify redirection. Un-
fortunately, since it has already handled redirection, it simply passes >> to the **cat**
command as a filename argument. Note the importance of knowing precedence here.

   ■ The C shell executes a subshell to process command substitution; that is, the
instance of the C shell that parses the command subsitution is distinct from the one that
evaluates the text inside command substitution marks. The following examples illustrate
this.
   Suppose you want to set a shell variable to a list of filenames. You type the command

```
% set flist = `ls -t ch10.[3-5]`
```

which uses command substitution to assign the list to variable **flist**. A subshell evaluates
(file-expands) **ch10.[3-5]**.
   As another example, suppose you want to edit a group of files containing pattern
maxprop. You use a shell variable **pat** to hold **maxprop**:

```
% set pat = maxprop
```

Now you execute the command

```
% vi `grep -l $pat *.c`
```

grep with the **-l** returns the names of all ***.c** files containing **maxprop**. With command
substitution, we use these filenames as arguments to the **vi** command. Note that we can
search for another pattern by just typing

```
% set pat = maxline
% !vi
vi `grep -l $pat *.c`
```

Thus command substitution marks can contain history commands, aliases, redirection,
pipe or background symbols, shell variables, and file expansion characters. Also, since
the history list contains the **vi** command with **$pat** unexpanded, we can assign new values
to it and use history to issue new commands.

Step 5: Execute Each Command

Once the C shell parses the command line, it must execute the command. This is where
it interfaces with UNIX, since it must tell UNIX what programs to execute and which
files to use for input and output.

10.2 THE FAMILY TREE: PARENT AND CHILD PROCESSES

To execute a command (such as **grep** or **ls**), the C shell calls another program. This section examines how the C shell uses UNIX system routines to do this. The method we describe here is not peculiar to the C shell, or even to shells in general, but it applies to any UNIX program that calls other programs.

To understand command execution, we must examine the basic unit of an executing program, the *process*. For example, the file **/bin/csh** is the executable code for the C shell itself. When you are using it, it runs as a system process. You type command lines, and the process parses them.

A process consists of program instructions, data areas, and the operating system structures required by UNIX. When the program finishes executing, the process goes away. We can think of a program as permanent (or as permanent as anything can be these days), whereas a process has a life cycle. It is created, it lives, and it dies. For example, when you login to UNIX, the login process creates a C shell process (that is, it executes **/bin/csh**). This process executes (lives) until you logout. As we have noted, each process has a unique systemwide process identification (PID).

A process also has a user and group identification to accommodate file access permissions. When you login to UNIX, it assigns your user and group identification to your C shell process. The **id** command (not available on BSD systems) displays this information:

```
% id
uid=202(sara) gid=50(project1)
```

Here **sara** has a user ID of 202 and a group ID of 50. (If your system does not have the **id** command, refer to Appendix F for the database files where this information is stored.) A process also has a current directory, a list of responses to signals (such as the interrupt signal), and a table of open files.

Each process includes program instruction and data areas. The program instruction area (also known as the *text* or *code space*) contains the executable instructions. More than one process can share it. A process's data area, however, is not shared; it includes the shell variables and environment data.

We've used both shell variables and environment variables in our shell scripts and from our login shell. The C shell variables (**ignoreeof, cdpath, term**) are part of the local data area. The environment variables (**PATH, HOME, TERM, EXINIT**) are part of the environment data area. UNIX copies the environment data for other programs. For example, the **vi** program uses environment variables **EXINIT, SHELL, TERM,** and **TERMCAP.**

Let's examine a typical C shell process as shown in step 1 of Figure 10-1. This process parses command lines. We label it with its name (**/bin/csh**). It contains program instructions and data. Although UNIX may treat these separately, we will consider them as one entity. We label the local data area as **VAR1** and the environment data area as **ENV.**

% grep maxprop *.c

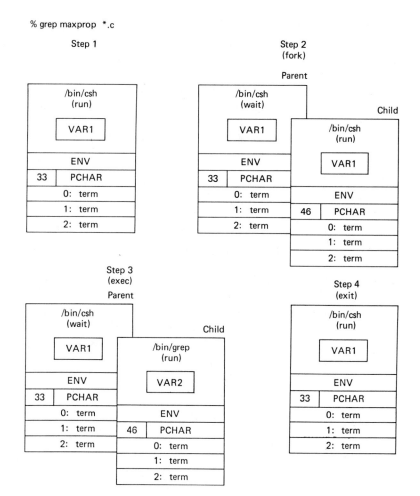

Figure 10-1

We also include slots (the process' open file table) for assigning the C shell's standard input, standard output, and diagnostic output files (labeled 0, 1, and 2, respectively). We call the assignments *file descriptors*. They are attached to the terminal by default (thus the label **term** in Figure 10-1). We refer to the rest of the process as **PCHAR** (process characteristics) and place the shell's process ID (**33** in this case) in this slot.

Let us now step through the C shell's execution of a command. We'll look first at UNIX commands and consider built-in commands (such as **cd**) later. Steps 1 through 4 of Figure 10-1 illustrate the execution of the command

```
% grep maxprop *.c
```

Process Creation (fork)

The C shell creates a new process to execute an external command. We refer to the original process as the *parent* and the new one as the *child*. If the parent process is a shell (in this case it is), we also refer to the child process as a *subshell* or child shell.

Here our login shell is the parent process. To run the **grep** command, it creates a child process by calling the UNIX *system routine* **fork**. System routines are resident in the UNIX operating system (kernel). We can execute kernel code by calling one of the system routines. **fork**, for example, duplicates the calling process. It copies everything: the program instructions, data, and all process characteristics. The child process is a snapshot of the parent at the time it called **fork**.

There are, however, two important differences between parent and child:

1. The child has its own process ID (PID) assigned by UNIX.
2. The child is aware of its relationship to the parent, as is the parent to the child.

fork results in two similar concurrently executing programs; it is the only way UNIX creates processes.

Step 2 of Figure 10-1 depicts process creation under UNIX. The child process (also labeled **/bin/csh**) is a duplicate of the parent. UNIX copies the local data area (**VAR1**), the environment data area (**ENV**), the process characteristics (**PCHAR**), and the table of open files. The child does, however, have its own process ID (**46**).

Executing a Command (exec)

Process creation is the first step in the execution of a UNIX command. In the next step, the child shell calls **exec** (another UNIX system routine distinct from the built-in command **exec**) to execute the command. This makes UNIX replace the calling program with the command's program and execute it. We call this an *overlay*. The number of processes stays the same. Whenever a process calls **exec**, UNIX overlays it with the called program. The new program then becomes the child process.

Step 3 of Figure 10-1 shows the calling of **exec**. Now the child process consists of the program data (labeled **VAR2**) and instructions for **/bin/grep**, the **grep** command. This replaces the program data and instructions of the child **/bin/csh**. However, the child's copy of the environment data (**ENV**), the process characteristics (**PCHAR**), and the open files are still intact.

The C shell performs this two-step sequence when it executes external commands like **grep**. Later in this chapter, when we look at redirection and subshells, we'll see why these steps are separate.

Waiting for the Command to Finish (wait)

While the child process (in our example, the **grep** command) is executing, the parent shell waits for it to finish. It does this by calling the UNIX system routine **wait**, which suspends it.

We label the **/bin/csh** program as waiting in steps 2 and 3. It no longer attempts to read commands, and the child process has sole access to our terminal. If the child must read input (such as a **mail** or **vi** command), it does not have to contend with the parent.

Similarly, **grep**'s output appears on the terminal without interference from the parent. The **wait** call synchronizes our input requests to the parent shell with the execution of subsequent commands.

The Command Finishes (exit)

The child process terminates by executing its last instruction, by an explicit termination call, or by some external event (such as pressing the interrupt key). UNIX notifies the waiting parent that its child has finished executing ("died"). The parent shell wakes up, stores the completion status in variable **$status**, and displays its prompt. We can now type a new command.

In most cases, a child terminates by using the **exit** system routine. This permits it to report a completion status to the parent. As noted earlier, UNIX commands use the completion conventions of 0 and nonzero for success or failure, respectively. UNIX passes this status to the waiting parent shell.

Step 4 of Figure 10-1 shows the parent process after the child process has called **exit**. The parent is now running, and the child process no longer exists.

Note that the **grep** command is independent of the mechanism (**fork** and **exec**) that UNIX and the C shell use to execute it. When a command runs as a child process, the program instructions read or write to a file descriptor, not to a hardware device. As we will see in the next two sections, this is a key to the implementation of redirection and pipes.

10.3 THE CHILD SHELL AS TRAFFIC POLICEMAN: REDIRECTION REVISITED

Redirection is one of the C shell's most elegant features. Now that you understand how the shell executes a command, let's see how it handles redirection.

Input/Output Redirection

The following command uses **tr** (translate characters) to convert file **srcfile** to uppercase letters. It places the result in file **destfile**.

```
% tr "[a-z]" "[A-Z]" < srcfile > destfile
```

This command uses both input and output redirection. Remember, **tr** is unaware that we redirected its input and output. It simply reads from standard input and writes to standard output.

The C shell handles redirection. When it reads the command line, it looks for special characters. Here, it finds the redirection symbols $<$ and $>$.

Figure 10-2 shows the steps required to execute a command involving redirection. In step 1, the parent C shell is running. In step 2, it **fork**s a child shell. The child shell inherits the parent shell's open files, including 0 (standard input), 1 (standard output), and 2 (diagnostic output).

Normally, these files are attached to the terminal. If we specify redirection, however, the child shell changes the file descriptors. In the current case, it uses UNIX system routines to close file 1 and open **destfile**. Since UNIX assigns the lowest available integer to the open file, it becomes file 1. File **destfile** is now the standard output. Similarly, the

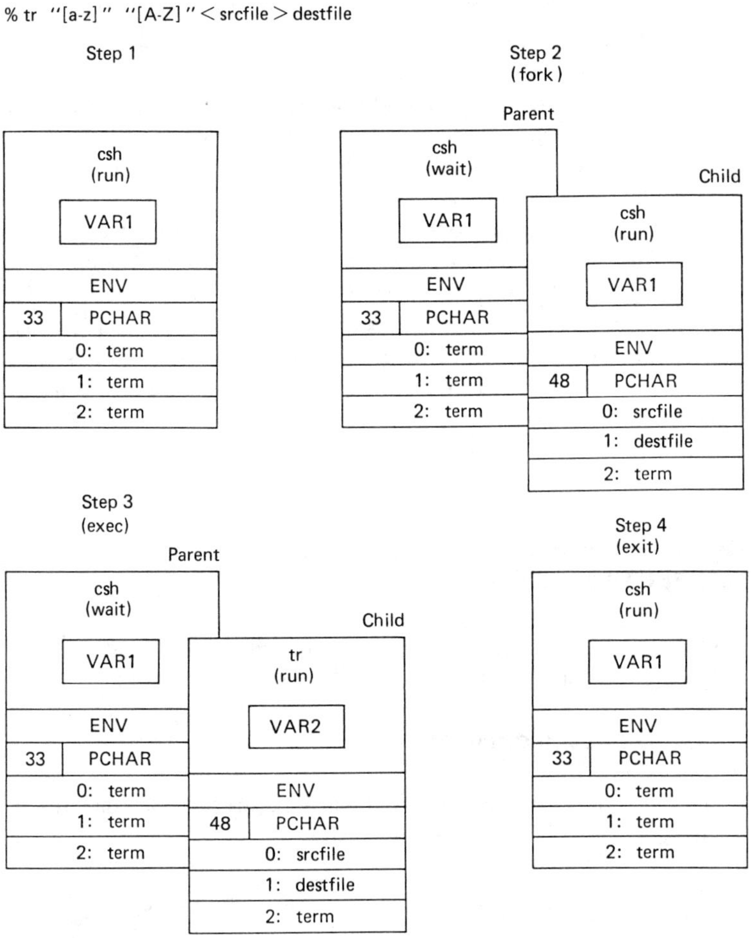

Figure 10-2

child shell closes file 0 and opens file **srcfile**. **srcfile** is now the standard input. Step 2 in Figure 10-2 reflects these new assignments.

The child shell now runs the **tr** program as depicted in step 3. It uses the **exec** system call to overlay itself; the **tr** command has access to its open files. When **tr** reads its standard input, it obtains the character stream from **srcfile**. Likewise, when it writes to standard output, the character stream goes to **destfile**. Note that **tr**'s diagnostic output is still attached to our terminal and that the parent shell's open files are unchanged.

When **tr** finishes, control returns to the parent shell, as shown in step 4.

Now that we understand how the C shell handles redirection, let's look at how it redirects diagnostic output and appends to existing files.

Standard and Diagnostic Redirection

This next command uses **find** to record the full pathname of any file called **spell** residing in the **/usr** file system. It redirects both standard and diagnostic output to file **paths**:

```
% find /usr -name spell -print >& paths
```

The shell goes through the steps outlined in Figure 10-2. In step 2, the parent shell **fork**s a child shell. In this example, the child shell closes file 1 (standard output) and opens file **paths**. It then closes file 2 (diagnostic output) and opens file **paths** again. When the **find** command writes either error information or pathnames, they go in file **paths**.

Steps 3 and 4 are the same as before. The child shell uses **exec** to run the **find** program. When it finishes, the child process disappears, leaving the parent process' file table unchanged (step 4).

Appending Standard Output

The next command appends the standard output of the disk usage command to file **fstatus**:

```
% du ~ >> fstatus
```

Here the child shell closes file 1 (standard output). After opening file **fstatus**, it seeks to the end of its current contents. Standard output from the **du** command will then appear there.

Redirection First

Knowing how (and when) the shell performs redirection helps us solve the following problem. We want to sort three files together: **dict1**, **dict2**, and **dict3**. We want to store the output back in **dict1**. We try the following command:

```
% sort dict1 dict2 dict3 > dict1
```

Unfortunately, we do not have **noclobber** set. The result is a new **dict1** without any data from the old **dict1** file! What happened?

When the shell parses the command, it recognizes the output redirection symbol. The parent shell creates a child shell, which performs the redirection. It closes file 1 (the standard output normally attached to the terminal) and opens file **dict1** for writing. However, the system destroys the contents of an existing file when it is opened for writing. We have just lost the contents of **dict1**.

Now the child calls **exec** to execute **sort**. **sort** then sorts its arguments: **dict1**, **dict2**, and **dict3**. But **dict1** is empty, so only **dict2** and **dict3** appear.

You should observe the following rule:

Do not use a filename as an argument and as the destination for redirection in the same command line.

How can we solve this problem? Fortunately, **sort** lets us specify an output file to which it writes only after doing its work. The command

```
% sort dict1 dict2 dict3 -o dict1
```

sorts the three files and puts the output in **dict1**. For commands that lack this option, use a temporary file. For example, the command

```
% cat dict1 dict2 dict3 > temp; mv temp dict1
```

concatenates files **dict1**, **dict2**, and **dict3** into a single file **temp,** then renames **temp** to **dict1**.

10.4 THE CASE OF THE COMMON ANCESTOR: PIPES REVISITED

The C shell implements pipes much like redirection by closing and opening file descriptors. With pipes, however, we have at least two cooperating processes.

Suppose we want to count the number of users currently on our dial-up lines. Assuming that these lines are on ports **tty5**, **tty6**, and **tty7**, we type the following command:

```
% who | grep "tty[5-7]" | wc -l
```

grep searches the output of the **who** command for lines containing **tty5**, **tty6**, or **tty7**. **wc** counts the number of lines it finds. We use two pipes to connect three commands.

Figure 10-3 shows the steps involved in executing this command. Step 1 shows the parent C shell process running. When it sees a pipe symbol, it creates a memory buffer using the **pipe** system routine. In this example, it creates two pipes, which we call (cleverly!) **pipe1** and **pipe2**. UNIX associates two file descriptors with each pipe, one for reading and one for writing. **pipe1** has file descriptors 3 and 4, **pipe2** 5 and 6.

Once the parent shell creates the pipes, it **fork**s a new process for each command. Step 2 shows the three new C shell processes (triplets!). Note that each has its own data areas and process characteristics. These new processes set up the file descriptors to make **who** write to **pipe1** through its standard output and **grep** read from **pipe1** through its standard input. Similarly, **grep** writes to **pipe2** through its standard output, and **wc** reads from **pipe2** through its standard input.

To do this, the first child shell closes file 1 (the standard output) and associates

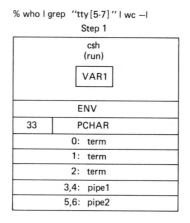

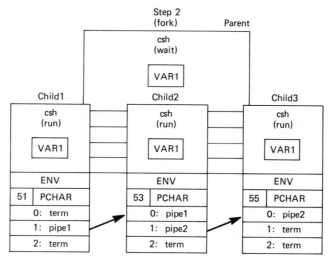

Figure 10-3

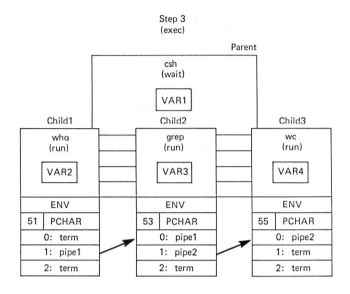

Step 3
(exec)

Step 4
(exit)

Figure 10-3 (*cont.*)

pipe1's write file descriptor with 1 using the UNIX system routine **dup** (duplicate a file descriptor). The second new child shell similarly closes file 0 (standard input) and associates **pipe1**'s read file descriptor with 0. Because a common parent shell created this pipe, the two processes share a data buffer. The second and third child shells do the same for **pipe2**. Step 2 shows the new file descriptor assignments to the pipes.

After the child shells set up the file descriptors, each calls its program using **exec**. Step 3 shows this mass action. The programs overlay the C shells, but the table of open files (including the pipes) remains intact.

The three commands in this example execute concurrently. The **who** command writes to **pipe1** until it finishes or the pipe fills. In the latter case, UNIX suspends **who** temporarily until **grep** removes data from the pipe and makes more room. Similarly, **grep** writes to **pipe2** until it finishes or the pipe fills. If either **grep** or **wc** attempts to read from an empty pipe, UNIX suspends it until data appears. Thus UNIX synchronizes commands connected by pipes. As with redirection, the mechanism is transparent to the commands themselves.

Step 4 shows the parent process after the three child processes finish. The parent shell must now remove each pipe it created in step 1. It does this by closing files 3, 4, 5, and 6. Note that the parent's standard files (0, 1, 2) never changed.

10.5 MEANWHILE, IN THE SIDE RINGS: BACKGROUND EXECUTION REVISITED

During normal command processing, the parent shell executes a **wait** system routine after **fork**ing the child shell. UNIX then suspends the parent process until the child finishes.

When a background command is issued, the parent does not wait for the child to finish executing. Let's see how the C shell implements this feature.

The following command compiles file **gets.c** in the background:

```
% cc -o gets gets.c &
[1]  163
%
```

As before, the parent shell parses the line and **fork**s a child shell. Since we specified background execution, the parent shell does not call **wait.** Instead, it simply reports the job number and PID (1 and 163, respectively) and then immediately displays the shell prompt. This allows us to execute commands while the **cc** command runs.

The parent and child shells still perform each step shown in Figure 10-1. The only differences are in steps 2 and 3. Here, the parent shell continues to run instead of waiting; that is, the parent and child processes run concurrently. UNIX still notifies the parent when a child process finishes. Because the child is a background task, its completion is not reported (unless we make arrangements such as having the terminal beep or sending ourselves mail). Berkeley versions of the C shell report the status at the next prompt.

Now that we understand how this works, let's examine the difference between the following command lines:

```
% budget_report& payroll_report&
[1]  164
[2]  165
% monthly.tot; sum.year &
[3]  166
```

The first command creates two concurrent background jobs: **budget_report** and **payroll_report**. Presumably, these are not interdependent. The shell reports two PIDs: 164 for **budget_report** and 165 for **payroll_report**.

The second command results in a single background job consisting of two sequential commands. Command **sum.year** will not execute until **monthly.tot** is finished. Here the C shell creates a single child process to create and execute (using **fork** and **exec**) the two commands. It is important to know which form to use when one task depends on another.

10.6 WHO'S ON FIRST? ALIASES AND BUILT-IN COMMANDS

Now let us describe how the C shell executes aliases and built-in commands.

Built-in Versus UNIX Commands

Since built-in commands (such as **cd**) are part of the C shell program, it executes them directly. There is no **fork** and **exec** step, hence no process creation. The C shell merely executes the code. Let's examine why **cd** must be a built-in command.

If **cd** were a UNIX command, the parent shell would **fork** a child shell to execute it. The child process would change the working directory and terminate. However, changes made in the child process affect only its environment. When it terminates, its environment disappears, and the parent shell's environment remains unchanged. With this arrangement, we could never change our working directory!

Thus commands that change the environment must be built into the C shell to avoid the process creation and program **exec** steps. Because there is no process creation, built-in commands run faster than external commands.

The Order of Things

Now that we see the difference between the C shell's execution of UNIX and built-in commands, let's examine aliases.

When the C shell reads a command line, it looks for possible aliases. It substitutes the definition for each one it finds. It then checks its list of built-in commands. It executes the internal code for each of these it finds. Finally, it looks for UNIX commands— commands that are not aliases or built in. It executes these by creating a process and going through the **fork** and **exec** sequence described earlier.

The order here is important. Since the C shell looks for aliases before it looks for built-in commands or UNIX commands, we can define aliases for existing commands and put aliases within aliases.

10.7 HAND-ME-DOWNS: CREATING SUBSHELLS

As we have noted, the C shell creates a child shell or subshell to execute commands that are not built in. Command groups and command substitution also result in subshells. This section looks at how these work in more detail.

Command Groups

By using parentheses, we can force the C shell to create a subshell. This allows us to change our environment temporarily while protecting the parent shell's environment.

The following example changes directory to **utils** and compiles program **gets.c**:

```
% pwd
/u/sara
% (cd utils; cc -o gets gets.c)
% pwd
/u/sara
```

Note that the current directory (**/u/sara**) is the same after the compile command finishes. To see why, let's analyze how the C shell executes this command.

The parent shell recognizes the parentheses used to form a command group. It **forks** a child shell containing a copy of its own code and data. The child shell thus has access to all shell variables and aliases.

The child shell now parses the command group. Since the **cd** command is built in, the child shell executes it directly without **fork**ing a new child shell. It changes the current directory to **utils**, but only within its environment.

The child shell then parses the compile (**cc**) command. Since this is not built in, it **forks** a new child shell, which uses **exec** to call the UNIX program **cc**. UNIX overlays the **cc** command on the new child shell and executes it. This child (or more precisely, grandchild) inherits the first child's environment; thus **cc** compiles **gets.c** in the **utils** directory. At completion, control returns to the first child shell.

The first child shell then **exits**. Now control returns to the original parent shell with its environment unchanged.

Command Substitution

Command substitution also makes the C shell create a subshell. In fact, subshell creation is precisely why command substitution works so well.

Recall, for example, the following command, which uses command substitution to produce a list of files for **vi**.

```
% vi `grep -l maxprop *.c`
```

Within the grave accent marks, we run a subshell that executes the **grep** command. **grep** searches for the pattern **maxprop** in our ***.c** files. Its output is a list of filenames. Let's analyze this command using Figure 10-4.

In step 1, the parent shell creates a pipe when it recognizes the grave marks indicating command substitution. In step 2, the parent shell **forks** a child shell that inherits the pipe mechanism. The child shell expands ***.c**. It then closes file descriptor 1 and associates the pipe's write descriptor with 1 instead. After setting up the pipe, the child shell calls

grep using **exec**. Step 3 shows both **grep** (child) and **csh** (parent) running. **grep** writes its standard output to the pipe, and the parent shell reads from it. When **grep** finishes, it **exit**s. In step 4, the parent substitutes the output from **grep** into the command line. The parent can now remove the pipe since it is no longer needed.

The parent continues parsing the command line as usual. In step 5, it creates another child shell and waits for its completion. This child shell acquires the argument list, including the filenames produced by the **grep** command. It then calls **vi** (using **exec**) and uses the argument list passed with the **exec** call (step 6). After **vi** finishes (step 7), the parent runs again.

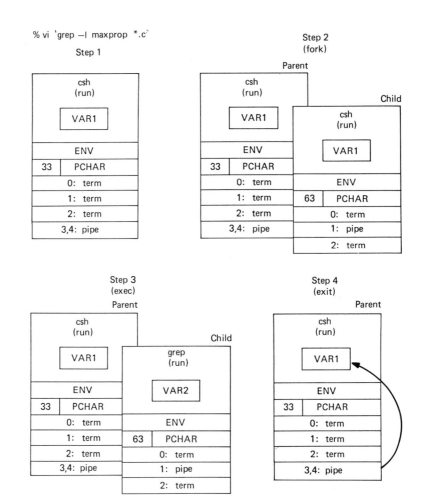

Figure 10-4

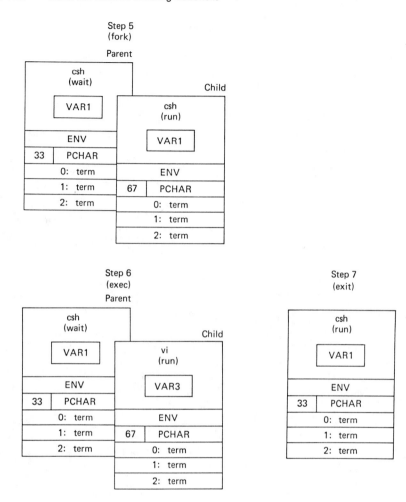

Figure 10-4 (*cont.*)

Subshells can also separate standard and diagnostic output. For example, the following **find** command looks for files named **spell** in the **/usr** file system. It writes pathnames to file **paths** and discards diagnostic output. (Recall that **/dev/null** is the "bit bucket.")

```
%  (find /usr -name spell -print > paths) >& /dev/null
```

Figure 10-5 illustrates how the shell executes this command. Step 1 shows the parent shell parsing the command line. It creates a child shell when it sees the parentheses (step

% (find /usr -name spell -print > paths) >& /dev/null

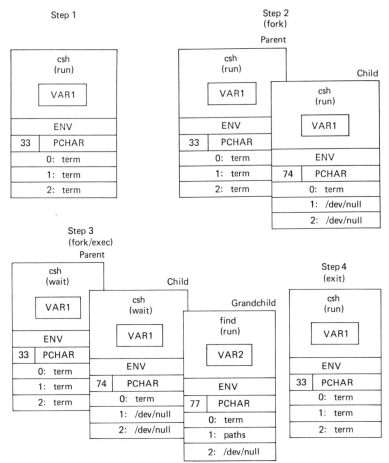

Figure 10-5

2). This child shell sees the special symbol >**&** for standard and diagnostic output redirection. It therefore closes file 1 and opens file **/dev/null**. It then closes file 2 and opens file **/dev/null** again. Now both standard and diagnostic output are attached to **/dev/null**.

The child shell parses the rest of the command:

```
find /usr -name spell -print > paths
```

It **fork**s a new child shell to handle output redirection (step 3). This new shell closes file 1 (attached to **/dev/null**) and opens file **paths**. Now file 1 is attached to **paths**, while file 2 remains attached to **/dev/null**. The new child shell then uses **exec** to call **find**. The

find command writes its standard output to **paths** and its diagnostic output to **/dev/null**.

Step 4 shows the parent process after **find** finishes and both child shells have **exit**ed. Again, the parent's open file table is unchanged.

10.8 STARTING OVER: EXECUTING NEW SHELLS

Our last topic is the creation of new C shells. One way to do this is by executing a shell script. The C shell handles scripts, like UNIX commands, using the **fork** and **exec** mechanisms. Note that this differs from just creating a subshell, which involves **fork** alone.

A subshell involves no initialization; it receives its data from the parent. When the C shell executes a script, however, the child shell overlays the program **/bin/csh**. This new program replaces the child shell's program data and instructions and begins executing. It must go through an initialization process much like the one the shell executes at login.

This section shows how the C shell executes shell scripts. In addition, we'll examine shell and environment variables in more detail. We'll discuss how new shells can gain access to login shell variables and aliases.

Executing Shell Scripts

Let's see what happens when we run the **loc** script (to find **echo2**'s pathname):

```
% loc echo2.c
```

Once the parent shell determines that **loc** is not an alias or a built-in command, it considers it an external command. It then **fork**s a child shell. The child shell calls **exec** to execute **loc**. Since **loc** is a C shell script, **exec** calls the program **/bin/csh**, using the script name and any arguments as the new argument list. Thus executing script **loc** works the same as if we had typed

```
% csh loc echo2.c
```

The important point here is that the child shell executes a new copy of the shell.

What initialization occurs? The new shell does not execute ~/**.login**, but it does execute ~/**.cshrc**. This means that scripts have access to alias and variable definitions included in our ~/**.cshrc** file. They do not have access, however, to ones created in our shell. Also, aliases and variable definitions are not available at all before the child shell executes ~/**.cshrc**.

After initialization, the new shell reads and executes the commands in the script. Thus the shell executes a script much like it executes a UNIX command (Figure 10-1). The only difference is that in step 3, the child shell overlays the **/bin/csh** program instead of **grep**. The arguments to **csh** are the shell script name and its argument list.

Escaping to New Shells

There are other ways to create new C shells. For example, we can "escape" from a utility (such as **vi** or **mail**) and enter a shell. Suppose we are editing in **vi** and we need to list the **.doc** files in our current directory. Instead of leaving **vi**, we temporarily escape it. We type the command

```
: sh
1%
```

and the C shell displays its familiar prompt. We issue our commands:

```
2% ls *.doc
3% !! | pr | lpr
4% exit
```

We list the files, then use **history** to send the listing through a formatter (**pr**) and to the line printer (**lpr**). After typing **exit,** we are back in **vi** at the same editing place.

    To do this, **vi fork**s a new process; it, however, is a copy of **vi** and not the C shell. The child process (**vi**) then uses **exec** to call the program **/bin/csh**. This new C shell overlays the child and begins executing. As in executing shell scripts, the new shell must initialize itself, which includes executing ~/**.cshrc**.

Aliases and Shell Variables

How do we communicate with new shells? Can we preserve shell variables and aliases across shells?

    Aliases and shell variables are local data in our current shell. If we create a command group (subshell) by using parentheses, for example, the subshell will recognize them. However, a new shell will not, since the **exec** system routine destroys local data (labeled **VAR1** in Figure 10-1) when it replaces the calling program with new local data (labeled **VAR2**). Thus the only way to pass aliases and shell variables to a new shell is through the ~/**.cshrc** file.

    What about the other direction? Variables or aliases defined in child shells (either subshells or newly executed shells) cannot be passed back to the parent. For example, the following command defines alias **nusers** in a subshell:

```
% (alias nusers 'who | wc -l')
```

The parent shell does not recognize this alias:

```
% nusers
nusers: Command not found.
```

Environment Variables

Since UNIX (not the C shell) maintains environment variables, they enjoy special treatment and recognition throughout the system. We have already given examples of programs besides the C shell using environment variables (**vi** uses **EXINIT** and **SHELL**, **mail** uses **SHELL**, etc.). When the shell calls a program using **exec**, UNIX copies the environment variables. The program overlays the child shell, destroying all local data, including the environment area. But UNIX then replaces the environment variables, giving the new program a current copy.

This is important to remember. It means that changes in the environment variables are passed on to other programs but, as with shell variables, not back to parent programs.

Suppose you create an environment variable called **TTYLINE** in your ~/**.login** file with the statement

```
setenv TTYLINE /dev/tty5
```

TTYLINE is available to subsequent programs; for example, a C program or a shell script may reference it. Changing **TTYLINE**'s value in a program, however, has no effect on its value in the parent shell.

10.9 PUTTING IT ALL TOGETHER

Now let's answer the questions raised at the beginning of the chapter.

1. Recall that the following two commands gave an error.

```
1% (date;set d = ~/projw/code;du -s $d; ls -l $d) >dstat
2% ls -ld $d
d: Undefined variable.
```

Although line 1 defines the shell variable **d**, it is undefined in line 2. This is because **$d** is defined only in the child shell created to execute the command group on line 1. When the child shell finishes, its program data (including **$d**) disappears.

2. Let us consider the problem of using an alias in a shell script. We defined the alias as follows:

```
% alias nu 'echo `who | wc -l`  users logged in'
```

Alias **nu** is available in our login shell, but not in the script **ustat**. Executing **ustat** results in the following error:

```
% ustat
Today is Wed Feb 20 10:37:18 PST 1985
nu: Command not found.
```

To use **nu** in a shell script, include it in your ~/.**cshrc** file. This makes it available to the new copy of the C shell that executes the script.

3. What happened to the file **compile_log**? The **pwd** and **find** commands reveal the answer:

```
1% pwd
/u/sara
2% (cd utils; cc -o gets gets.c) >>& compile_log
3% pwd
/u/sara
4% find . -name compile_log -print
/u/sara/compile_log
```

We display the current working directory (commands 1 and 3) before and after the command group (command 2). The working directory is unchanged. Command 4 uses the **find** command to display the full pathname of file **compile_log**. We see that it is in directory /**u/sara**—not in subdirectory **utils**.

Although the parent shell creates a child shell when it sees the parentheses, the child shell does not execute the command group until after it handles redirection. Here we request redirection of standard output and diagnostic output to file **compile_log**. Since we have not yet changed the working directory, the child shell opens the file in the directory /**u/sara**. After setting up redirection, the child shell executes the command group. The **cd** command affects only the child shell; the output from **cc** goes to the file /**u/sara/compile_log** instead of to the terminal. When the command group finishes, the child dies. The parent shell's current directory is unchanged.

One final question: Why did the UNIX developers choose to separate the **fork** and **exec** steps instead of providing a single routine? Here are three major reasons:

1. Sometimes it is necessary to duplicate a process without subsequently executing a new program (as when the C shell creates a subshell for command substitution).
2. The child process can perform tasks after the **fork** and before the **exec** (as when the child shell manipulates file descriptors for redirection and pipes).
3. The calling program can skip the duplicating step (as when the C shell uses the built-in command **exec** to call a menu program from ~/.**login**).

10.10 HINTS AND CAUTIONS

■ Remember that piped commands run concurrently. Although functionally equivalent to the pipe command in Section 10.4, the following commands execute quite differently:

```
% who > tmp1; grep "tty[5-7]" tmp1 > tmp2;\
wc -l tmp2; rm tmp1 tmp2
```

Each command in the group runs as a separate process, executing sequentially. Moreover, this implementation requires disk space for files, whereas pipes use a data buffer. In general, piping commands is faster and more efficient.

■ We can use subshells to create local shell variables within alias definitions as follows:

```
% alias nu '(set n = `who | wc -l`; echo $n users logged in)'
```

Alias **nu** (number of users) reports the number of users currently logged in. Because we placed its definition in parentheses, we create a subshell each time it is called. This arrangement makes **$n** local, so we do not have to worry about conflicting uses. When the alias command finishes, **$n** disappears along with the entire child shell.

■ Be careful when using aliases in command substitutions. If the alias contains a command substitution as well, the C shell will not be able to execute the command. Suppose we included the following alias for **cd** in our ~/**.cshrc** file (we're using a C shell version that excludes the predefined variable **cwd** and wish to maintain it ourselves):

```
alias cd 'cd \!*; set cwd = `/bin/pwd`; setenv CWD $cwd'
```

The command

```
% set flist = `cd book; echo ch*`
```

produces an error ("core dump"!) since we've embedded command substitution marks by using the **cd** alias.

■ Be careful when using C shell variables to build strings of executable commands. Suppose we set a shell variable to a command that uses pipes. The command

```
% set com = 'ls -l | grep "^d" '
```

uses **com** to store a command string that lists directory names. We would like to execute this command by just typing **$com**. Here is the result:

```
% $com
| not found
grep not found
"^d" not found
```

What's wrong? Because the C shell parses pipes before expanding variables, it doesn't recognize the pipe symbol here. Instead, it passes the strings |, **grep**, and " ˆd" to **ls** as filename arguments. Can we still use this shell variable as a command?

Yes. From the command line we can use the built-in command **eval** (on BSD versions), which parses **$com** in the current shell:

```
% eval $com
```

or we can type

```
% echo $com | csh
```

which pipes the text **ls -l | grep "ˆd"** to the standard input of **csh**. This works because the new program **csh** interprets the pipe symbol. If we define **$com** in a shell script, we can use a here document as follows:

```
/bin/csh << EOF
    $com
EOF
```

Essentially we expand **$com** and then force a different shell to parse the command.

■ We have described the use of the **source** command to test modifications to setup files (such as, ~/.**cshrc**). This built-in command prevents the process creation step we've seen with UNIX commands. **source** makes the parent shell read and execute the commands in file ~/.**cshrc** directly. This means that any alias definitions, variable settings, or working directory changes will affect the current shell.

■ The C shell also has a built-in command (**exec**) that prevents the shell from performing process creation. From our login shell, we can use this command to overlay our C shell with another program to create an alternative user interface to UNIX. When we exit this program, UNIX logs us out. Section 11.7 contains a sample menu program for this application.

TABLE 10-1 UNIX PROCESS CONTROL SYSTEM ROUTINES

fork	UNIX duplicates the calling process (the parent). The new process inherits all the parent's process characteristics except the PID.
exec	UNIX overlays the calling process with the named program. The open files, PID, environment variables, etc., remain intact.
wait	UNIX suspends the calling process until its child finishes executing.
exit	UNIX removes the calling process and notifies the waiting parent process.

TABLE 10-2 UNIX FILE MANIPULATION SYSTEM ROUTINES

creat, **open**	UNIX creates a new file or opens an existing file and assigns the lowest available file descriptor.
close	UNIX closes a file and releases the associated file descriptor.
pipe	UNIX creates a data buffer and assigns the two lowest available file descriptors: one for reading the pipe, one for writing.
dup	UNIX duplicates a file descriptor by assigning the lowest available file descriptor to an already open file.

10.11 KEY POINT SUMMARY

Knowing the C shell's parsing order is helpful. For example, it tells us that shell variables cannot contain redirection symbols because redirection processing occurs before variable substitution. Shell variables may, however, contain file expansion symbols. Similarly, alias definitions may contain most other features: I/O redirection, pipes, background execution, and variable, command, and filename substitution.

The C shell executes built-in commands directly. It executes external commands using a **fork** (creation) and **exec** (execution) step. This results in a child process that inherits the parent's characteristics, including environment variables and open file tables. Table 10-1 summarizes the UNIX process control system routines.

The C shell executes aliases first, then built-in commands, followed by external commands. Aliases can contain special characters (pipe and redirection symbols, etc.) and can contain built-in as well as external commands and other aliases.

To handle command substitution and command groups, the C shell creates a subshell with the **fork** system call. All the parent's data (shell variables, environment variables, etc.) are available to the subshell. To execute shell scripts, the C shell creates a new shell, by making the program **/bin/csh** replace the process that calls it. New shells can access shell variables and aliases only through the ~/**.cshrc** file.

UNIX makes a copy of the environment variables for programs (including shell scripts) called with **exec**.

The C shell handles redirection and pipes by manipulating the standard file descriptors in the child shell. Table 10-2 summarizes the UNIX file manipulation system routines.

11

Example C Shell Scripts

This chapter contains a collection of C shell scripts. They illustrate typical application areas as well as provide useful tools. You can use them as models for writing your own scripts or simply incorporate the interesting ones in your tool box.

We have tried to make these scripts portable. We've run them on both Berkeley 4.2BSD UNIX and a System III–based UNIX (XENIX). Since these systems have different versions of the C shell, there were some discrepancies. In general, our texts will run under both versions. This means that occasionally we had to refrain from using special techniques (such as pattern matching) available only in the Berkeley version. Where common versions were difficult to provide, we present the text for the Berkeley version and describe the modifications necessary for XENIX.

The description of each script includes discussions of its motivation and use as well as sample output. We also explain the overall approach and each command line.

We wrote all the scripts except **bd** and **which**. These were generously contributed by Marty Gray and Peter Kessler, respectively.

The examples cover a wide range of applications. Script **ccpb** compiles C programs in the background. **loc** helps find files in a large directory system. **usage** provides a brief help facility. **tutor** is a vocabulary drill tool, and **dosget** allows the use of file expansion characters when transferring files from MS-DOS to XENIX. **bd** detects changes in key files to monitor system security. **menu** provides a menu-driven user interface. C programmers will find **search** useful for keeping track of program identifiers (especially in large projects). **which** will straighten out the confused UNIX user who has custom versions of UNIX commands. Finally, **pushd** and **popd** implement the directory stack commands available in Berkeley versions of the C shell.

11.1 WHILE THE SHOW GOES ON: COMPILING C PROGRAMS
IN THE BACKGROUND (ccpb)

Compiling C programs often takes a while, so you may want to do it in the background. Moreover, compile errors normally appear on the terminal (via diagnostic output), and they may fill your screen. The command

```
% cc -o esttax esttax.c >& esttax.out &
[1] 131
```

sends compile errors to the file **esttax.out** in the background, but it provides no notification of completion. Besides, it's long and clumsy to type.

The **ccpb** script handles all these problems. All you must provide is the name of either the C source file or the executable file. For example,

```
% ccpb esttax &
[1] 133
```

compiles **esttax.c** and puts the output in file **esttax**.

Alternatively, you can type

```
% ccpb esttax.c &
[1] 135
```

if you feel more comfortable typing the **.c** suffix. You can even create the following alias to avoid typing **&** each time:

```
% alias ccpb 'ccpb \!*&'
```

ccpb can also compile programs in other directories. For example, the command

```
% ccpb accnt/invent
[2] 146
```

compiles **invent.c** and stores the executable file **invent** in directory **accnt**.

How does **ccpb** notify us when it's done? It provides both a beep and the message

```
You have new mail.
```

The beep is handy when we're using the editor. If we are typing commands, **mail** reports the completed job. In either case, **cc**'s output appears in our mailbox.

Here's the text for **ccpb**:

```
        % num ccpb
    1   # ccpb - compile c programs in the background
    2   #       ccpb produces an executable object file named
    3   #       "file". The argument should take the form
    4   #       "file.c" or "file". It sends mail to the user when
    5   #       the compile finishes.
    6   # Usage: ccpb file &
    7
    8   nohup                               # allow to run after log off
    9   set com = $0                        # get command name
   10   if ($#argv != 1) then
   11       echo2 "Usage: $com:t filename"  # only 1 argument allowed
   12       exit 1
   13   endif
   14
   15   set program = $argv[1]              # save program name
   16   if ($program:h != $program) then    # not in current dir
   17       cd $program:h                   # change directories
   18       set program = $program:t        # only use filename
   19   endif
   20
   21   if ($program:r != $program) then    # does argument have .c
   22       set program = $program:r        # don't use extension
   23   endif
   24
   25   set tf = /tmp/$com:t.$$             # set up temporary file
   26   cc -o $program $program.c >& $tf    # compile; store output
   27                                       # in temp file
   28   # check status to see if compile was successful:
   29   if ($status == 0) then
   30       echo $program.c: No errors. >> $tf
   31   endif
   32
   33   mail $USER < $tf                    # mail results to user
   34   rm -f $tf                           # remove temp file
   35   beep                                # ring the bell
```

Line 8 calls **nohup** so that **ccpb** can run after you logout. Line 9 saves the program name in **com** for later use in creating a temporary file.

Lines 10 through 13 check for a single argument. Line 15 saves the program filename in **program** for readability. Lines 16 through 19 use pathname modifiers to determine whether the filename contains a header directory. Let's see how this works.

If we type

```
% ccpb accnt/invent
[3] 176
```

line 16 is true. This is because **$program:h** is **accnt** and **$program** is **accnt/invent**. Line 17 changes directories to **accnt**, and line 18 assigns the filename **invent** (using **:t**) to **program**. **invent** compiles in the **accnt** directory.

If, on the other hand, we type

```
% ccpb invent
[4] 185
```

$program and **$program:h** are the same. Since line 16 is false, no change of directory occurs.

Lines 21 through 23 use a similar technique to remove a **.c** extension. The **:r** modifier lets us examine the filename up to but not including the extension (**.c**). Suppose we type

```
% ccpb invent.c &
```

Then line 21 is true, since **$program:r** is **invent** and **$program** is **invent.c**. Line 22 assigns **invent** to **program**. If we had typed just **invent**, however, line 21 would be false, and **program** would be left unchanged. In either case, **program** ends up containing the filename with no extension.

If your version of the C shell has the **:e** variable modifier (e.g., 4BSD), change line 21 to

```
21 if ($program:e == c) then  # .c included?
```

As an exercise, verify the following command:

```
% ccpb accnt/invent.c
```

In this case, **ccpb** changes directories and removes the **.c** extension.

We need a temporary file to hold **cc**'s output for the mail. Line 25 defines this file using **$com:t** (filename only) and the script's process ID in the **/tmp** directory.

Line 26 calls the **cc** command, putting a **.c** after **$program**. We redirect both standard and diagnostic output to temporary file **$tf**.

Since the **cc** command returns 1 if it finds errors, we check **status** when it finishes. Compile errors appear in **$tf**. If there are none, **$status** is 0, and line 30 simply puts "No errors" in **$tf**.

Line 33 uses **$USER** to mail ourselves the result of the compilation. (You may need to use **$LOGNAME** instead.)

Line 34 removes the temporary file, and line 35 produces the beep (see Section 7.1). We assume that **beep** is installed in one of the directories in **$path**.

ccpb doesn't check for mistyped filenames, since **cc** reports them and returns nonzero status. **ccpb** still mails us the error. Suppose we type **estax** instead of **esttax**. The mail file would contain

```
estax.c
cc: can't open estax.c
```

11.2 QUICK AND EASY FIND: LOCATE A FILE (loc)

The UNIX **find** command is a powerful utility with many options. However, it can be difficult to use. Its most common function is to search the file system for a file and display its pathname. This can be handy for both newcomers and users with huge numbers of files or poor memories.

For example, to find the file **meeting.notes**, we use the following command:

```
% find ~ -name meeting.notes -print
/u/sara/misc/meeting.notes
```

where ~ (our home directory) is the starting place for the search, **meeting.notes** is the name of the target file, and **-print** says to display the full pathname.

find allows file expansion characters, but we must quote them so that the shell doesn't expand them. To find all **.c** files in our file system, for example, we type

```
% find ~ -name "*.c" -print
/u/sara/book/ch9/scripts/tenv.c
/u/sara/book/ch11/test/echo2.c
/u/sara/gtools/getc.c
```

To search the entire file system, we use **find** with / (the root) as the starting pathname. Since **find** reports any directory it can't search, this may produce many annoying error messages as well as the target filenames:

```
% find / -name "*tty*" -print
find: cannot open /usr/spool/at
find: cannot open /usr/spool/uucp/.XQTDIR
find: cannot open /usr/spool/uucp/.XFDDIR
/bin/stty
/bin/tty
/dev/tty
/dev/tty00
```

find writes the target filenames to standard output and the error messages to diagnostic output. Furthermore, **find** does not use **status** to indicate whether it found the target file; instead, **status** is always 0. Some versions of **find** don't even report failure to find the target file.

The **loc** script simplifies the use of **find** and solves these problems. It does not make **find** execute more quickly (in some cases, the result takes even longer), but it is much easier to use. Just compare the lengths of the commands! **loc** discards **find**'s error messages and returns a nonzero status when the search is unsuccessful. Our home directory is **loc**'s default starting point, but an option allows an alternate directory.

For example, to locate the file **meeting.notes**, we type

```
% loc meeting.notes
/u/sara/misc/meeting.notes
```

To search for **.c** files, we type

```
% loc "*.c"
/u/sara/book/ch9/scripts/tenv.c
/u/sara/book/ch11/test/echo2.c
/u/sara/gtools/getc.c
```

Finally, to search the entire file system for **tty** files, we specify the root directory as the first argument and the target filename as the second argument:

```
% loc / "*tty*"
/bin/stty
/bin/tty
/dev/tty
/dev/tty00
```

Note that **find**'s error messages no longer appear on the terminal.

If **loc** cannot find the target file, it displays an error message and returns nonzero status:

```
% loc message2
loc: Can't find message2.
% echo $status
1
```

Here's the text for **loc**:

```
     % num loc
  1  # loc: quick and easy find
  2  #       Assumes home directory unless directory specified.
  3  # usage: loc [dir] filename
  4  #
  5  set noglob                              # prevent file expansion
  6  set com = $0                            # save command name
  7  if ($#argv < 1 || $#argv > 2) then      # check arguments
  8      echo2 "Usage: $com:t [path] filename"# only 1 or 2 allowed
  9      exit 1                              # error exit
```

```
10  endif
11
12  if ($#argv == 2) then                # if 2 then path specified
13      set p = $argv[1]
14      shift                            # remove first argument
15  else
16      set p = $HOME                    # use home dir as default
17  endif
18
19  if (! -d $p:q) then                  # check for directory
20      echo2 "$com:t: No directory $p"
21      exit 1                           # error exit
22  endif
23
24  set tf = /tmp/$com:t.$$              # set up temp file
25
26  # throw away diagnostic output; standard output in $tf
27  ((find $p -name $argv[1] -print|tee $tf)>/dev/tty)>& /dev/null
28
29  if (-z $tf) then                     # no output from find
30      echo2 "$com:t: Can't find $argv[1]."  # failure message
31      rm -f $tf                        # remove temp file
32      exit 1                           # error exit
33  endif
34  rm -f $tf                            # remove temp file
35  exit 0                               # normal exit
```

Line 5 sets **noglob** to disable file expansion. Line 6 saves the command name in **com** for later use.

Lines 7 through 10 verify that **loc** has either one or two arguments. If there are two, the first is the starting search path, and the second is the filename. In this case, line 13 sets **p** to the starting pathname, and line 14 shifts the argument list (making the target filename the first argument). If we specify only one argument, line 16 makes the search start at **$HOME**.

Line 19 checks whether the starting search directory exists. If it does not, **loc** reports the error and exits with nonzero status.

Line 24 defines a temporary file for **loc** to use. Its name is derived using the process ID.

Line 27 does the real work, using the **find** command with embedded command groups. Let's examine this closely, since it illustrates several interesting techniques.

First, we do not need to quote the filename argument (**$argv[1]**), since **noglob** is set. Next we use a command group to separate standard and diagnostic output. We send diagnostic output to **/dev/null** (i.e., discard it). What about standard output? Our **find** statement is as follows:

```
find $p -name $argv[1] -print | tee $tf
```

By piping **find**'s output to the **tee** command, we save a copy of the standard output in **$tf**. Unless we also redirect standard output, it will be discarded as well. The command

```
(find $p -name $argv[1] -print | tee $tf) > /dev/tty
```

does the job. We must redirect standard output back to the terminal (**/dev/tty**) because the outer command group already redirected it to **/dev/null**.

Why use this roundabout method? We could redirect the standard output to a file, then list its contents when **find** finishes. This technique, however, produces output only after the search ends. Our method lets us interrupt **loc** when the pathname we are interested in appears.

Why send a copy of standard output to **$tf**? Remember that **find** does not use status to indicate whether its search succeeded. Therefore, the only way we can determine this is by examining the standard output. If there is none, **find** was unsuccessful. Otherwise, file **$tf** will contain data.

Line 29 checks whether file **$tf** has zero length. If it does, **find** failed, and line 30 displays an error message. We then remove the temporary file and exit with error status (lines 31 and 32). If **$tf** does not have zero length, however, **find** located pathnames. Line 34 removes the temporary file, and line 35 exits with zero status (success).

A word of caution: **loc**'s output cannot be redirected or piped. Since we redirect **find**'s output to **/dev/tty**, it always appears on the terminal. After all, the alternative (writing the pathnames to a file) makes us wait longer. As an exercise, try modifying **loc** so that you can redirect or pipe its output.

11.3 A SIMPLE HELP UTILITY: LEARNING UNIX COMMANDS (usage)

Most UNIX users find command syntax difficult to remember. Suppose we attempt to search a file **manuscript** for the pattern **Permission**. We type the following:

```
% grep manuscript Permission
grep: can't open Permission
```

We have the arguments in the wrong order. **grep** wants the pattern first, then the target filenames. Similarly, suppose we try to split a formatted document into pages. We type

```
% split 66 manuscript
cannot open input
```

Here we forgot to type the dash in front of the optional line length argument.

It would be convenient to have a help facility that shows the correct syntax. The **usage** script does this. For example, after mistyping the **split** command, we can simply type

```
% usage
split: Usage split [-n] [filename]
split: If no input file given, reads from standard input
```

to display proper usage for the latest command.

usage can also provide this information for a specific command. For example, we might type

```
% usage loc echo
loc:  (locate filename) Usage: loc [start-path] filename
echo: Usage: echo [-n] ⟨strings⟩  (strings may use variable,
echo:          file expansion)
```

usage displays information on commands **loc** (a shell script) and **echo.**

usage has a database containing information about commands. Of course, it reports an error if we ask about a command that is not in the database.

We can add new commands to the database at any time. We store it in a public directory (**/usr/pub/usage**).

Before we go through the script, consider the following problem. How does **usage** determine the last command? (If you know the answer, go to the head of the class.)

We can use the history and alias mechanisms to obtain this information. The last command can be referenced as word 0. For example, if we type

```
5% du -s ~
2584 /u/sara
  .  .  .
```

we can later display the command name with

```
19% echo !5:0
du
```

!5 refers to command line 5, and 0 is the first word (the command name).

But how can a script obtain this information? We cannot use history commands in a shell script. Why not? Remember that we execute a brand new copy of the **/bin/csh** program to read and execute a script. **history** starts over, and we can't reference history commands from the previous shell.

The alias mechanism lets us reference the history list correctly. We define an alias that grabs the previous command's name (using **!-1:0**) and passes it to the **usage** script. Here's the alias definition for **usage:**

```
% alias usage '/usr/local/u \!-1:0 \!*'
```

When we type **usage,** we run the alias first, not the script. (We therefore name the script **u** and store it in **/usr/local** to avoid confusion.) What about the rest of the definition? Let's illustrate it with an example.

Suppose we try to remove the **menudefs** directory:

```
% rmdir menudefs
rmdir: menudefs not empty
```

We then type

```
% usage
rmdir: (remove directories ) Usage: rmdir directory(s)
rmdir:        directory(s) must be empty
rmdir:        use rm -r to remove nonempty directories
```

usage reminds us to type **rm -r** to remove **menudefs**.

How do we call script **u**? The **usage** alias picks up the previous command's name only (**rmdir** in this case). Since the C shell stores commands in the history list before expanding aliases, the **usage** command appears after **rmdir**. To refer to **rmdir**, we must access the history list with the **!-1:0** notation (meaning the command before the previous command). Here's our **usage** command after alias substitution:

```
/usr/local/u rmdir
```

In this case the **u** script has only one argument since we called **usage** with no arguments (∖!* is null).

Suppose we type

```
% usage rm rmdir
rm: (remove files/directories) Usage: rm file(s)
rm: rm -r dir(s) removes nonempty directories
rmdir: (remove directories ) Usage: rmdir directory(s)
rmdir:        directory(s) must be empty
rmdir:        use rm -r to remove nonempty directories
```

instead of **usage** by itself. In this case, our command after alias substitution is

```
/usr/local/u rmdir rm rmdir
```

The **u** script now has three arguments. The first (**rmdir**) is from the previous command; the second and third are from the **usage** command. The alias definition uses ∖!-1:0 to make the previous command's name argument 1 and ∖!* to place **usage**'s arguments after it.

How does the **u** script handle both cases? It simply looks at its argument list. If there is only one argument, **usage** had no arguments initially; if there are more, however, **u** ignores the first one and processes the rest.

Now that we understand how it works, let's go through the script. Here's the text:

```
      % num /usr/local/u
 1    # usage: prints a usage message for the
 2    #         command(s) specified
 3    # Usage: usage [command(s)]
 4    #
 5    set com = $0                          # save command name
 6    set udata = /usr/pub/usage            # command data base
 7
 8    if ($#argv == 0) then                 # at least 1 argument
 9        echo2 "Usage: $com:t [tcommand(s)]"
10        exit 1                            # error exit
11    endif
12
13    if ($#argv != 1 ) shift               # remove first argument
14
15    foreach ucom ($argv[*])               # search data base
16        grep "^${ucom}:" $udata||\
17            echo2 "$com:t: No usage info for $ucom."
18    end
```

Line 6 sets **udata** to the name of the usage database. Its format is

```
command: ⟨text⟩
```

Note that colons separate **command** and **⟨text⟩**. **command** identifies the command name and is at the left. **⟨text⟩** describes the use of the command. A command may have many lines of text.

Lines 8 through 11 make sure that the script has at least one argument. Line 13 determines whether we are considering the last command. If there is more than one argument, the first one contains the previous command's name, and we discard it using **shift**. If **$#argv** is 1, however, we leave the argument list unchanged.

The rest of the script is just a **foreach** loop based on the argument list (**$argv[*]**). Lines 16 and 17 use **grep** to search the database (**udata**) for the pattern "ˆ**${ucom}:**". This is the command name preceded by ˆ, a special **grep** character indicating the beginning of the line. We need to insulate **ucom** with braces so that the C shell won't expect a variable modifier (e.g., **:h** or **:q**).

grep displays each line containing this pattern. We use the conditional command operator ‖ to execute the **echo** command (line 17) if **grep** fails. This happens when the target command is not in the database. (*Note:* In XENIX you must use **&&** instead of ‖ in line 16.)

Here's a fragment of the database:

```
% cat /usr/pub/usage
cp: (copy file) Usage: cp f1 f2; or cp [ -r ] f1 ... fn d2
rm: (remove files/directories) Usage: rm file(s)
rm: rm -r dir(s) removes nonempty directories
```

```
rmdir: (remove directories ) Usage: rmdir directory(s)
rmdir:          directory(s) must be empty
rmdir:          use rm -r to remove nonempty directories
grep: (search for patterns) Usage: grep ⟨pattern⟩ [file(s)]
grep: grep reads from standard input if no file arguments
split: Usage split [-n] [filename]
split: If no input file given, reads from standard input
```

These entries need not be ordered, and a command may have several entries.

Note that the **usage** command will fail if it's the first command (event number 1). This is because the alias tries to reference the previous command, but there isn't one.

11.4 LEARNING NEW VOCABULARY: LANGUAGE TUTOR (tutor)

This section presents a simple drill and practice tool for learning vocabulary in a foreign language. It displays a word (in either language), waits for you to type the equivalent in the other language, and then shows the correct answer. Although you can learn Japanese vocabulary (our sample language) this way, the tool is no substitute for a year in Tokyo. It is, however, a lot cheaper.

The shell script reads an ASCII file one line at a time. It expects the line to consist of two words: a prompt and an answer. Here is a partial listing of our Japanese-English dictionary:

```
    % num dict1
1   akai red
2   aoi blue
3   aruite-kudasai please:walk
4   ashi leg
5   atama head
6   chairoi brown
7   eki train:station
```

If there is more than one word in either language, we separate them with colons (e.g., **train:station** for **eki** in line 7). This format makes it easy to divide the line into prompt and answer words from the C shell.

Let's run through a sample session with file **dict1**:

```
% tutor dict1
akai ?
```

Argument **dict1** specifies the dictionary file.

The **tutor** program reads the first line of the file and displays the first word followed by a question mark. Here it displays **akai**, meaning red. We type the response:

```
akai ? red
red
aoi ?
```

The **tutor** script displays the correct translation (**red**) and then proceeds to the next Japanese word, **aoi**. (**tutor** does not check the response—it just gives the correct answer.) This continues until the script reaches the end of the dictionary file or we type **q** for quit.

Once we've mastered the words in **dict1**, we can try another file. We can also specify more than one file. Here we use file expansion to gives ourselves a final examination with the command

```
% tutor dict?
```

We can make the English word the prompt with the **-r** (reverse) option:

```
% tutor -r dict1
red ?
```

Now **tutor** displays **red** and we must reply **akai**.

Here's the text for script **tutor**:

```
1    #
2    # Tutor: teaches a vocabulary list
3    #        reads vocabulary list from files in argument list
4    # Form of input is:
5    #        word1 ⟨white space⟩ word2
6    # Multiword items should be separated with
7    # punctuation (e.g., : or _).
8    #
9    # By default tutor prompts with word1 and displays word2
10   # as answer. To reverse this, use the -r (reverse) option.
11   # Usage: tutor [-r] file(s)
12
13   set noglob                          # prevent file expansion
14   set com = $0
15   unset reverse                       # reset reverse flag
16
17   if ($#argv) then                    # at least one argument?
18       if ("$argv[1]" == "-r") then    # reverse option?
19           set reverse                 # set reverse flag
20           shift                       # remove from command line
21       endif
22   endif
23
23
```

```
24   if ($#argv == 0) then                         # No arguments?
25       echo2 "Usage: $com:t [-r] dictionary_file(s)"
26       exit 1
27   endif
28
29   if ($?reverse) then                           # reverse order?
30       set prompt = 2                            # prompt word is second
31       set answer = 1                            # answer word is first
32   else
33       set prompt = 1                            # assign prompt word
34       set answer = 2                            # assign answer word
35   endif
36
37   foreach f ($argv)                             # loop over input files
38       @ nl = 1                                  # initialize line number
39       while (1)                                 # infinite loop
40           # read a line from the file:
41           set words = `sed -n $nl,${nl}p $f`
42           if ("$words" == " ") break            # null means EOF
43           @ nl++                                # increment line number
44           echo -n "$words[$prompt] ? "          # display prompt word
45           set response = $<                     # get response
46           if ("$response" == q) break           # quit this file
47           if ("$response" == c) continue        # go to next item
48           echo $words[$answer]                  # display answer word
49       end # while
50   end # foreach
```

Line 13 sets **noglob** to prevent file expansion, and line 14 saves the command name in **com**. We use variable **reverse** as a flag. Line 15 resets it. Lines 17 through 22 determine if the first argument is **-r**, indicating the reverse option. If it is, we set variable **reverse** and shift out the argument. Lines 24 through 27 make sure the script has at least one argument.

Lines 29 through 35 set **prompt** and **answer**. If **reverse** is set, **$prompt** is 2 (the second word) and **$answer** is 1. Otherwise, we use word 1 for the prompt and word 2 for the answer.

Lines 37 through 50 form a **foreach** loop to process each dictionary file specified in the argument list. Line 38 initializes the line count (variable **nl**) to 1 each time. Lines 39 through 49 form an "infinite" **while** loop. The only exit is via a **break** in line 42 or 46. The loop reads one line (**nl** contains the line number) from the dictionary file (**$f**). We use the UNIX **sed** (stream editor) utility and assign **sed**'s output to the wordlist variable **words**. A null string indicates the end of file, and the **break** causes **tutor** to get the next file (in the **foreach** loop). Line 43 increments the line count so that next time around **sed** will read the next line.

Line 44 uses **$prompt** to index into **words**. We use **echo** with **-n** to prevent a carriage return and double quotation marks to preserve the space, quote the question mark, and allow variable expansion. This displays the vocabulary word. Line 45 then reads a line of input from the terminal using **$<**. (If your C shell does not include **$<**, replace it with `` `gets` ``.)

We check **response** for two values. Typing **q** terminates the **while** loop with **break** (and we proceed to the next file, if there is one). Typing **c** (continue) transfers control to the top of the **while** loop (line 39). This prevents **tutor** from displaying the answer (line 48).

tutor doesn't check for mistyped filenames but leaves this task for **sed**. In this case **sed** writes an error message to the diagnostic output (it appears on your terminal), returning null to **$words**.

11.5 CUSTOMIZING A STANDARD XENIX UTILITY: GETTING FILES FROM A DOS DISK (dosget)

XENIX has utilities that transfer UNIX files to and from MS-DOS disks. The utility that copies files is called **doscp** (DOS copy). For example, to copy file **proj.doc** from a DOS-formatted floppy disk in drive **A**: to the current directory, we type

```
% doscp A:proj.doc .
```

Similarly, to transfer several files from the DOS disk to our file system, we type

```
% doscp A:proj1.dat A:proj2.dat A:proj3.dat .
```

This copies files **proj1.dat**, **proj2.dat**, and **proj3.dat** to our current directory.

doscp does not allow file expansion characters, but our **dosget** script does. We must quote the characters, however, since we are not matching files in the UNIX file system. To copy our three files, for example, we type

```
% dosget "proj[1-3].dat"
Copying files to directory /u/sara/data
copying proj1.dat
copying proj2.dat
copying proj3.dat
```

dosget displays the current directory and each file it finds to copy. Similarly, we type

```
% dosget "*.doc"
Copying files to directory /u/sara/manual
copying files.doc
copying dir.doc
```

```
copying commands.doc
copying scripts.doc
```

to copy all **.doc** files.

dosget assumes a DOS disk in floppy drive A. (If your computer has more than one floppy drive, you can default to drive A, but allow an option for an alternative drive.) Second, it always copies the files to the current directory.

dosget has an interactive mode, which asks about each file before copying it. To copy the entire disk interactively, for example, we type

```
% dosget -i "*"
Copying files to directory /u/sara/book/ch11
copy bookc? y
copying bookc
copy outline? y
copying outline
copy ccpb.doc? n
copy loc.doc? n
copy tutor.doc? y
copying tutor.doc
```

Now **dosget** prints each filename and copies it only if we type **y**.

We can also specify more than one file argument, as follows:

```
% dosget "*.jan" "*.lst"
Copying files to directory /u/sara/accntg
copying payroll.jan
copying genledg.jan
copying expenses.jan
copying janreport.lst
```

This command copies all files ending in **.jan** or **.lst**.

Here's the text for **dosget**:

```
% num dosget
1   # dosget: copies MS-DOS disk files to XENIX current directory.
2   #    Allows file expansion characters for target filenames.
3   #    Uses dosls to generate filenames and doscp for the copy.
4   #    Reads from drive A only.
5   #    Interactive mode (-i) prompts the user for each file.
6   # Usage: dosget [-i] file(s)
7
8   set noglob                          # turn off file expansion
9   unset ic                            # reset interactive flag
```

```
10
11    if ($#argv) then                        # check for at least one argument
12        if ("$argv[1]" == "-i") then    # interactive option?
13            set ic                           # set interactive flag
14            shift                            # shift flag out of command line
15        endif
16    endif
17
18    if ($#argv == 0) then                    # check for correct number
19        echo2 "Usage: dosget [-i] file(s)"   # of arguments
20        exit 1
21    endif
22
23    set flist = `dosls A:|tr "[A-Z]" "[a-z]" `  # get file list
24    if ($#flist == 0) exit 1                     # exit if no files found
25
26    echo "Copying files to directory `pwd` "    # current directory
27
28    foreach arg ($argv[*])                       # loop over argument list
29        foreach f ($flist)                       # get lower case filenames
30        switch ($f)                              # examine current filename
31            case $arg:                           # is it the one we want?
32                if ($?ic) then                   # interactive copy?
33                    echo -n "copy $f? "          # yes, request copy
34                    set resp = gets`             # get response
35                    if ($resp != 'y') continue   # no, get next name
36                endif                            # of interactive copy
37                echo copying $f
38                doscp A:$f $f                    # copy to dir
39            endsw                                # end of switch
40        end                                      # end of filename loop
41    end                                          # end of arg loop
```

Line 8 sets **noglob** to prevent file expansion. Line 9 initializes the interactive flag **ic**. Line 11 verifies that at least one argument exists. If so, line 12 tests whether the first argument is **-i**. We quote both **$argv[1]** and **-i** to keep the C shell from confusing the option with the file inquiry operators. If **$argv[1]** is **-i**, line 13 sets **ic** and line 14 removes the option from the argument list. Lines 18 through 21 check whether there is still at least one argument.

Line 23 generates a list of files and assigns them to a wordlist variable (**flist**) using command substitution. The command

```
dosls A:  |  tr "[A-Z]" "[a-z]"
```

uses **dosls** to create a list of the filenames on the DOS disk. Since these names are all uppercase, we translate them to all lowercase by piping the output to **tr** (translate). We then assign the pipe's output to **flist**. If there are no files, **$#flist** is 0, and line 24 **exits**.

Line 26 displays the current directory by using **pwd** in an **echo** command.

Now we construct an embedded **foreach** loop. The outer loop (line 28) uses the argument list. Remember, it may contain any number of arguments, including file expansion characters. These remain unexpanded, however, since we set **noglob**. The inner **foreach** loop (line 29) uses the directory list in **flist**. This loop will be executed for each file on the DOS disk. The C shell assigns the next filename from **flist** to variable **f**. We then use it in a **switch** statement (line 30). The **case** statement contains the command line argument. Since the C shell's **case** statement allows pattern matching, we can compare the argument (stored in variable **arg**) with **$f**, the filename. If they match, we execute lines 32 through 38. We use the **switch** statement for pattern matching because the XENIX C shell lacks the pattern matching operators.

Line 32 checks whether **ic** is defined (**$?ic** is true if it is). In interactive mode, lines 33 through 35 display the prompt

```
copy filename?
```

and read an input line using **gets**. If the input is not **y**, a **continue** command returns control to line 29. If it is **y**, lines 37 and 38 display the message

```
copying filename
```

and call the **doscp** command to transfer the file to our current directory.

In the noninteractive mode, we skip lines 33 through 35 and just display the copying message and transfer the file.

11.6 LOOKING FOR CHANGES: MONITORING SYSTEM SECURITY (bd)

Security is an important issue for time-sharing systems, networked systems, or systems with remote access. How do you detect unauthorized changes in key files such as the password file or login program?

The **bd** (backdoor) script can help. It detects alterations of important files by going through a list that includes both automatic entries and ones you suggest. We call the user-supplied file list the *base* files. The others we call *SETUID* files.

A SETUID file allows the user who executes it to have the same permissions as its owner. For example, to change our password, we must modify the system password file. We use the **passwd** command (a SETUID file) for this because it temporarily gives us the permissions of **root**, its owner. We can identify a SETUID file from its long listing. For example, the command

```
% ls -l /bin/passwd
-rws--x--x 1 root bin 15554 Oct 3 12:59 /bin/passwd
```

shows the permission bits and owner for the password command. The permission for owner is **rws**; the **s** (instead of **x**) indicates a SETUID file.

Unauthorized alteration can indicate an intrusion into a superuser SETUID file. The clever intruder can gain superuser powers by replacing a standard SETUID program with his or her own code. If this occurs, changing passwords is ineffective; the administrator must restore the system from a known valid source.

One way to detect file alteration is by periodically calculating a checksum. The UNIX **sum** command sums all characters in the input stream. If any character changes, the sum changes. The **-r** option (not available on BSD) produces position dependence. Let's see why this is important.

Suppose we calculate a checksum for the combined **/bin/passwd** and **/bin/csh** files. The commands

```
% cat /bin/passwd /bin/csh | sum -r
05340 134
```

and

```
% cat /bin/csh /bin/passwd | sum -r
57746 134
```

show that the order is important. The first number is the checksum integer, and the second is the block count.

Why is position dependence important? If we include a password along with a file's content, even someone with detailed knowledge of **sum**'s operation cannot make the altered file's checksum the same as the good one's. Since the password is not stored in the system (or in **bd**), it is a good safeguard against tampering. Thus **bd** prompts for a password and uses it in the checksum calculation.

In addition to validating root-owned SETUID files, **bd** also checks a base list. This contains files that are likely targets for intruders. An altered **login** program, for example, might record users' passwords for an intruder to read. Typical files in a base list include **/unix** (the operating system), **/bin/sum** (the checksum program), **/bin/csh** (the C shell), **/bin/sh** (the Bourne shell), and **/etc/login** (the login program).

How do we run **bd**? First, it must always run in superuser mode (**#** prompt), since it must access files and directories that are readable only by **root**. We must run it initially when we know all files are unaltered. We use **bd**'s expanded option to record the checksums for each file. Be sure to print the output on paper and keep it in a safe place. Don't pin it to the bulletin board over your desk.

Let's look at how we run **bd**.

```
# bd
Enter password for checksum generation:
Enter password again, please:
Do you want an expanded checksum listing (y,n): y
```

bd prompts for a password. It won't appear on your terminal. You will be asked to enter the password twice so that **bd** can report a typing error.

bd now locates all **root** SETUID files. It reports how many it found, including the base files.

Next **bd** calculates the checksum and displays the permission, links, owner, group, size, last modification date, and name for each file. Here's part of a typical output:

```
18 base and SETUID files to verify
41520 -rw-r--r-- 1 bin  bin   106350 Oct 11 11:44 /unix
20190 -rwx--x--x 1 bin  bin     6672 Aug 31 1984  /bin/sum
12939 -rwx--x--x 1 bin  bin    52850 Aug 31 1984  /bin/csh
04131 -rwx--x--x 2 bin  bin    29391 Oct 11 11:44 /bin/sh
00036 -rwx------ 1 bin  bin    16678 Aug  3 1984  /etc/login
16629 -rws--x--x 3 root root   10272 Aug 31 1984  /bin/cp
  . . .
Checksum total of all files is -22218
```

The first number on the left is the checksum. The last line is the total checksum for all files. It may be positive or negative.

In unexpanded mode, **bd** provides the overall checksum without the details.

If the checksum has changed, you may have a corrupted file. In this case, rerun **bd** with an expanded listing to compare each file's checksum with its initial value.

Here's the text for **bd**:*

```
       % num bd
   1   # bd: test of selected files and set user id root files.
   2   #
   3   # bd tests for alteration all SETUID files with owner
   4   # as root as well as a selected list of base files.
   5   # This script prompts for a password and must
   6   # be run in superuser mode.
   7   #
   8   # The file list in baselist should contain otherwise
   9   # nonqualified files you want tested.
  10
  11   set baselist = (/unix /bin/sum /bin/csh /bin/sh /etc/login)
  12
  13   # get a password; turn off echoing
  14   onintr tty                          # trap interrupts
```

*This script was written by Marty Gray and is used by permission.

```
15    stty -echo                                    # turn off echo
16    echo -n "Enter password for checksum generation: "
17    set password = `gets`
18    echo ""
19    echo -n "Enter password again, please: "
20    set p2 = `gets`
21    stty echo                                     # turn on echo
22    echo ""
23    onintr                                        # trap no longer needed
24    if ($p2 != $password) then
25        echo2 bd: Mismatched passwords
26        exit 1                                    # error status
27    endif
28
29    # expanded checksum option
30    echo -n "Do you want an expanded checksum listing (y,n): "
31    @ expand = (`gets`  == y)
32
33    # here we get a list of SETUID files with root (0) as owner
34    set sulist = `find / -user 0 -perm -4000 -print`
35
36    # combine lists
37    set list = ($baselist $sulist)
38    echo "$#list base and SETUID files to verify"
39
40    # get checksum for each file in $list prepended by $password
41    set checksum = 0
42    foreach file ($list)
43        set sum = ` echo $password | cat - $file | sum -r`
44        if ($expand) then
45            echo $sum[1] " `ls -l $file`  "
46        endif
47        @ checksum = ($sum[1]  + $checksum)
48    end
49
50    echo "Checksum total of all files is $checksum"
51    exit 0
52
53    tty:                                          # restore tty
54        stty echo                                 # turn on echo
55        echo ""                                   # display carriage return
56        exit 1                                    # nonzero exit
```

Line 11 defines the base list.

Lines 14 through 27 handle the password. Line 14 prepares to trap interrupts. This prevents the terminal from being left in echo-off mode. Line 15 uses **stty** to turn off echoing on the terminal. Line 16 displays the prompt, and line 17 reads a line (use $<

in BSD). Line 18 provides a carriage return (since the **-echo** feature prevented it when you terminated your password entry). Lines 19 through 21 request the password a second time. Lines 24 through 27 compare the two passwords and **exit** if they don't match. Line 23 restores interrupts to the default setting.

Line 30 prompts for the expanded option. Line 31 uses command substitution to read a response and make expand 1 (true) if the input is **y**.

Line 34 uses **find** to locate all files with the SETUID bit on (**-perm -4000**) whose user (owner) is **0** (**root**). Using command substitution, we assign the output of **find** to **sulist**.

Line 37 creates a new wordlist variable by concatenating **$baselist** and **$sulist**. Line 38 reports the number of elements in this list, **$#list**.

Lines 41 through 48 generate the checksums. Line 41 initializes **checksum** to 0. Line 42 uses a **foreach** loop with **$list** to process all filenames. Line 43 combines the password with the target file and pipes the result to **sum** (with the **-r** option). The - option for **cat** reads from the standard input first and concatenates the text with any file arguments. This puts the password in front of the file's contents.

If you requested expanded output, line 45 displays the checksum and the long listing of the file. **$sum[1]** is the checksum, and **ls -l** (using command substitution) produces the listing. Line 47 adds the current file's checksum to the running total (**checksum**). The arithmetic assignment command @ updates **checksum**.

Line 50 prints the total checksum. Line 51 **exits** with 0 (normal) status.

Lines 53 through 56 process interrupts. Line 54 restores the terminal, and line 55 displays a carriage return. Line 56 **exit**s with nonzero status.

11.7 A FRIENDLY USER INTERFACE: SIMPLE MENU PROGRAM (menu)

The script **menu** replaces the C shell with a menu program. **menu** shows how easy it is to modify the UNIX interface. This approach allows people to use a UNIX program without knowing anything about UNIX or the shell.

Since we want UNIX to execute the menu program automatically at login, we put an **exec** statement in the user's **.login** file:

```
exec /usr/accntg/menu
```

exec executes **/usr/accntg/menu** without creating a subshell. The menu script replaces **/bin/csh**. When the user exits, UNIX logs the user out.

Alternatively, the following statements provide the option of running the **menu** script or a C shell. Put them at the end of your **.login** file.

```
# prompt for special menu program for testing
echo -n "Menu? "
if (`gets` == y) then
```

```
        exec /usr/accntg/menu
endif
```

This arrangement can also help you test the **menu** script.

After you've logged in and the shell has executed **.login**, the following menu appears:

	Menu Options

---

a	Accounting Package
g	General Ledger
p	Payroll Package
f	Filer
w	Word Processor
q	Quit Menu

Enter your selection ⟶

The cursor remains at the arrow while the program waits for a response. **menu** reads a single character (no carriage return). The user can type **a**, **g**, **p**, **f**, **w**, or **q** (or the uppercase equivalents). Anything else is reported as an error.

A legal request results in the execution of a package. After the package exits, the **menu** reappears.

This script is like the **menu** program in Chapter 7. The main difference is that this version requires only a single character input.

Here's the text for **menu**:

```
     % num /usr/accntg/menu
 1   # Menu: general menu interface
 2   #
 3   # Usage: menu
 4   #
 5   set com = $0
 6   set screen = /usr/accntg/screen      # text for menu display
 7   set ac = /usr/accntg                 # accnt programs dir
 8
 9   while (1)
10       cat $screen                      # display menu
11       # display prompt
12       echo -n "                           Enter your selection  ⟶   "
13       stty raw                         # put tty in raw mode
14       set answ = `getch`               # read single character
15       stty -raw                        # return tty to normal
16       echo ""
17       echo ""
18       echo ""
```

```
19          switch ($answ)                          # look at character
20                  case [aA]:
21                      $ac/accntg                  # accounting package
22                      breaksw
23                  case [gG]:
24                      $ac/genledg                 # general ledger package
25                      breaksw
26                  case [fF]:
27                      $ac/filer                   # filer
28                      breaksw
29                  case [pP]:
30                      $ac/payroll                 # payroll package
31                      breaksw
32                  case [wW]:
33                      $ac/wordpro                 # word processor
34                      breaksw
35                  case [qQ]:                      # exit menu
36                      exit 0
37                      breaksw
38                  default:
39                      echo2 $com:t\: No program for $answ
40                      breaksw
41          endsw
42      end
```

Line 5 saves the command name in **com** for error messages. Line 6 defines the filename containing the screen display. We place it in a separate file (**/usr/accntg/screen**) rather than in the script itself. This lets us change the menu by modifying just the screen file.

Line 7 sets **ac** to the accounting directory.

Line 9 uses an "infinite" **while** loop to display the menu. This lets us redisplay the screen after running a program. Line 36 exits the loop if we type **q**.

Line 12 displays the input prompt. We put it in **menu** rather than in the screen file so that we can easily control the placement of the cursor. **echo** with **-n** places the cursor just right of the arrow. At this point **menu** is waiting for a single character input.

How does **menu** handle a single character? Normally, UNIX buffers terminal input. A read command (such as **gets** or **$<**) does not terminate until we type a carriage return. To return a single character we must use a C program such as **getch.c** (see Appendix D). We must also tell UNIX not to buffer input while this program runs.

getch reads a character from standard input and writes it to standard output. Line 14 calls it from the shell using command substitution.

How do we tell UNIX to allow a single character read? Terminals are normally in "cooked" mode (the opposite of "raw," of course). Raw mode prevents processing by the terminal interface driver; that is, nothing special happens for such keys as RETURN, interrupt, and BACKSPACE. Line 13 uses **stty** (set terminal) to enter raw mode to read the single character (line 14). Line 15 restores buffered input.

Lines 16 through 18 display three blank lines.

Lines 19 through 41 use a **switch** statement to process the input. We allow characters to be uppercase or lowercase letters by using pattern matching in each **case** statement. A **q** or **Q** causes an **exit** at line 36. The default label (line 38) checks for improper input. The **breaksw** in line 37 is not necessary; it's included for completeness.

What happens if we interrupt **menu**? Normally, pressing the interrupt key terminates a script. However, here the terminal is in raw mode, so the interrupt key is treated like any other character. The shell transfers control to the default-label response, and **menu** prints the error message in line 39.

11.8 THE SEARCH IS ON: PATTERN SEARCHING MADE EASY (search)

This section presents an example script written to do a specific job. Though we may use it many times, we would probably not install it in a public tools directory. Knowing this allows us to accept some rigidity in the script in exchange for making it faster or easier to use.

search locates patterns in a large group of files. It returns the pattern name followed by all filenames and line numbers containing the pattern. It's handy for cross-referencing words in a group of files.

Suppose we are involved in a large software project that includes many C source files. Frequently, we must list all occurrences of a variable name. Perhaps we need to know where it's defined or how it's referenced. Here's how we would run **search** to find the variables **pnum** and **error**:

```
% search pnum error
pnum
inventory/add.c:37:        pnum = error[5];
inventory/scan.c:18:        char *pnum;

error
inventory/add.c:37:        pnum = error[5];
inventory/change.c:6:       char *error[NERR];
```

search tells us that **scan.c** declares **pnum** in line 18 and **add.c** references it in line 37. Similarly, **change.c** declares **error** in line 6 and **add.c** uses it in line 37. All files are in directory **inventory**.

You may also use other types of patterns with **search**. Suppose you want to know which files declare a function **calc**. You use **search** as follows:

```
% search "float calc"
float calc
agents/headr1.h:12:        float calc();
agents/screen.c:86:        float calc(n)
```

search reports that the header file **agents/headr1.h** declares the function in line 12; the function code starts at line 86 of **agents/screen.c**. We use double quotation marks to preserve the space in the pattern.

search lets us specify many patterns at once. Since it is intended for a particular project, we don't have it require a list of files to search. Instead we create a file called **pgm.files** in the current directory. It contains all pertinent filenames. Here's a sample list:

```
% cat pgm.files
agents/headr1.h
agents/headr2.h
agents/*.c
inventory/header.h
inventory/screens.c
report/screen?.c
```

Note that the list contains **.c** and **.h** files as well as filenames using file expansion characters (**?**, *****). The files can be in different directories. We can change the list at any time.

Here's the text for **search**:

```
      % num search
 1    # search:  searches for patterns in requested files.
 2    #          Assumes a file called pgm.files in the current
 3    #          directory. Uses grep to look for specified
 4    #          patterns in each file. Reports filename and
 5    #          line number where pattern is found.
 6    # Usage:  search pattern(s)
 7
 8    set com = $0
 9    if ($#argv == 0) then            # must have at least 1 argument
10        echo2 "Usage: $com:t pattern(s)"
11        exit 1
12    endif
13
14    set flist = `cat pgm.files`      # get list of files
15
16    foreach pattern ($argv[*]:q)     # loop over patterns
17        echo ""                      # extra line for readability
18        echo "$pattern"              # display pattern (quote it)
19        grep -n "$pattern" $flist    # search all files for pattern
20    end
```

Lines 8 through 12 ensure the existence of at least one argument. Line 14 uses command substitution to generate the list of files, and we store it in a wordlist variable (**flist**). Lines 16 through 20 are a **foreach** loop based on the argument list. Each time through the loop, we assign the next argument to variable **pattern**. We use **:q** to quote the wordlist and double quotation marks to quote **pattern**. This prevents file expansion and allows other special characters in the pattern (spaces, redirection symbols, etc.).

Line 19 uses **grep** with the **-n** option for the search. This reports the filename, line number, and text containing the pattern.

11.9 KEEPING IT TOGETHER: WHICH COMMAND DO I GET ANYWAY? (which)

One reason for the C shell's popularity is that it allows customization. For example, we can hide discrepancies in versions of UNIX or the C shell by creating aliases and using C shell variables to mimic the missing features. Consider the differences between the C shell in Berkeley version 4.2BSD and in XENIX.

XENIX lacks the predefined variables **$user** and **$cwd**. It calls the Berkeley **ls** program **/bin/lc** and uses **/bin/ls** to refer to the AT&T version. XENIX's built-in **echo** command uses \c to prevent a carriage return, whereas Berkeley's **echo** uses **-n**. XENIX also lacks the built-in commands **pushd**, **popd**, and **dirs**.

How can we overcome these inconsistencies? We create a shell variable **$user** to be the same as **$LOGNAME**. We define an alias for **cd**, which keeps **$cwd** current. We alias the **ls** command to **/bin/lc** to get our favorite **ls** program. We create an alias for **echo** to call the program **/bin/echo**. Now we can use **-n** for compatibility, although we are sacrificing performance (the built-in **echo** executes faster than **/bin/echo**). Finally, we create aliases and scripts for **pushd**, **popd**, and **dirs** (see Section 11.10).

However, all this customization can produce confusion. Which command is the system executing anyway? If we have many aliases or private versions of standard commands in our tools directory, we may want to know which ones are active (particularly after a vacation or a long project wrap-up). We must remember that the C shell searches the **$path** directories *in order*—the first **ls**, **who**, or **cc** command it finds is the one we get. The more command customization we do, the more likely we are to get confused between a standard command and a custom alternative.

Of course, we can always obtain the answer manually. We first check our list of aliases for the command. Next we check each directory in our **path** variable (in order). The first executable file we find is the one the C shell executes. This is a tedious process.

The shell script **which** helps with this problem. It tells us which command we have and whether it's an alias, a command in our local directory, or somewhere else. Let's look at some examples.

```
% which echo tutor2 ls
/bin/echo
./tutor2
/bin/lc
```

echo is the program **/bin/echo**, and **tutor2** is a file in our local directory. When we type **ls**, we are running the **/bin/lc** program.

Let's look at **cd** and **pwd**:

```
% which cd
cd: aliased to cd !*; set cwd = `/bin/pwd`;setenv CWD $cwd
% which pwd
pwd: aliased to echo $cwd
```

which reports their alias definitions.

which cannot detect built-in commands; for example,

```
% which history set
no history in /bin /usr/bin /usr/local /usr/sara/bin .
no set in /bin /usr/bin  /usr/local /usr/sara/bin .
```

which reports the same thing for nonexistent commands.

which is also useful for reporting the active command during system modification. Suppose we are modifying our **loc** script. We copy it from **/usr/local** to our own working directory:

```
% cp /usr/local/loc .
```

We modify and test it. Our modifications, however, don't work. **which** tells us whether we are running the old version or the new one.

```
% which loc
/usr/local/loc
```

Though we thought we were running the new version of **loc** in our current directory, we're still running the old one. This is because **/usr/local** appears before **.** in our **$path** variable. To test the local copy, we specify the directory name:

```
% ./loc testfile
```

Here's the text for **which**:*

```
      % num which
   1  #
   2  #
   3  #      @(#)which.csh     4.2     (Berkeley)           83/02/14
```

*This script was written by Peter Kessler and is used by permission of the Regents of the University of California.

```
 4    #
 5    #       which : tells you which program you get
 6    #
 7    set noglob
 8    foreach arg ( $argv )
 9        set alius = `alias $arg`           # get the alias, if any
10        switch ( $#alius )                 # how many words?
11          case 0 :                         # none -- no alias
12              breaksw
13          case 1 :                         # one word in alias
14              set arg = $alius[1]
15              breaksw
16          default :                        # more than one word
17              echo ${arg}: "               " aliased to $alius
18              continue                     # get next command
19        endsw
20        unset found                        # reset found
21        if ( $arg:h != $arg:t ) then       # qualifying path?
22            if ( -e $arg ) then
23                echo $arg                  # file exists
24            else
25                echo $arg not found        # file doesn't exist
26            endif
27            continue                       # get next command
28        else                               # no qualifying path
29            foreach i ($path )             # check each path dir
30                if ( -x $i/$arg && ! -d $i/$arg ) then
31                    echo $i/$arg           # found it! display
32                    set found
33                    break                  # get out of foreach
34                endif
35            end
36        endif
37        if ( ! $?found ) then              # did we find it?
38            echo no $arg in $path          # no: report failure
39        endif
40    end
```

Line 7 sets **noglob** to prevent file expansion. The rest of the script consists of a **foreach** loop. Inside it we check whether the command has an alias and whether it exists.

Line 9 sets variable **alius** to the command's alias. There are three possibilities:

1. No alias exists and **$#alius** is 0 (lines 11 and 12).
2. The alias consists of a single word (another command). In this case we save the expanded alias instead of the original command word (lines 13 through 15) because we're going to look this up in the **path** variable.

3. The alias consists of more than one word. In this case we simply display the text and get the next command word (lines 16 through 18).

Line 21 uses the **:h** and **:t** modifiers to check if the command has a qualifying pathname (a directory header). If so, line 22 makes sure it exists and displays its pathname; otherwise, line 25 reports an error.

If the command does not have a qualifying path, we must search each directory in **$path** until we find the file. Line 29 sets up a **foreach** loop for this. Line 30 makes sure that the file is executable and that it is not a directory (using the **-x** and **-d** file inquiry operators). If the expression in line 30 is true, we display the full pathname, set variable **found**, and use **break** to exit the inner **foreach** loop (lines 31 through 33). If we don't find the file in any path directory, **found** remains undefined. This makes the **if** statement in line 37 print the diagnostic message in line 38.

A few notes about **which**: This script can be implemented only in the C shell, since it examines the alias list. Furthermore, it cannot be run with a fast startup (i.e., **csh -f**). Recall that the **-f** option prevents the C shell from reading the ~/.**cshrc** file. Hence, none of the aliases are defined. Also, **which** does not report aliases defined in the current shell (ones that are not in the ~/.**cshrc** file) or follow changes in the **path** variable.

11.10 ALL IT'S STACKED UP TO BE: DIRECTORY STACKS (pushd, popd, dirs)

Using the C shell often requires switching among several directories. You may be developing software or solving system problems that use files in different directories. Instead of typing their names with **cd** each time, you'd like a way to store them and recall them whenever you want.

This section shows you how to keep track of multiple directories using a *stack* (a structure whose most recently entered item is at the top). The C shell has three built-in commands for maintaining a directory stack: **pushd**, **popd**, and **dirs**. We use these in place of **cd** for changing directories. Once we "push" frequently visited directories on the stack, we can switch among them easily. It is especially easy to travel between two directories (**pushd** with no arguments) or to go to the *n*th directory on the stack (**pushd +n**). We use **popd** with no arguments to remove the top directory or **popd +n** to remove the *n*th directory. **dirs** simply displays the directory stack.

Unfortunately, only BSD versions of the C shell have this mechanism. This section shows how to use these commands and how to implement them using aliases and C shell scripts. You can then include them in your C shell environment if you're running on a non-BSD system.

Suppose we frequently work in directories **proj1**, **proj1/test**, and **proj1/doc** all under our home directory. We sign on and change to directory **proj1** using **pushd**:

```
% pushd proj1
/u/sara/proj1 /u/sara
```

pushd pushes **proj1** and displays the current directory stack. We see two directories on the stack: **/u/sara/proj1** is at the top (the leftmost position), followed by the home directory, **/u/sara**.

After doing some work here, we change to subdirectory **test**. Again, we use **pushd**:

```
% pushd test
/u/sara/proj1/test /u/sara/proj1 /u/sara
```

Now **test** is at the top, followed by **proj1** and the home directory.

When its time to work in subdirectory **doc**, we give the following command:

```
% pushd ../doc
/u/sara/proj1/doc  /u/sara/proj1/test /u/sara/proj1 /u/sara
```

(We use **../doc** since both **doc** and **test** are subdirectories of the same parent, **proj1**.) Our directory stack now contains four entries; **/u/sara/proj1/doc** is at the top. If we need to return to **test**, we type

```
% pushd
/u/sara/proj1/test /u/sara/proj1/doc /u/sara/proj1 /u/sara
```

This changes to directory **test** and switches the top two entries of the stack. Similarly, we can return to **doc** with the same command:

```
% pushd
/u/sara/proj1/doc  /u/sara/proj1/test /u/sara/proj1 /u/sara
```

What if we want to change to directory **proj1**? We have two choices. We can either "rotate" the stack so that **proj1** is at the top, or we can "pop" the stack. We use the first method when we want to keep **doc** and **test** on the stack:

```
% pushd +2
/u/sara/proj1 /u/sara  /u/sara/proj1/doc /u/sara/proj1/test
```

The C shell starts counting stack entries at 0; thus we refer to **proj1** with **+2** (you must include the **+**). **pushd** places **proj1** at the top, rotating the other directories to maintain their order.

We use the second method when we no longer need to reference **doc** and **test**. Let's use **pushd +2** to return to the previous state and then pop the stack twice:

```
% pushd +2
/u/sara/proj1/doc  /u/sara/proj1/test /u/sara/proj1 /u/sara
% popd
/u/sara/proj1/test /u/sara/proj1 /u/sara
% popd
/u/sara/proj1 /u/sara
```

Each time **popd** removes the top directory and changes to the next one in line.

We can also remove a directory that's not at the top. Suppose we're in directory **doc** and the stack is as follows:

```
% dirs
/u/sara/proj1/doc /u/sara/proj1/test /u/sara/proj1 /u/sara
```

To remove directory **test** from the stack, we use **popd +1** (remember to start at 0):

```
% popd +1
/u/sara/proj1/doc  /u/sara/proj1 /u/sara
```

Now the stack contains three entries and we remain in directory **doc**. This is useful for removing nonexistent directories (ones that were deleted from the file system but still remain on the stack).

If we enter a new shell by executing a shell script or the **csh** command, the directory stack starts over, with the current directory as the sole entry on the stack. When we return to our login shell, the stack is as it was.

To implement these three commands, we need to consider the following requirements:

1. The commands must run in the current shell since we will be changing the working directory.
2. **pushd** and **popd** are too complicated to implement as aliases; we must use scripts.
3. We must be able to pass arguments to **pushd** and **popd** from our current shell.

Recall, we use **source** to execute a script in the current environment. We define aliases, then, for **pushd** and **popd** that call scripts with **source**. However, we cannot pass arguments to a "sourced" script. But we can use the alias mechanism to save the arguments to the alias in a variable. Since the shell executes our script directly, it will recognize any variables we define. Let's look at the aliases for **pushd** and **popd** (these go in our ~/.**cshrc** file):

```
alias pushd 'set args = (\!*); source /usr/local/pushd'
alias popd 'set args = (\!*); source /usr/local/popd'
```

We define a wordlist (**args**) to contain the alias's arguments. We then call the scripts with **source**. We now reference the script's argument list with **args** instead of **argv**. We store the scripts in /**usr**/**local** for public access.

The scripts depend on additional initializations. The following **cd** alias maintains a shell variable **cwd**, an environment variable **CWD**, and the top directory stack entry, **dstack[1]**. (If your C shell lacks **pushd** and **popd**, it also lacks the predefined variable **cwd**.) The **chdir** alias is the same, except that it does not manipulate **dstack**. (The C shell built-in command **chdir** is just an alternate name for **cd**.) We put the following aliases in our ~/.**cshrc** file (being sure to put alias **cd** on one line):

```
alias cd 'cd \!*; set cwd = `/bin/pwd`;set dstack[1] = $cwd;
                setenv CWD $cwd'
alias chdir 'chdir \!*; set cwd = `/bin/pwd`; setenv CWD $cwd'
```

With these aliases we can still use **cd** to change directories. **cd** replaces the top stack entry with the new directory name. For example, here we use **cd** to change to the parent directory:

```
% dirs
/usr/sys/source /usr/include /u/sara
% cd ..
% dirs
/usr/sys /usr/include /u/sara
```

Scripts **pushd** and **popd** call **chdir** instead of **cd** to change directories. This avoids **cd**'s manipulation of **dstack**.

We must also define **cwd**, the directory stack wordlist, and the alias to display it (also in our ~/.**cshrc** file):

```
set cwd = $CWD
set dstack = ($CWD)
alias dirs 'echo $dstack'
```

The **CWD** environment variable saves the current working directory for new shells. It must be initialized to ~ (the home directory) in the systemwide C shell startup file (/**etc**/ **cshrc** is a typical name). We initialize **dstack** to the current working directory. When we log in, **dstack** contains the home directory. The **dirs** alias simply echoes the **dstack** wordlist.

Let's examine the scripts **pushd** and **popd** now. We implement the following forms:

pushd directory	Push **directory** on stack.
pushd +n	Rotate **n**th entry to top.
pushd	Switch top two entries.
popd +n	Remove **n**th entry from stack.
popd	Remove top entry.

Both **pushd** and **popd** allow one or no arguments only. The scripts use **chdir** to check the validity of the directory. That is, if the directory doesn't exist or the permission is bad, **chdir** will display an error message and terminate the script. We therefore always attempt the **chdir** command before modifying the stack variable.

Here's the text for **pushd**:

```
  % num pushd
1   # pushd - push directory on stack
2   #
```

```
 3    # pushd                                exchange first 2 dirs
 4    # pushd name                           push name on stack
 5    # pushd +n                             rotate stack n times
 6    #
 7    # Note: this script must be called via an alias using source
 8    #       it assumes aliases for cd, chdir, pushd, popd, dirs
 9
10    switch ($#args)
11       case 0:                       # no arguments
12          if ($#dstack < 2) then     # check stacksize
13             echo "pushd: No other directory."
14             exit 1
15          endif
16          chdir $dstack[2]           # change directory
17
18          set temp = $dstack[2]      # exchange first 2
19          set dstack[2] = $dstack[1]
20          set dstack[1] = $temp
21
22          echo $dstack               # display stack
23          breaksw
24       case 1:                       # 1 argument
25          switch ($args[1])
26             case +[1-9]:            # only allow +1 through +9
27                                     # get number in usable form
28                @ n = 1
29                set notfound
30                while ($?notfound)
31                   switch ($args[1])
32                      case +$n:
33                         unset notfound
34                         breaksw
35                      default:
36                         @ n++
37                   endsw
38                end
39                @ n++
40                if ($n > $#dstack) then   # check stacksize
41                echo "pushd: Directory stack not that deep."
42                   exit 1
43                endif
44
45                chdir $dstack[$n]                # change directory
46                while ($n > 1)                   # rotate
47                   set temp = $dstack[1]         # stack n
48                   shift dstack                  # times
49                   set dstack = ($dstack $temp)
50                   @ n--
51                end
```

```
52                    echo $dstack                    # display stack
53                    breaksw
54               default:
55                    chdir $args[1]
56                    set dstack = ($cwd $dstack)   # push name
57                    echo $dstack                    # display stack
58               endsw
59               breaksw
60          default:                                  # more than 1 argument
61               echo "pushd: Too many arguments."
62               exit 1
63     endsw
```

Lines 10 through 63 contain a **switch** statement on the number of arguments. We check for 0 (line 11), 1 (line 24), and anything else (line 60). **pushd** with no arguments attempts to exchange the top two entries. Lines 12 through 15 make sure there's at least two entries in **dstack**. Line 16 changes directory to the second entry (**$dstack[1]** is the top, or first, entry). If **chdir** is successful, lines 18 through 20 exchange the stack. Line 22 displays the stack. We then exit the script (by falling through the rest of the code).

If there is one argument, we use a **switch** statement to determine whether the argument is of the form **+n** (line 26) or a directory name (line 54). We limit the **+n** form to **+1** through **+9**. If the argument is numeric, we must discard the **+** in order to use its value in an arithmetic statement. We use a **switch** statement (line 31) within a **while** statement to count the number of times it takes to match the number. After incrementing **n** (line 39), it refers to the **dstack** entry that is to be at the top. (*Note:* Although this loop lacks elegance, it is preferable to using the UNIX utility **expr** to extract the number. Since **expr** is not a built-in command, it is too slow to use here. Most of the time we will have no more than three or four directories on the stack anyway.)

Lines 40 through 43 make sure that **dstack** contains at least that many entries. Line 45 changes to the **n**th directory. Lines 46 through 51 rotate **dstack** **n** − 1 times using the **shift** command and placing the first entry at the end each time. Line 52 displays the modified stack.

Lines 55 through 57 push a named directory on the stack. We change directories to the new entry and use **$cwd** to place it on the directory stack. We don't use **$args[1]** because this might contain a relative pathname. All directory entries in **dstack** must have absolute pathnames because we need to reference them from any directory.

Here's the text for **popd**:

```
    % num popd
    1  # popd - pop directory from stack
    2  #
    3  # popd                    pop top directory
```

```
 4  # popd +n                        pop nth directory
 5  #
 6  # Note: this script must be called via an alias using source
 7  #       it assumes aliases for cd, chdir, popd, pushd, dirs
 8
 9  switch ($#args)
10     case 0:                                # no arguments
11        if ($#dstack <= 1) then             # check stacksize
12           echo "popd: Directory stack empty."
13           exit 1
14        endif
15        chdir $dstack[2]                     # change directory
16        shift dstack                         # pop stack
17        echo $dstack                         # display stack
18        breaksw
19     case 1:                                 # 1 argument
20        switch ($args[1])
21           case +[1-9]:                      # only allow +1 through +9
22                                             # get number in usable form
23              @ n = 1
24              set notfound
25              while ($?notfound)
26                 switch ($args[1])
27                    case +$n:
28                       unset notfound
29                       breaksw
30                    default:
31                       @ n++
32                 endsw
33              end
34              @ n++
35              if ($n > $#dstack) then        # check stacksize
36              echo "popd: Directory stack not that deep."
37           exit 1
38              endif
39
40              while ($n < $#dstack)          # pop the nth entry
41                 @ next = $n + 1
42                 set dstack[$n] = $dstack[$next]
43                 @ n++
44              end
45              @ n--
46              set dstack = ($dstack[1-$n])
47
48              echo $dstack                   # display stack
49              breaksw
50           default:
51              echo "popd: Bad directory."
52              exit 1
```

```
53              endsw
54              breaksw
55         default:                                    # more than 1 argument
56              echo "popd: Too many arguments."
57              exit 1
58    endsw
```

The structure of **popd** is similar to that of **pushd**. Again, we use a **switch** statement to check the number of arguments. No arguments (lines 11 through 18) requests removal of the top entry. Lines 11 through 14 make sure there are at least two entries. Line 15 changes to the new directory, and line 16 executes **shift** to discard the top. Line 17 displays the new stack.

If there is one argument (line 19), it must be of the form **+n**. As with **pushd**, we allow only **+1** through **+9** and use the same code to extract the number from the argument (lines 23 through 34). (For the same reason, we refrain from using **expr**.) Lines 35 through 38 make sure **dstack** has enough entries. Lines 40 through 45 pop the entry.

The default label (lines 50 through 52) means the argument was not in the correct form (**+n**).

These scripts emulate the Berkeley built-in commands, with two exceptions:

1. We allow only **+1** through **+9** for the **+n** argument form.
2. We display the full pathname for the home directory instead of ~.

In addition, you may want to include the following aliases to save on typing:

```
alias pd pushd
alias pd2 'pd +2'
alias pd3 'pd +3'
alias pd4 'pd +4'
```

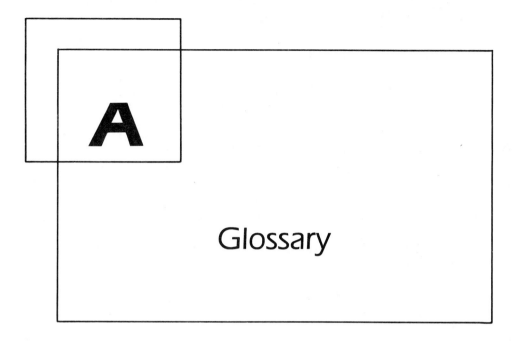

Glossary

. (dot)   the name of the current directory

.. (dot-dot)   the name of the parent directory

absolute pathname   a pathname that starts at the root (with /)

alias   the C shell mechanism that substitutes a command line for a single word. A command line may consist of one or more words.

argument list   the list of words from the command line that the C shell passes to a command

background job   a job that the shell does not wait for. It usually runs independent of user interaction and terminal input/output.

bit bucket   the file **/dev/null.** Characters written here are "thrown away."

built-in command   a command whose code is internal to the C shell; the C shell does not execute an external program.

child process   the process created when a program (the parent) executes the **fork** system routine

command group   one or more commands executed within a subshell

command substitution   substituting the output of a command for the command itself

current directory   the directory to which all relative pathnames refer. Simple filenames (i.e., with no pathname header) refer to the current directory by default.

debugging   correcting errors in a program or procedure

detached (job state)   continuing to run after the user logs out

diagnostic (error) output   output written to file descriptor 2. A command's error messages are usually written to the diagnostic output.

directory   a UNIX file that contains names of other files or directories. A directory is an intermediate node in the file system.

directory stack   a data structure that stores each current directory a user enters, keeping the most recent one on top. **pushd** and **popd** use a directory stack.

done (job state)   finished normally

environment   the set of characteristics describing a user's UNIX work area. The characteristics include the open files, the user and group identification, the process identification, and environment variables.

environment variable   a variable that is exported automatically to subsequent programs. Environment variables are defined with the **setenv** command.

EOF   the character indicating the end of a file. From the keyboard, this is usually **control-D.**

escaping   removing the special meaning from a character or string; also called *quoting*

event   past command stored in the history list

exit status   See *status*.

export   to pass the value of a variable to another program. UNIX exports the environment variables.

extension (variable modifier)   the part after the **.** in a pathname

file   a stream of bytes stored under a unique pathname

file and device independence   using filenames and device names in commands equivalently; e.g., **who > out** and **who > /dev/lp.**

file descriptor   the number UNIX assigns to an open file

filename   a set of characters that refer to a file. Any characters are legal, but it is best to choose from the alphanumeric character set, dot, and underscore. 4BSD filenames may contain up to 255 characters; all other versions are limited to 14.

filename expansion   matching filenames in the specified directory according to the following rules, * matches any character sequence including null, **?** matches any single character, **[ ]** delimit a set of characters, **[n-m]** matches the range of characters **n** through **m** inclusive, ~ matches the home directory, and { } delimit different parts in a common pathname.

filter   a program that reads data from the standard input, processes it, and writes it to the standard output. Filters are typically used in pipe constructions.

flag   a program option, typically indicated with a single letter preceded with a -

foreground job   a job that must be completed or interrupted before the shell will accept more commands

fork   the system routine that creates a new process by duplicating the calling (parent) process

full job control   the set of job control features available in 4BSD and later. These include suspending and restarting foreground and background jobs, the **jobs** and **notify** commands, and enhanced terminal control for background jobs.

group ID   a numeric identification designating the group to which a user belongs. The number corresponds to an entry in the **/etc/group** file.

header (variable modifier)   the directory containing the filename

here document   in-line input in a shell script redirected to another command

history list   storage place for past commands

home directory   the user's default working directory (specified in the **/etc/passwd** file)

input   data read by a command

interrupt   a signal, typically generated at the keyboard. It causes the currently executing process to terminate unless special action was taken by the process to handle the signal.

interrupt handler a set of statements that is executed upon receipt of an interrupt

inverted tree structure the hierarchical structure of the UNIX file system: The root is the single node at the top; subdirectories are intermediate branches, and files are terminal branches, or leaves.

job a command line. It may consist of one or more processes and may execute in the foreground or in the background.

job number on systems with full job control, the number that uniquely identifies a job within a C shell session

job states See *suspended, terminated, done, detached.*

link an entry in a directory (i.e., a filename) that points to an existing file. Hard links may not point across file systems. Symbolic links (4BSD only) may.

lock file a file whose existence prevents some function (e.g., access to a common database, printing device, or other shared facility)

metacharacter a character with a special meaning (e.g., > denotes output redirection in the C shell)

modifier See *variable modifier.*

node a branch in the UNIX file system. Nodes may be intermediate (and thus themselves contain nodes; these are always directories) or terminal (these are files).

output data produced by a program

overlay to replace a process with another process. The environment of the process remains intact, but the instructions and local data are replaced.

parent directory the directory above the current directory; the directory one level closer to the root

parent process the originator of the **fork** call that caused the creation of a process

parsing order the order in which the C shell evaluates a command line and instigates any special mechanisms (history, alias, etc.)

password a special code word known only by the user that allows the user to login to UNIX. A user's password is stored in encrypted form in the **/etc/passwd** file.

pathname   the names of all the directories that must be traversed to reach a given destination (file or directory)

pathname qualifier   See *variable modifier*.

pipe   a connection that allows one program to get its input directly from the output of another program

predefined variable   a shell variable defined and maintained by the C shell. These variables may be used in shell scripts and commands.

prepend   to append to the front

process   a program that is being executed or is waiting to be executed

process ID   an integer that uniquely identifies a process within the system

quoting   See *escaping*.

range checking   checking whether a value is between specified upper and lower bounds

recursion   defined in terms of itself; calling a procedure within itself.

redirection   designating the source or destination of input or output to be a named file or device

redo   repeating the latest command

relative pathname   a pathname within the current directory (e.g., **../src** or **doc/intro**)

remembered pattern   a string of characters derived from a previous command

root   the initial single node of the file system hierarchy

root (variable modifier)   the full pathname except the final **.** (dot) and extension

script   a shell procedure or program

search path   the ordered list of directories (stored in **$path**) that the C shell searches to find commands

shell   the command interpreter for UNIX

shell variable   an identifier that can hold one or more strings of characters

signal   an interprocess communication device that by default causes the receiving process to terminate

standard error   See *diagnostic output*.

standard input   file descriptor 0. This is usually the default input for a program.

standard output   file descriptor 1. This is usually the default output from a program (excluding error messages).

status   the state in which a program exits. By convention, 0 indicates a successful exit, nonzero indicates an error.

subdirectory   a directory that exists within another directory; any directory other than the root

subshell   the shell process created when the shell executes the **fork** system call. All local data are preserved.

suspend   to stop a foreground job (with **control-Z**) or a background job (using **stop**) temporarily.

suspended (job state)   temporarily stopped (execution may resume)

system routines   the set of procedures resident in the UNIX operating system callable by the user

tail (variable modifier)   the final filename only (no directory specifiers)

terminated (job state)   permanently stopped

user ID   the number associated with each username. This number is stored in the **/etc/passwd** file.

variable expansion   replacing the variable identifier with its associated string or strings in a shell command line

variable modifier   symbol referring to part of a variable, usually under the assumption that its value is a pathname. See also *root, tail, extension, header*.

word   a string separated by blanks, tabs, or C shell special characters >, <, |, **&, ;,**), (

wordlist variable　a C shell variable consisting of more than one word. In the assignment statement, the list of words must be put in parentheses.

working directory　See *current directory*.

B

Predefined C Shell Variables

This appendix describes the C shell's predefined variables. We use the notation **set/unset** for variables that are set and unset only (ones that have no set value). Refer to Section 9.2 for examples. In addition, we implement the following notation to distinguish differences in the versions:

    *BSD versions only
    **non-BSD versions

argv   argument vector
    Wordlist variable containing the argument list passed to shell scripts. Contains the empty string ( ) by default.

cdpath   change directory path
    Wordlist variable containing the full pathnames of alternate directories to search for arguments to **cd** (and **pushd** and **popd**). Unset by default.

**child   child process
    Contains the process ID of the most recently invoked background process. When the process terminates, variable **child** is undefined. Unset by default.

*cwd   current working directory
    Contains the full pathname of the current working directory.

echo   echo mode (set/unset)

When set, each command is displayed just before execution. Commands reflect history, alias, command, filename, and variable substitutions. Unset by default. May enable in a script with the **csh -x** option.

histchars   history substitution characters

Contains the two history substitution characters. If unset, these characters are ! ˆ .

history   history list size

Contains the number of past commands the shell will store in the history list. Unset by default.

home   home directory

Contains the full pathname of the user's home directory. This variable is initialized by the C shell from the environment variable **HOME.**

ignoreeof   ignore end-of-file character (set/unset)

When set, the shell will not terminate by reading an end-of-file character from the keyboard (i.e., **control-D**). To logout, use the **logout** command. To exit a child shell, use the **exit** command. Unset by default.

mail   mail file

Wordlist or single variable containing the pathnames where the C shell checks for mail. If the first word is numeric, the shell checks for mail in that many seconds. The default interval is 10 minutes. If the mail variable contains more than one mail file, the mail message is "New mail in **file_name**"; otherwise the message is "You have new mail." Unset by default, and the shell uses mail file **/usr/spool/mail/**$USER (or $LOGNAME).

noclobber   don't clobber files (set/unset)

When set, the shell prevents redirection commands from overwriting an existing file. It also prevents append commands from creating a file. Use **!** to override the **noclobber** option on a single command. Unset by default.

noglob   don't allow file expansion (set/unset)

When set, filename expansion is inhibited. Unset by default.

nonomatch   no error on nonmatching file expansion characters (set/unset)

When set, a command containing file expansion characters that do not match any files does not produce an error. If no files match, the command is invoked with the characters unexpanded. When unset, the shell reports an error and does not invoke the command. Unset by default.

*notify   notify of job completions (set/unset)
> When set, the shell notifies users of job completions asynchronously. When unset, notification is just before the prompt. Unset by default.

path   command path list
> Wordlist variable containing the pathnames the shell should search to find commands. The C shell sets path to (**. /bin /usr/bin**) by default. The C shell maintains **path** and the environment variable **PATH** together.

prompt   C shell prompt
> Contains the C shell prompt string. Default value is **'% '**. Use the history command character **!** to include the event number (i.e., **set prompt = '\!% '**).

*savehist   save commands in history list
> Contains the number of commands the shell should save upon logout. The shell places these commands back into the active history list automatically at login without executing them. The commands are stored in file ~/**.history.** Unset by default.

shell   default shell file
> Contains the full pathname of the default shell. The shell invokes this program to execute shell scripts. Default value is **/bin/csh.**

status   last command status
> Contains the completion status of the last invoked command. Built-in commands return 0 if successful and 1 if unsuccessful.

*term   terminal ID
> Contains the name of the terminal type. Initialized by default to the value in file **/etc/ttytype** corresponding to the **tty** line.

time   automatic timing control
> Contains the maximum number of seconds in CPU time the shell allows a command to consume without reporting usage statistics. Unset by default.

*user   user's name
> Contains the user's login name. The shell initializes it from the environment variable **USER** (or **LOGNAME**).

verbose   verbose mode (set/unset)
> When set, the shell displays the command after history substitutions but before alias, command, filename, and variable substitutions. May be invoked in shell scripts with the **csh -v** option. Unset by default.

C

Built-in C Shell Commands

This appendix describes the C shell's built-in commands. The C shell executes these commands in the current shell. We only include commands that are used interactively. Refer to your C shell documentation for a complete list. We use the following notation to indicate differences in versions:

*BSD version only
**non-BSD versions

alias	Displays the list of currently defined aliases and their meanings.
alias name	Displays the definition of alias **name.**
alias name wordlist	Defines **alias name** to be **wordlist.** Use history commands to pass arguments (e.g., **!*** is all the arguments and **!ˆ** is the first argument).
*bg	Executes the current job in the background.
*bg %job	Executes the job specified by **%job** in the background.
cd	With no argument, changes directory to the user's
cd name	home directory. Otherwise, changes directory to
chdir	**name. chdir** is equivalent to **cd.**
chdir name	

*dirs	Displays the directory stack.
echo wordlist	Displays its arguments using history, variable, and
*echo -n wordlist	filename expansion. With **-n**, prevents the carriage
**echo wordlist \c	return. In other versions, **\c** in the argument list prevents the carriage return.
*eval arg . . .	Reads the argument list and executes the arguments in the current shell. This allows the generation of commands using variable or filename expansion; normally parsing occurs before this expansion.
exec command	Executes **command** without **fork**ing a new shell. UNIX overlays current shell with the command.
exit	The current shell terminates. The shell returns **expr**
exit (expr)	as **exit** status to the parent shell.
*fg	Executes the current job in the foreground.
*fg %job	Executes the job specified by **%job** in the foreground.
foreach name (wordlist)	Sets variable **name** to each value in **wordlist** and
. . .	executes the commands between the **foreach** and
end	matching **end** statement using this value of **name.**
glob wordlist	Displays **wordlist** using history, variable, and filename expansion. Puts a null character between words and does not include a carriage return at the end.
*hashstat	Displays statistics indicating how successful the hash table has been at locating commands.
history	Displays the history list.
*history n	Displays the last **n** lines of the history list.
*history -r n	Displays the last **n** lines of the history list in reverse order.
*history -h n	Displays the last **n** lines of the history list, leaving off the event numbers.
*jobs	Lists the active jobs.
*jobs -l	Lists the active jobs and their process IDs.
*kill %job	Terminates the job specified by **%job.**
*kill -sig %job	Sends signal **sig** to the job specified by **%job.**
kill pid	Terminates the process identified by **pid.**
kill -sig pid . . .	Sends signal **sig** to process **pid.**
*kill -l	Lists the signal names.
*limit	Lists all currently imposed resource limits.
*limit resource	Lists the current limit for **resource.**
*limit resource maximum-use	Sets a limit of **maximum-use** for **resource** for each individual process (and any subprocesses).
*login	Terminates the login shell and invokes the program **/bin/login.**

logout	Terminates the login shell. This command must be used if **ignoreeof** is set.
nice	Adds 4 to the current priority for the shell (and all subsequent commands).
nice +number	Adds **number** to the current priority for the shell (and all subsequent commands).
nice command	Executes **command** at priority 4 (4 added to the default priority).
nice +number command	Executes **command** at priority **number** (number added to the default priority).
nohup	Ignores the hangup signal in the current shell.
nohup command	Ignores the hangup signal for **command.**
*notify	Notifies user immediately on change of status of the current job.
*notify %job	Notifies user immediately on change of status of job **%job.**
*popd	Pops the top directory off the directory stack and changes directories to the new top.
*popd +n	Pops the **n**th directory off the directory stack.
*pushd	Exchanges the top two directories and changes directories to the new top.
*pushd dir	Puts directory **dir** on the directory stack and changes to it.
*pushd +n	Puts the **n**th directory on the top and changes to it.
rehash	Rebuilds the internal hash table.
repeat count command	Repeats **command count** times.
set	Displays the list of currently defined C shell variables and their values.
set name	Sets variable **name** to the null string.
set name = word	Sets variable **name** to the single word **word.**
set name[n] = word	Sets the nth word of **name** to **word.**
set name = (wordlist)	Sets the variable **name** to **wordlist.**
setenv name value	Sets environment variable **name** to **value.**
source name	Executes C shell script **name** in the current shell.
*source -h name	Reads commands from script **name** and places them in the current history list without executing them.
*stop	Stops (suspends) the current job (which is running in the background).
*stop %job	Stops the job specified by **%job** (which is running in the background).
*suspend	Stops the current shell (analogous to typing **control-Z** for foreground jobs).
time	Displays a summary of the time used by the current shell and its children.

time command	Displays a summary of the time used by executing **command.**
umask	Displays the current value for **umask.**
umask value	Sets the value of **umask** to **value.** UNIX uses the **umask** value to set the permissions for newly created files and directories.
unalias pattern	Removes all alias definitions matched by **pattern.**
unhash	Disables use of the internal hash table.
***unlimit**	Removes all resource limitations.
***unlimit resource**	Removes limitations for **resource.**
unset pattern	Releases all C shell variables matched by **pattern.**
***unsetenv pattern**	Releases all environment variables matched by **pattern.**
wait	Waits for all background jobs to complete. (This command can be interrupted.)
while (expr)	As long as **expr** evaluates to nonzero, the C shell executes the commands between the **while** and matching **end** statements.
. . .	
end	
***%job**	Brings the specified job into the foreground.
***%job &**	Continues the specified job in the background.
@	Displays the values of all C shell variables.
@ name = expr	Sets the variable **name** to value of **expr. expr** can contain numeric operators.
@ name[n] = expr	Sets the **nth** word of variable **name** to value of **expr.**

D

C Programs for **echo2**, **getch**, and **gets**

This appendix contains the C source code for the following utility programs:

echo2   Writes its argument list to standard error. Option **-n** prevents a new line.

getch   Reads a single character from the standard input and writes it to the standard output.

gets   Reads a single line from the standard input and writes it to the standard output.

You can call the programs from the C shell, either in scripts or interactively.

Examples

```
# getch (read a single character)
echo -n "Enter a character: "     # prompt
stty raw                          # allow single character
set r = `getch`                   # read single character
stty -raw                         # return terminal to default
# gets (read a line)
echo -n "Enter a value: "         # prompt
set val = `gets`                  # read a line

# echo2 (write to standard error)
if ($val > 10) echo2 "Illegal value -- try again"
```

echo2

```
/* Echo2 - writes characters to standard error
          Option:    -n    do not append newline
*/
#include <stdio.h>

main(argc, argv)
    short argc;
    char *argv[];
{
    short nl = 1;                        /* set newline flag on */

    if (strcmp(argv[1], "-n") == 0) {
      nl = 0;                            /* request no newline */
      argc--;                            /* decrease arg count */
      argv++;                            /* move to next arg */
    }

    while (--argc) {                     /* loop through the args */
        fputs(*++argv, stderr);          /* put the word out to std err */
        if (argc > 1)                    /* put a space between words */
            putc(' ', stderr);           /* except for the last word */
    }
    if (nl)                              /* append newline? */
        putc('\n', stderr);
}
```

getch

```
/* getch -- read a single character from standard input */

main()
{
    int c;

    c = getchar();                 /* get a char from standard input */
    putchar(c);                    /* write a char to standard output */
    return (0);                    /* return with good status */

}
```

gets

```
/* gets - Read a line from standard input */
#include <stdio.h>

main()
{
    int c;
    while ((c = getchar()) != '\n' && c != EOF)
        putchar(c);
    putchar('\n');
}
```

Installation

Include ~/**bin** directory in your **$path** variable. Compile and install these utilities in your ~/**bin** directory with the following sequence of commands:

```
% cc echo2.c -s -o echo2
% cc getch.c -s -o getch
% cc gets.c -s -o gets
% cp echo2 getch gets ~/bin
% rehash
```

The compile option **-s** strips the symbol table from the output file. Option **-o** names the output file (the next argument). The **rehash** command rebuilds the internal hash table so that the C shell will "find" these newly installed commands.

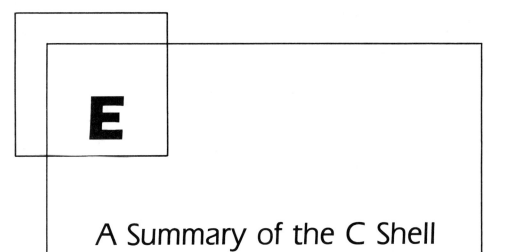

E

A Summary of the C Shell

Notation

stdin	standard input
stdout	standard output
stderr	standard error
str, str1, str2	strings
cmd	command or command group
var	shell variable
expr	expression

Special Characters for Issuing Commands

Character(s)	Meaning
;	Separate commands.
( )	Group commands.
|	Pipe **stdout** to **stdin**.
|&	Pipe **stderr** and **stdout** to **stdin**.
&&	Execute next command only if previous one is successful.
||	Execute next command only if previous one fails.
&	Execute in background.

Input/Output Redirection

Character(s)	Redirects
`<`	`stdin`
`>`	`stdout`
`>&`	`stdout` and `stderr`
`>!`	`stdout` (override `noclobber`)
`>&!`	`stdout` and `stderr` (override `noclobber`)
`>>`	append `stdout`
`>>&`	append `stdout` and `stderr`
`>>!`	append `stdout` (override `noclobber`)
`>>&!`	append `stdout` and `stderr` (override `noclobber`)
`<< str`	Read input lines until `str` is encountered at the beginning of a line.

Filename Expansion and Pattern Matching

Character(s)	Meaning
`*`	Match zero or more characters.
`?`	Match any single character.
`[list]`	Match any character in `list`.
`[lower-upper]`	Match any character in range between **lower** and **upper**.
`str{str1,str2,...}`	Expand different parts with common **str**.
`~`	your home directory
`~user`	home directory of **user**

Quoting

Character(s)	Meaning
`` `cmd` ``	Execute **cmd** and substitute output (command substitution).
`\c`	Escape character **c** (take literally).
`'str'`	String characters taken literally.
`"str"`	Allow command substitution and variable substitution.

Special Characters That Must be Escaped

Character(s)	Meaning
space	command argument separator
tab	command argument separator
RETURN	command argument terminator
$	variable identifier
* [ ] ? { } ~ -	file expansion
< > & !	redirection
! ^	history
|	pipe
;	command delimiter
( )	command group
\ ' "	quoting
`	command substitution
&	background execution

Shell Variables

Variable modifiers apply to the following (replace **var** with **argv** to refer to command line arguments):

$var	value of **var**
${var}	value of **var**, insulate **var** string
$var[i]	value of **ith** word from **var** wordlist
${var[i]}	value of **ith** word from **var** wordlist, insulate **var** string
$var[*]	same as **$var**
$var[n-m]	words **n** through **m** from **var** wordlist
${var[n-m]}	words **n** through **m** from wordlist, insulate **var** string
$var[$#var]	last word from **var** wordlist
$var[[$#var]]	last word from **var** wordlist, insulate **var** string
$i	same as **$argv[i]** (**i** restricted to 1–9)
$*	same as **$argv[*]**
$#var	number of words in **var**
${#var}	number of words in **var**, insulate **var** string

Variable modifiers do not apply to the following:

$0	name of script file
$?var	1 if **var** is defined; 0 if not
${?var}	1 if **var** is defined; 0 if not; insulate **var** string
$$	process ID of parent shell
$< (BSD only)	Substitute a line from **stdin**.

Variable Modifiers

Character(s)	Meaning
: **r**	root name
: **h**	header name
: **t**	tail
: **e** (BSD only)	extension
: **gr**	Extract root names from wordlist.
: **gh**	Extract header names from wordlist.
: **gt**	Extract tail names from wordlist.
: **ge** (BSD only)	Extract extension names from wordlist.
: **q**	Quote.
: **x**	Quote and expand into separate words.

History List Recall

Format: **command [word] [modifier]**

Command	From History List
! **N**	command **N**
! !	last command
! -**N**	**N**th command from last one
! **str**	last command starting with **str**
! ? **str** ?	last command with **str** anywhere in command line
! ? **str** ?%	Produce argument from last command with **str**.
! { **str1** } **str2**	last command with **str1**, append with **str2**
ˆ **str1** ˆ **str2** ˆ	Substitute **str2** for **str1** in last command.

Word	Command
: **0**	command name
: **n**	**n**th word
: ˆ	first word
: **$**	last word
: %	word matched by ? **str** ? search
: **n-m**	**n**th through **m**th words
: -**n**	0 through **n**th words
: **n-**	**n** through next-to-last word
: **n∗**	**n** through last word
: ∗	1 through last word

Modifier	Meaning
: h	pathname head
: r	pathname root (no extension)
: t	pathname tail
: e (BSD only)	pathname extension
: q	Quote wordlist.
: x	Quote individual words.
: &	Repeat previous substitution.
: s/str1/str2/	Substitute str2 for str1.
: g[hrtes]	Modify all words in wordlist using specified modifier.
: g&	Repeat previous substitution globally.

Job Control (BSD only)

Format: **command [job_number]**

Command	Meaning
bg	Run job in background.
fg	Run job in foreground.
kill [signal]	Terminate (or send signal).
stop	Suspend background job.
notify	Notify when status of job changes.
jobs	List active jobs.
jobs -l	List with process IDs.
^Z	Suspend foreground job.

Job Number	Meaning
PID	process ID
%	current job
%N	job N
%str	job with str as command name
%?str	job with str anywhere in command string
%-	previous job

Operators

Operators are listed in order of decreasing precedence.

Operator	Meaning
( )	change precedence
~	1's complement
!	logical negation
* / %	multiply, divide, modulo
+ -	add, subtract
<< >>	left shift, right shift
== !=	string comparison
=~ !~	pattern matching (BSD only)
&	bitwise "and"
^	bitwise "exclusive or"
|	bitwise "inclusive or"
&&	logical "and"
||	logical "or"

Assignment Operators

Operator	Meaning
++	increment
--	decrement
=	assignment
*=	Multiply left side by right side and update left side.
/=	Divide left side by right side and update left side.
+=	Add left side to right side and update left side.
-=	Subtract left side from right side and update left side.
^=	"Exclusive or" left side to right side and update left side.
%=	(modulo) Divide left side by right side and update left side with remainder.

File Inquiry Operators

Format:　　**(operator filename)**

Operator	True If
-d	file is a directory
-e	file exists
-f	file is a plain file
-o	user is owner
-r	user has read access
-w	user has write access
-x	user has execute access
-z	file has zero length

C Shell Programming

Shell scripts

\#   comment

First Line of a Script

\#   Execute C shell.
\#!/bin/sh (BSD only)   Execute Bourne shell.
\#!/bin/csh -f (BSD only)   fast C shell startup

Conditional Statements

```
if (expr) command

if (expr) then
     command(s)
endif

if (expr) then
     command(s)
else
     command(s)
endif

if (expr) then
     command(s)
else if (expr) then
     command(s)
. . . . .
else
     command(s)
endif
```

Looping and Control

```
foreach var (wordlist)
     command(s)
end

while (expr)
     command(s)
end
```

break	Exit from innermost loop.
continue	Continue with next iteration of innermost loop.
shift name	Shift variable **name** one position.
shift	Shift variable **argv** one position.
goto label	Branch to **label**.

Selection

```
switch (str)
case pat1:
     command(s)
breaksw
case pat2:
     command(s)
breaksw
.  .  .  .  .
default:
     command(s)
breaksw
endsw
```

Interrupts

onintr label	Branch to **label** if interrupt occurs.
onintr -	Ignore interrupts.
onintr	Default interrupt handling (terminate shell script).

Special Files

File	Meaning
/etc/cshrc	C shell executes commands in current shell at login before ~/.cshrc (XENIX only).
~/.cshrc	C shell executes commands in current shell during C shell startup.
~/.login	C shell executes commands in current shell during login after ~/.cshrc.
~/.logout	C shell executes commands in current shell during logout.

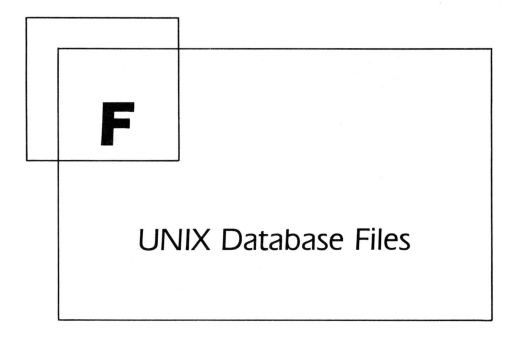

UNIX Database Files

UNIX maintains several database files to initialize C shell predefined variables and UNIX environment variables. You will find it useful to know the format of these files and how the system uses the data. We'll examine the following files:

/etc/passwd
/etc/group
/etc/ttytype
/etc/termcap
/etc/cshrc

All users may look at (read) these files. You can even read the UNIX password file (**/etc/passwd**). Don't worry, UNIX stores the passwords in an encrypted form.

/etc/passwd

The **/etc/passwd** file contains a single line of information for each user. Each line is divided into fields separated by colons according to the following format:

```
user:password:userid:groupid:comment:home:program
```

user is your login name. **password** contains your login password (encrypted, of course). **userid** is a unique number that UNIX assigns to your username. UNIX uses this **userid** instead of your username for storing file and directory ownership. Likewise, **groupid** is a unique number that UNIX assigns to your default group. The corresponding group name is stored in **/etc/group**. The comment field contains personal or administrative information (your name, for example). **home** contains your home directory. **program** is the default shell (or any program) that the login process executes when you login.

To examine your own password file entry, type the following command:

```
% grep "^$USER" /etc/passwd
sara:9vlKMPVf8MBYc:202:50:sara jones ext 322:/u/sara:/bin/csh
```

You may need to use **$LOGNAME** on your system. In this example, we show user name **sara**. We have a **userid** of 202 and a **groupid** of 50. Our default directory is **/u/sara**, and we login to a C shell (**/bin/csh**).

The following predefined C shell variables take their values from the **/etc/passwd** file:

```
home      /u/sara
shell     /bin/csh
```

Similarly, the system defines these environment variables from the **/etc/password** file:

```
USER=sara
HOME=/u/sara
SHELL=/bin/csh
```

Although you may examine */etc/passwd* at will, you cannot modify (write to) it. UNIX provides utilities that allow you to change your password entry in a controlled manner. For example, the **passwd** command allows you to change your login password. Only system administrators (superusers), however, can modify the other fields. Many UNIX systems provide additional utilities, like **adduser** and **rmuser**, to add and remove users in the password file.

/etc/group

This file contains a database of groups and their respective members. Like the password file, each line is divided into fields separated by colons according to the format

```
group:password:groupid:user,user,...
```

group is a group name followed by an optional password. The third field is the **groupid** code, and the last field is a list of usernames belonging to the group.

From the password file, we see that **sara** is a member of group 50. To find out the group name and the group members, we type

```
% grep :50: /etc/group
pgm1::50:sara,marty,ann
```

The name of group 50 is **pgm1**. It has three members: **sara**, **marty**, and **ann**. There is no password associated with this group.

Most UNIX systems (except Berkeley BSD versions) provide the **id** command to display your user and group ID codes. For example,

```
% id
uid=202(sara)  gid=50(pgm1)
```

shows that **sara** (**userid** 202) is a member of group **pgm1** (**groupid** 50).

You may be a member of more than one group. The command

```
% grep $USER /etc/group
pgm1::50:sara,marty,ann
pgm2::51:gail,sara,kellen
```

shows that **sara** is a member of two groups, **pgm1** and **pgm2**. As illustrated, the group members can be different in each group.

When you login, UNIX puts you in your default group as specified in the **/etc/passwd** file. Most UNIX systems (except BSD versions) allow you to change groups with the **newgrp** (new group) command. For example, the command

```
% newgrp pgm2
```

changes the current group to **pgm2**. The **id** command reflects the group change:

```
% id
uid=202(sara)  gid=51(pgm2)
```

BSD systems check **/etc/group** for your group affiliation when you use the **chgrp** (change group) command. UNIX checks file and directory access permissions according to the new group (here **pgm2** instead of **pgm1**). You can therefore use groups to implement less restrictive permission settings. Let's see how this works.

Suppose group **pgm1** is developing a large software project. We set up a working directory with the following commands:

```
% umask 7
% mkdir /u/A/proj1
% ls -ld /u/A/proj1
drwxrwx--- 2 sara    pgm1    32 Apr 20 10:39 /u/A/proj1
```

Using **umask**, we set the permission of all directories to be 770 (**rwxrwx---**) and all subsequent files to be 660 (**rw-rw----**). This gives any group member of **pgm1** the same permission status as the owner (**sara**). Any user in the group can then modify the files.

Suppose **marty** (a member of **pgm1**) changes groups. He will no longer be able to modify (or even access) files in the **/u/A/proj1** directory (or in any subdirectories).

/etc/ttytype

When you login to UNIX, the login process looks up your port in the terminal type file (/**etc/ttytype**) to see what kind of terminal you are using. It uses this to set the **TERM** environment variable. This file has the following format:

```
termtype port
```

There is one line per port in /**etc/ttytype**, with each field separated by a space. The first field is the terminal type (e.g., **adm3a**, **vt100**, **dialup**, **patchboard**). The second field is the line or port identification. For example, in the following system, the **console** is a **tvi920** terminal, **tty01** is an **adm3a**, and **tty02** is a dial-up line:

```
% cat /etc/ttytype
tvi920 console
adm3a tty01
dialup tty02
```

If the terminal has a dedicated line (that is, if it is hard-wired), the login process automatically sets the **TERM** environment variable. However, if the port is a dial-up line, a network line, or some other line with an indeterminate terminal type, the login process can only assign a generic terminal ID. In this case we can use the **tset** command to tell the system what type of terminal we're using. This is especially useful when we are apt to use many different ports and terminals for accessing the same UNIX system.

For example, if we always sign on to the UNIX system using the **adm3a** on line **tty01** (a hard-wired line), we let UNIX use the value stored in /**etc/ttytype**.

However, suppose we use a **vt100** to dial up; otherwise, we use the console port (a **tvi920**). In this case we use **tset**, as follows:

```
tset - -m 'dialup:vt100'
```

This says to map (**-m**) a dial-up port to a **vt100** terminal; otherwise, use the default mapping in /**etc/ttytype**. The **-** option says to send the terminal name to the standard output. This allows us to use command substitution and assign the terminal type to **TERM**. The command

```
setenv TERM `tset - -m 'dialup:vt100'`
```

in our **.login** file sets **TERM** appropriately.

/etc/termcap

The **vi** editor (and other cursor-control utilities) are terminal-independent because of a "terminal capabilities" file (/**etc/termcap**). When you use **vi**, for example, it scans /**etc/termcap** for your terminal type ($**TERM**) to initialize specific terminal characteristics (cursor motion, clear to end of line, etc.). The format for this file is

```
termn1|termn2:\
  :capdef:capdef:
```

termn1 and **termn2** are different terminal names for the same **termcap** entry, separated by |. There may be several names. The backslash character indicates that the capability definition continues to the next line. Colons separate the fields of capability definitions (**capdef**) for that terminal entry. Refer to **termcap(5)** in your UNIX documentation for the details to these **capdef** definitions.

When we give a terminal type identification to define **TERM**, we may use any of the names in the */etc/termcap* file. For example, an entry in */etc/termcap* may look like

```
cT|tvi912|tvi920|tvi:\
  :al=\EE:am:bs:ce=\Et:cm=\E=%+ %+ :cl=\E*:co#80:dc=\EW:dl=\ER:\
  :ei=:ho=^^:im=:ic=\EQ:in:li#24:nd=^L:pt:se=\Ek:so=\Ej:up=^K:
```

where **cT**, **tvi912**, **tvi920**, and **tvi** are all allowable abbreviations for a **Televideo** display terminal.

Cursor-dependent utilities (e.g., **vi**, **curses**) use the **TERMCAP** environment variable to identify the **termcap** file. The default pathname is

```
TERMCAP    /etc/termcap
```

You may create your own database of **termcap** entries and set **TERMCAP** to the appropriate filename. Refer to "Hints and Cautions" in Chapter 9 for an example of this technique.

/etc/cshrc

This is a systemwide startup file for all users who run the C shell. The C shell executes commands placed in this file before executing the user's **.cshrc** file. Only the superuser can modify this file.

For example, the following commands may appear in this file:

```
% cat /etc/cshrc
umask 027
setenv TZ PST8PDT
setenv CWD ~
```

This defines a default **umask** code of 027 for each user and sets the **TZ** environment variable to Pacific Standard Time. This eliminates the need to include these statements in each user's **.cshrc** or **.login** file. We also initialize the **CWD** environment variable to the user's home directory (~). Refer to Section 9.6 for the **cd** alias definition that relies on **CWD**'s initialization. (*Note:* The name of this file may be different on your system— */etc/cshprofile*, for example. Furthermore, some systems may not have a systemwide C shell startup command file.)

G

The C Shell Under XENIX

This appendix describes the C shell under XENIX. We present the differences between this version and the C shell under UNIX 4BSD. In general, the XENIX C shell is a subset of the 4BSD C shell. In some cases you can implement the missing features by creating aliases or scripts or defining variables. We provide these. In other cases the differences are just alternate implementations (e.g., the built-in **echo** command).

History List

The XENIX C shell does not include the following built-in commands relating to the history mechanism:

source -h	place commands in history list but don't execute
history -h	print history list without line numbers
history n	print last **n** commands
history -r	print history list in reverse order

In addition, it does not implement the **savehist** predefined variable. Therefore, you cannot save your history list across login sessions. Also, you cannot use the **:e** modifier with history list arguments.

Use the **tail** command to implement **history n**. For example, the following command prints the last five history commands:

```
% history | tail -5
```

Shell/Environment Variables

The XENIX C shell uses the command **env** instead of **printenv** to print the environment variable list. It does not include the **unsetenv** command to remove an environment variable (there is no way to do this).

The XENIX C shell uses environment variable **LOGNAME** instead of **USER**, and it does not include the predefined shell variables **user**, **term**, **cwd** (current working directory), **notify** (notify of job completion), or **savehist** (save history list). Place the following statements in your **.cshrc** file to implement variables **user**, **term**, and **cwd**:

```
set user = $LOGNAME
set term = $TERM
alias cd 'cd \!*; set cwd = `/bin/pwd`; setenv CWD $cwd'
```

This also requires the following statement in **/etc/cshrc** (systemwide C shell startup file):

```
setenv CWD ~
```

The XENIX C shell also provides you with the **child** shell variable (this doesn't exist in 4BSD). Use this to access the process ID of the most recent background process.

As with history arguments, the XENIX C shell does not support the **:e** modifier for shell variables.

Command Differences

XENIX includes both the **ls** command (AT&T version) and the **lc** command (4BSD version). Under 4BSD, only **lc** is supplied, and it is called **/bin/ls**. Therefore, if you prefer to use this version under XENIX by typing **ls**, you need to install the following alias:

```
alias ls /bin/lc
```

The XENIX C shell has a built-in **echo** command as well as one in **/bin**. They are not the same. The built-in version uses \c in the argument string to suppress a new line instead of the **-n** option. For example,

```
echo "Please input a number:\c "
```

displays the same prompt using the built-in version. The command

```
/bin/echo -n "Please input a number: "
```

uses the version in **/bin**. The program in **/bin** allows you to write to the error output using the **-e** option. (This provides the same function as **echo2**.) For example,

```
/bin/echo -e "Bad filename"
```

writes the message to the error output. To use the **/bin/echo** program instead of the built-in **echo**, put the statement

```
alias echo /bin/echo
```

in your ~/.**cshrc** file. Be warned, however, that this runs slower than the built-in version.

Directory Stacks

The XENIX C shell does not include the built-in commands **pushd**, **popd**, and **dirs**. See Section 11.10 for shell scripts and aliases that implement these commands.

Operators

The XENIX conditional command operators (**&&** and **||**) have the opposite meaning from BSD. For example, the BSD command

```
grep fritz /etc/passwd > /dev/null && echo fritz is a user
```

informs you that **fritz** is a user only if his name appears in the system password file. Under XENIX, you must use the following command:

```
grep fritz /etc/passwd > /dev/null || echo fritz is a user
```

Note that **&&** and || used as logical operators are the same under both versions. The command

```
if ($#argv < 3 || $#argv > 5) then
   echo Error: number of args must be between 3 and 5.
   exit 1
endif
```

executes the same in both XENIX and BSD environments.

The XENIX C shell does not include the pattern matching operators =~ and !~. The BSD statement

```
if ($argv[1] =~ *.c) then
   echo $argv[1]:r is a C program
endif
```

must be written in XENIX as

```
switch ($argv[1])
  case *.c:
    echo $argv[1]:r is a C program
    breaksw
endsw
```

Shell Scripts

In BSD, you may include a directive in your shell script to perform a fast shell startup. For example, the C shell executes the following script (called **build**) without reading the ~/**.cshrc** file:

```
% cat build
#!/bin/csh -f
. . . . . .
```

The XENIX C shell does not recognize this directive. Instead, you can use an alias to call the C shell with the **-f** (fast startup) option, as follows:

```
alias build '/bin/csh -f ~/bin/build'
```

Input from the Terminal

The XENIX C shell does not include the built-in directive **$<** for reading standard input. Instead, use **gets** or **line** with command substitution. The statement (under BSD)

```
set input = $<
```

reads a line of input and stores it in variable **input**. The commands

```
set input = `gets`
set input = `line`
```

show the equivalent function using **gets** and **line** respectively.

Job Control

The XENIX C shell does not implement full job control, which includes the commands **bg**, **fg**, **jobs**, **limit**, **notify**, **stop**, and **unlimit** (see Appendix C for their descriptions) and the predefined shell variable **notify**. Job control under XENIX allows background execution (using **&**) and provides the **ps**, **kill**, and **nohup** commands.

Special Files

In addition to the standard C shell special files ~/.**cshrc**, ~/.**login**, and ~/.**logout**, the XENIX C shell provides file /**etc/cshrc**. This is a systemwide startup file that the C shell executes once at login time before reading the ~/.**cshrc** file. It is useful for initialization tasks that should be done before executing ~/.**cshrc**. (We use it to initialize variable **CWD**.)

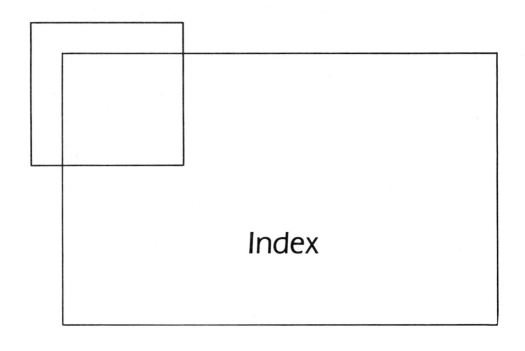

Index